Lands of the Curry Leaf

To my family and yours, this book is dedicated to any one and every one who reads and cooks from it. Make these recipes your own, and cook with love for your loved ones.

Born in London to an Austrian mother and Sri Lankan father, Peter Kuruvita spent much of his childhood in Sri Lanka before moving to Australia with his parents. Here he began his career as a chef, which has taken him from Sydney to prestigious restaurants in London, the USA, Fiji, the Hayman Islands and Bali. Home in Australia, Peter brings his signature style and focus on seafood to Noosa Beach House on the Sunshine Coast. Memories of an idyllic childhood spent in Sri Lanka inspired his first book, *Serendip*, published in 2009. This was followed by Peter's first TV series, *My Sri Lanka*, and by three subsequent TV series: *Island Feast*, *Mexican Fiesta* and *Peter Kuruvita's Coastal Kitchen*. Peter has worked as an ambassador for Dilmah Tea for many years, and also hosts culinary tours of Sri Lanka for World Expeditions.

Lands
of the
Curry
Leaf

A vegetarian food journey
from Sri Lanka to Nepal

PETER KURUVITA

MURDOCH BOOKS
SYDNEY · LONDON

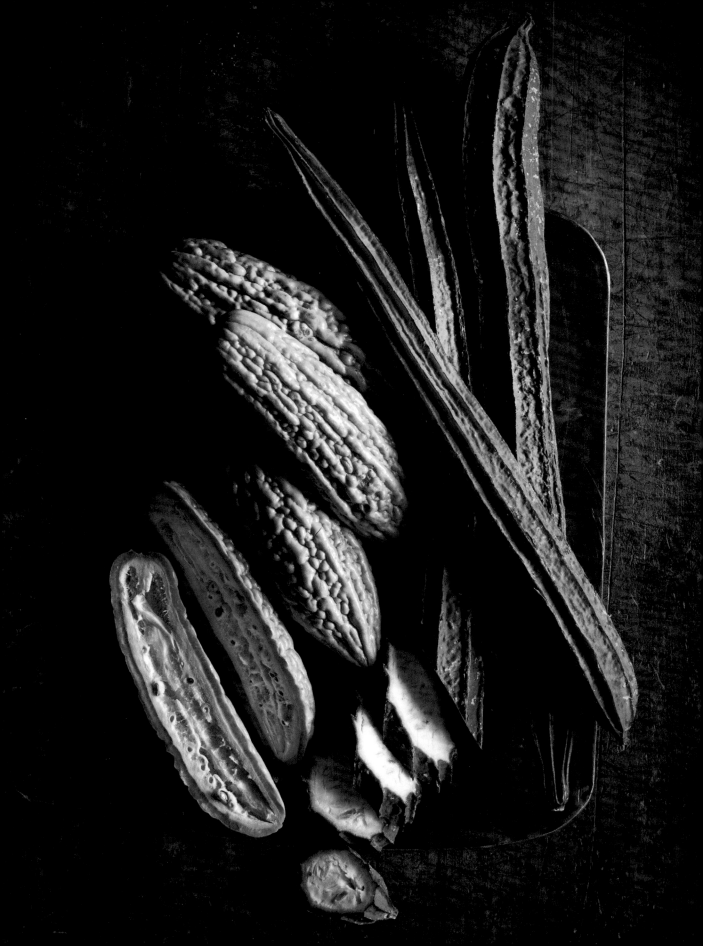

Contents

Ayubowan!

(A traditional Sri Lankan greeting, meaning 'long life'.)

To say this collection of recipes, gathered from across the subcontinent, is deeply personal would be an understatement. Food and the memories of food — who it was eaten with, the taste, the location, the physical need, and the emotional associations they carry — are my lifeblood. A culture of food and friendship flows through my veins. This is the culture of the subcontinent, where a curry leaf tree grows in the garden of just about every home.

When we look back at our personal histories, there are very clear moments and events that create our food stories. At the age of four, my Austrian mother lost her mother in very tragic circumstances, as do many during times of war. It set in motion the story of a woman of great independence, who left for London, alone, at the tender age of seventeen. Soon afterwards she met my dad, who was from Sri Lanka. He had ridden to London with three friends on his Indian motorcycle with side car in 1952 to see the coronation of Queen Elizabeth, and had stayed on to study engineering. And that was it. The connection. The immersion. A beautiful clash of cultures. Where my story began.

My earliest food memory is of my father feeding me with his fingers. Little balls of rice and dhal delivered on rough, cracked hands that smelt and tasted of the diesel from his engineering workshop. And my grandmother, in our kitchen in Sri Lanka, cooking with other women, all so passionate about food and produce; all teaching me that there is so much more to food than just filling our bellies.

Growing up, food and cooking were simply natural extensions of self. The ingredients, family and food collided in ways that make it difficult for me to imagine how one could exist without the other. There were no recipes: just conversation and a reliance on the senses. The art of watching. The fragrant smells. The heat, the flavours, the feelings of respect for food and where it came from, and an indescribable energy that swirled and buzzed around the kitchen like spices tempered in a pan.

The food in this book is the culmination of my upbringing and my travels through the subcontinent. I've brought together recipes that reflect the diversity of the regions, their landscape, their history and my life. This is the food I grew up with. I have done my best to distil the local colour, quite literally, into the local flavour; to express the energy and the excitement of the region's cuisines and hopefully to expand your flavour repertoire.

These recipes are also a reflection of the changing dialogue about what we eat. They are a celebration of all things vegetable and their growing prominence at our tables. I want to show you how they can be the star. As the Sri Lankans are fond of saying, you can 'curry anything' — and I want you to embrace the idea of a meal where flesh is not the main event. Vegetables and grains and pulses can shine. And here they do. Very brightly.

Cooking with vegetables is a very natural thing for me. My grandmother was a vegan all her life and Sri Lankans would usually have only one piece of meat, if any, in their meals, along with lots of different vegetable curries. Growing up in Sri Lanka, I was exposed to a multitude of vegetables, pulses and grains, and saw how these elements are celebrated in the subcontinent's different cuisines. I am not a vegetarian, but I do love vegetables. They can become such a complete and joyous meal, and my motivation — far above those associated with choice based on taste, environmental or moral reasons — is just to cook with more vegies.

The time is right. There is increased availability of a wider range of vegetables (including exotic and heirloom varieties) and a better understanding of how to grow them or source them sustainably. I hope this book contributes to a heightened interest in vegetarian food within your weekly recipe repertoire.

Writing a book brings a lot of pressure. A desire for honesty, for accuracy, and ultimately for usefulness. From the first to the last page, this is not a cookbook for your coffee table. This is a cookbook for your kitchen. I hope it becomes well-thumbed, splattered with oil and smelling faintly of curry, cumin and a heady mix of spices. I hope its pages are filled with ticks, additions and your own personal edits as my recipes become yours.

My history with food, like these dishes, is layered — where flavours and experiences build upon each other to create a foundation for family, for sharing, and celebrating the flavours of a truly phenomenal and diverse region of the world.

I am honoured to have the opportunity to share a piece of myself with you: the food that I grew up with; the food that shaped me and everything that I do to this day. I hope it becomes part of your full pantry, warm home, celebrations, family gatherings and happy everyday routines. Essentially, I hope this food, my food, becomes part of the fabric of your life.

Peter Kuruvita

Feasting in the Footsteps of My Father

Food is about family for me. As is my somewhat insatiable desire for travel. Dad had this spirit that made the impossible seem possible, and because of that I have been fortunate enough to travel widely and experience much, both with my family as a small boy, and now as a chef and television presenter.

My travels across the subcontinent have been exhilarating, intense, frightening, awe-inspiring and, without a doubt, palate-expanding. The adventure started for me at the tender age of four-and-a-half, when we packed up our London life into a blue Austin minibus, purchased second hand from the *Thunderbirds* film set, and set off on the treacherous overland track for Sri Lanka.

Mum kept a diary of our travels. In 1968 she noted:

Necessity — as well as a healthy hunger for adventure — decided we would go overland on the now famous track from London to Colombo. It would cost us £800/– to go by ship but only £450/– to go overland. We hoped we would be able to start a new life, a better one for all of us, in Ceylon — the birthplace of Wick, my husband. He also wanted the boys to have a real home, one with roots that reach back many centuries, and experience the respect and place of honour his family enjoyed in their society.

Mum documents our intrigue and natural interest in food throughout the trip. There is a sense of awe in even the humblest of foodstuffs, and this is something I carry with me to this day and hope to convey through this book. It is also why I think vegetarian food is so important. You can take the truly simple, the truly basic —

from legumes and other starches, as well as vegetables and fruits — and turn them into a breathtaking and complete meal.

THE SUBCONTINENT

While traditionally the 'subcontinent' is most often taken to refer to India, Sri Lanka, Pakistan and Bangladesh, in this book I've also included the countries of Bhutan, Nepal and Afghanistan. As my mother wrote in her travel diary on that overland trip: 'Hospitality is legendary in the subcontinent, and the Middle and Far East — it is a basic lifeline in harsh environments.' I want to showcase some of this truly remarkable hospitality and food culture and explore the goldmine of flavours on offer in these less charted territories.

Across the subcontinent, from remote tribal villages to frenzied capital cities, food is the central principle of life, and connection is realised through cooking. It is in these culinary microcosms that I discovered indigenous vegetables, chutneys, flat breads, curries and unusual grains, and legion dishes I might never have otherwise experienced. I cannot detail them all, but here are some of the regions whose hospitality we will sample on our vegetarian culinary journey across the subcontinent.

AFGHANISTAN

My first and only time in Afghanistan was in 1969, when we drove along the border on our way to Sri Lanka. (These days, news of the famous annual Dakar rally always inspires me to repeat my father's journey with my own family, but this time from Australia to London via Sri Lanka. I even bought a BMW GS800 30th anniversary–model motorcycle to make the journey on. Sadly, the war in Afghanistan put my dreams on hold.)

Afghan cuisine is steeped in ritual and a sense of hospitality that has miraculously survived war, invasion and upheaval. I have never forgotten my father saying Afghans are the most beautiful people and the ultimate hosts. Afghanistan's culinary specialties reflect its ethnic diversity and geographic proximity to neighbouring Tajikistan, Uzbekistan, Pakistan, Turkmenistan and Iran (formerly known as Persia).

Persia contributed saffron, pepper, garam masala (cardamom, cinnamon, cloves, cumin, nutmeg), mint, coriander and cooking with sabzi (spinach or green herbs); Mongolian influences can be seen in the amazing dumplings and noodles; from India came chillies, originally via Central and South America. But Afghan cuisine has a style of its own. Fatty dishes are an important fuel in this nation of harsh landscapes and freezing winters, with oil used liberally and mutton fat traditionally added to many dishes.

Bread is eaten with virtually everything, possibly because Afghan food is largely based on the country's main cereal crops, such as wheat, maize, barley and rice. (Before turmoil became a byword for the country, Afghanistan was referred to as 'the ruler of the rice world', in a region where reputations can be made or lost with rice.) Dairy products, nuts, native vegetables, fresh and dried fruits are also widely used.

Essential flavours: Basmati rice, bread, cardamom, dried fruits, dried mint, yoghurt.

The role of vegetables: In Afghanistan, as in neighbouring Iran and Pakistan, basmati rice is so valued that it is the centre of the dish: any meat or vegetables are the accompaniment. Afghanistan is a difficult place to be a vegetarian, with lamb a regular and ready hero, although its proximity to India does make it more accepting of vegetable-only food, leaving space for liberal use of spices. But scratch the surface and there are lip-smackingly delicious vegetarian foods across Afghanistan — and as with many cultures of the subcontinent, it is in the sides and extras, such as chutney, or chatni, where the vegetable is truly on display. Qorma-i-sabzi is a very popular vegetarian dish comprised of spinach (sabzi), parsley, coriander and spring onions, served with basmati rice. There is also qorma-i-tarkari, made with cauliflower, baby carrots and potatoes, cooked with a blend of dill, turmeric and cumin.

INDIA

India is a challenging country to travel, but equally as wondrous, no matter how long you are there. When your plane, train or bus leaves the Indian border there is a romance and intrigue that beckons your return. I would love to spend three months in the desert town of Pushkar, learning how to play the tabla — one of the most beautiful drums in the world.

India is a country of extremes with a diversity of cuisine that belies belief. Indian food is regionally specific: the north favours richer food with lots of ghee, meat and wheat; while the south features intense, more tropical flavours, coconut milk and rice. But it is the clever use and blending of spices (whether used whole, or toasted then ground) that creates an intensity and depth of flavour that defines Indian cuisine.

Even four millennia ago, inhabitants of the north's fertile Indus Valley were using ingredients that characterise the cooking of the region now: cereals and basmati rice, pulses, dairy, and spices such as mustard and fenugreek. Across the fields of Uttar Pradesh and eastern Rajasthan, northward through the Punjab, and up into mountainous Kashmir, ancient cooking techniques survive, too. The north-eastern states are dramatically different from the rest of India. Connected to the subcontinent by a mere thread of land, most of the population traces its ancestry back to bordering Bhutan, China and Myanmar. Pork and bamboo feature prominently, as do salty fermented foods that speak more of South-East Asia than the subcontinent as we have come to know it.

The eastern Indian states are home to fruitful plains crisscrossed by waterways. After the monsoon season, fields are blanketed with mustard flowers, whose seeds yield pungent cooking oil, and gardens are rich with vegetables. Where the Ganges finally flows into the Bay of Bengal, freshwater fish and rice are the foundation of the cuisine; further south, many hundreds of kilometres of coastline yield prawns and a bounty of other seafood.

In the west the landscape is a romantic tale of extremes, ranging from sparse stretches of desert to a vibrant coast. In the state of Gujarat it is the thali (a meal of various dishes composed in a compartmentalised tray) that holds legendary status. Continue south and the lush Maharashtra and Goa abound with seafood and fresh produce, and coconut-enriched sauces are used with joyous abandon.

Essential flavours: Black mustard seeds, coriander seeds, cumin, dhal, garam masala, turmeric, black salt, asafoetida.

The role of vegetables: India is where the vegetarian reigns supreme. Vegetarianism is often assumed as the norm, encouraged or imposed by religion and caste. Although meat eating does occur across the country, India has one of the world's lowest rates of per capita meat consumption. The use of vegetables is varied, exciting and prominent. Animal-based ingredients (other than milk and honey) such as lard, gelatine and meat stock are not used in the traditional cuisine.

The only rule of thumb people follow is respect and tolerance for each other's preferences; there is a lovely absence of policing your neighbour's plate. The first question in any restaurant is, 'Veg or non-veg?'

SRI LANKA

Growing up in my home country, food was my world, and the education passed down to me by my grandmother and aunties will remain with me forever. Part of this knowledge was as much about understanding the health qualities of different foods as anything else. Ask any Sri Lankan and they will know the Ayurvedic qualities of the food they eat, but all will say they don't know *how* they have this knowledge. It is just a part of life.

With influences from Arab traders, Malay navigators, Portuguese, Dutch and British colonists, and South Indian neighbours, Sri Lanka is a culinary paradise. Thanks to its tropical climate, fresh fruit, vegetables and spices are in abundance and all are used in many ways. Freshness is key, with households regularly shopping more than once a day for produce.

The sound and smell of mustard seeds and curry leaves popping in hot oil is Sri Lanka to me — it is the kind of musty heat not necessarily suited to the timid eater, for whom coconut, herbs and mellow spices are king. Most Sri Lankan cooking features unapologetically punch-you-in-the-face, get-the-adrenaline-pumping flavours. But the heat is more an intensity of spice than actual physical 'chilli heat'. Making liberal use of local fruit, such as coconut and jackfruit, seafood and an arsenal of spices, Sri Lankan cooking delivers an abundance of incredible dishes and flavour combinations, from sweet caramelised onion relishes and bitter melon, to spicy scraped coconut and curry with rice, and desserts sweetened with palm sugar.

Many families have a curry leaf tree and grow vegetables, some of which are indigenous to Sri Lanka, such as murunga (drumstick tree). These are used in curries and accompaniments, and their leaves are a popular addition to the famous crab curry.

Every meal comes with rice. One Sinhalese greeting translates as, 'Have you eaten rice?' A simple meal might consist of rice, a sambal made with chilli, pickles or chutney (to wake up the tastebuds), and at least one vegetable curry or dhal. There might also be a huge range of meat-based, vegetable and seafood dishes. Sri Lankan banquets are incredibly colourful, with curries that range from yellow to deep brown, contrasting with the vibrant greens of the vegetables, and the bright hues of sambal.

Essential flavours: Chutneys, pickles and sambals, coconut and coconut oil, curry leaves, curry powders, fenugreek, goraka (gambodge), Maldive fish (cured tuna), pandan leaf.

The role of vegetables: Vegetarianism is prominent in Sri Lankan cuisine, as it is in Indian. However, Sri Lanka is a country where tastes in meat eating, and food in general, are more varied than you would find even across Europe's multi-faceted populations.

PAKISTAN

For a long time, Pakistan to me meant cricket. In the 70s and 80s, when Pakistan and the West Indies were champions of the sport, I used to watch cricket with my dad, more for his memories than the game itself. He'd had so many adventures in his life and certain moments brought out these memories, which were generally about food and the people. He'd start with a sentence like, 'I used to know this Pakistani fella who could cook one hell of a biriyani,' and he'd go on to describe the flavours and colours of the food.

This was the beginning of my education in tolerance. My dad was no saint, but he found something good in all people. It is worth looking for, because when you are patient and understanding you can learn a lot. A way to connect with anyone is to ask about food and their family — this always makes their eyes light up. Sharing memories of childhood and food, in my opinion, could make peace everywhere. The same emotions live in all of us.

Pakistani cuisine is the lesser-known food of the subcontinent, perhaps because this region of magical mountains is known as the difficult child of South Asia — abundant in beauty, as much as it is plagued by political instability. The food is rich in tradition and full of marvellous and diverse dishes influenced by a blend of Indian, Far Eastern and Middle Eastern cooking techniques, which create a distinctive mix of complex flavours. Spices are king and are used cleverly and consistently. The cuisine incorporates elements from neighbouring India, Afghanistan and Iran and is heavily influenced by the largely Muslim population.

Essential flavours: Cardamom, chaat masala, cumin, dhal, dried plums, dried pomegranate, garam masala, ghee, saffron.

The role of vegetables: It is more a social nuisance to be vegetarian in Pakistan than anything else, because the breadth of vegetables and the delicious ways they are cooked are plentiful and varied. Eating out, most of the non-meat choices are full of staples such as grains, rather than vegetables. As in many Islamic countries, it is very difficult to find meals free from meat, but if you pull the meat from most recipes you end up with some truly spectacular vegetarian offerings. The vegetable is the foundation upon which you build your dish.

NEPAL

To me, Nepal is wondrous. It is full of ancient stories and beautiful temples, not to mention the world's most magnificent mountain range. I have travelled the dangerous narrow winding roads between Kathmandu and Pokhara on the roof of a bus, the driver travelling at breakneck speed and the ground dropping away hundreds of metres below us. I have walked to Annapurna Base Camp and swum in the Pokhara Lake while looking at the Himalayas above. The people are rugged and strong. My dad told me tales from World War II of the Gurkha soldiers: they were fearless and their enemies were petrified of them. As mountaineers, they have no match. I have vivid memories of children of the hill stations, skipping up steep stairs on the way to school, while we trekkers huffed and puffed our way upwards in their dust. Sherpas with no shoes jogged past us, carrying cases of beer on their heads, so that the beers would be cold when we triumphantly arrived at Base Camp. One old man carried a hefty tree stump on his head, while puffing on a cigarette.

A blend of Indian and Tibetan influences, Nepalese cuisine is simple, subtle and satisfying. Lentils and rice form the base of most meals, with herbs, vegetables and meats adding a mix of fresh and smoky flavours.

Common and widely loved dishes include spicy potato salad (aaloo ko achar), which is one of the freshest and cheapest dishes to prepare, vegetable pakoras, which are enjoyed with a typical Nepali-style tomato pickle (golbheda ko achar), and potato with bamboo shoots and black-eyed beans (aaloo tama), in which the sourness of the bamboo is all-important.

Essential flavours: Nepal's valley regions could be another state of India, with all the northern Indian flavours. In the highlands of Nepal, cheese and chilli and slightly more Asian flavours prevail, with touches of Tibet and Bhutan.

The role of vegetables: Dhal bhat (dhal and rice) and vegetables are the lifeblood of the cuisine. While the range and availability of vegetables is relatively limited due to the harsh environment and geography, the Nepalese have managed to work out their nutritional requirements and developed their cuisine accordingly. Vegetable dishes are focused on energy-dense, nutrient-rich foods, such as potatoes, cabbage, cauliflower, leafy greens, sprouts and pulses.

BANGLADESH

Bangladeshi cuisine really came to the forefront for me when a wave of Bangladeshi students migrated to Australia. Many worked in hospitality, eagerly gaining 900 hours of kitchen experience so they could apply for permanent residency. Some did it for the visa, but others were like me: driven by memories of their parents' and grandparents' kitchens; keen to be chefs and contribute to culinary tapestry of flavours of their new home. In Sydney, when we asked our kitchen hands to cook staff meals, incredible biriyanis were made and proud conversations took place about the bountiful seafood in the Bay of Bengal. It made for good stories and tasty staff meals.

The Bengal borders were witness to two prolific forced migrations: once in 1947 during the partitioning of British India and Pakistan, and again in 1971 with the formation of Bangladesh. Upwards of 13 million people were shifted each time, meaning Bangladesh is home to more than 135 ethnic groups and now shares borders with India and Myanmar, with influences from China, Thailand and Laos. The historical partitioning of India is still raw, and can be seen at its ugliest on Bangladesh's northern border with India.

It is safe to say that the cuisine of Bangladesh is diverse and eclectic — a delicious clash of the spicy rich curries of India, the garlicky sweet sauces of China, and the bright herb-filled salads and soups of Thailand. There's nothing quite like it.

Essential flavours: Ghee, milder chillies (such as Kashmiri chillies), cardamom, cloves, cinnamon, lime, tamarind, leafy greens.

The role of vegetables: Given its close proximity to India, vegetarianism is quite widely accepted in Bangladesh, and vegetables feature quite prominently in Bangladeshi cuisine.

Rice is the main staple, often served with strong aromatic curries, which include eggs, potatoes, tomatoes and eggplants. A variety of spices and herbs, along with mustard oil and ghee, are used in Bangladeshi cooking. As in many countries across the subcontinent, dhal and breads, from naan to paratha, play an important role at the table.

BHUTAN

Spice is king across Bhutan. Chillies are an essential part of nearly every dish and are considered so important that most Bhutanese people would not enjoy a meal that wasn't hot with spice.

Influenced by Tibetan, Nepalese and Indian food, Bhutanese cuisine is all about red rice (the only rice that grows at high altitude), buckwheat and meat, as well as warming and fortifying soups and stews during the harsh cold winters.

Bhutanese red rice has been grown for thousands of years at 2500 metres (8000 feet) in the fertile soil of the Paro Valley, irrigated by 1000-year-old glacier water, rich in trace minerals. It is perhaps the most unique rice we have ever encountered. With more potassium than commercial sports drinks and a significant amount of magnesium, this quick-cooking wholegrain is a nutritional and culinary superstar.

In Bhutan, red rice is frequently paired with mushrooms and hot chillies. It is perfect for those dishes in which rice holds the place of honour: pilaf, risotto, stir-fry, salad, pudding, or simply steamed to accompany vegetable, seafood and meat dishes.

Vegetables commonly eaten include spinach, pumpkin, turnip, radishes, tomatoes, river weed, onions and green beans. Grains such as buckwheat and barley are also cultivated in various regions of the country, depending on the local climate.

Essential flavours: Chilli, red rice, cheese, potatoes, dried beef, pork, sichuan pepper.

The role of vegetables: Due to the harsh conditions in many areas of Bhutan, vegetables can be scarce in the winter. Lom, which are turnip leaves, are one of the few vegetables that can be dried and preserved for eating throughout the year (the turnips themselves are fed to livestock). Spinach, green beans, onions, pumpkin (winter squash), radishes, cucumber, tomatoes, river weed and bitter melon are also eaten.

Clockwise from top left: The family in Colombo with Aunty Miri and Uncle Kenny, setting off on another adventure; Peter with his brother and parents, dressed-up and heading out in Colombo; Peter at Annapurna Base Camp with a Sherpa; Chatting with an Indian street person (all people are worthy of attention); Peter's wife, Karen, on the India–Nepal border; Travelling through Afghanistan in 1969.

The Subcontinental Pantry

The following ingredients are useful to have on hand in your kitchen when cooking recipes from across the subcontinent. Most are now widely available. For more information on specific spices, see pages 20–25.

ALEPPO PEPPER is adored for its slightly fruity flavour and mild chilli kick. Deep red in colour, this chilli variety is usually sold as crushed dried flakes. If unavailable, use smoked paprika.

BANANA FLOWER Found in Asian markets, banana flower, or kere kafool, tastes like artichoke and is used in salads and curries.

BANANA LEAVES These large pliable leaves are used in Asia to wrap foods for steaming or baking. They help retain moisture and infuse a mild flavour into food. They're also used as disposable plates.

BASIL SEEDS, SWEET Also called tukmaria, sabja, kasa kasa and falooda seeds, these tiny black seeds are full of fibre and widely used in sweet drinks. They are reputed to have many health benefits, including antioxidant, antibacterial, antiviral and antifungal properties.

BAY LEAVES Fragrant bay leaves, or tez patta, lend a refreshing, slightly spicy, herbal intensity to dishes. The recipes in this book always use fresh bay leaves.

BESAN Besan, or chickpea flour, makes a toothsome batter for fritters, and adds a nutty flavour to sweets and salty snacks.

CAYENNE PEPPER A type of finely ground chilli powder, with a heat level of about 8 out of 10. It is blended from a mix of different dried long hot (usually red) chillies, to give a consistent heat.

CHILLIES Most people are attracted to subcontinental food for two reasons: lots of flavour, and lots of heat! If you're after the heat, you should know a thing or two about chillies. It can often be hit or miss when it comes to chillies: sometimes you'll buy a batch that isn't very spicy, and sometimes they'll be eye-watering. The only way to tell is to break the chilli in half and dab it on your tongue.

Don't worry, you'll soon get used to it, and it's much better than putting too much in your dish and ruining it. Confusingly, each individual chilli variety can be known by many names, but here are the types most commonly found in Indian and Asian grocery stores.

Dried chillies Look for dried chillies that are soft, pliable and deeply coloured (brick reds, mahogany and black). They should be fragrant, and feel firm but fleshy, like a raisin or prune. Any that are dry, dusty or brittle are probably old, with little flavour. Dried red chillies are dried mature Serrano chillies. Nearly maroon in colour, they're great fried and added into tempered spices.

Fresh green chillies are known as unripe Serrano chillies, but I call them Indian green chillies; they are also called jwala chillies. Select ones that are bright green, crisp, plump, unwrinkled and unbruised. They add a herbal heat to stews and chutneys, and are also eaten raw as a condiment to spice up a meal.

Red chillies These are ripe Serranos; I call them Indian red chillies. Do not confuse either the unripe green Serranos or the ripe red Serranos with the long green and red chillies sold in supermarkets, and served in most restaurants. They make a great garnish and add a mild spice, but do not have the complexity of flavour due to their mass production. Toasting the dried red Indian chillies retains their scarlet tinge and brings out their spice, adding a punch to Indian dishes.

COCONUT In its many forms, coconut is key to so much cooking across the subcontinent. In Sri Lanka, the coconut palm is referred to as a gift of the gods. Every part of the tree is used — in building, for utensils, right down to the milk, the oil and of course the flesh. Finely grated in sambals and mallungs, added to curries and baked into sweet delights, it is the quintessential Sri Lankan ingredient.

Coconut aminos are a sauce made from coconut sap. Rich, salty and slightly sweet, you can use it as you would a tamari or soy sauce.

Coconut butter is the flesh of the coconut, ground into a butter. It's creamier than coconut oil, and makes a great dairy-free spread.

Coconut cream is the thick, creamy liquid that comes from the first pressing of the grated meat of a fresh coconut. It is incredibly rich, with an almost spreadable consistency. It is similar to coconut milk, but contains less water, giving it a thicker, paste-like texture. Use it much as you would coconut milk, in all types of sweet and savoury dishes.

Coconut flakes are the flaked dried meat of the coconut. They can be enjoyed raw or lightly toasted and make a great textural addition to recipes.

Coconut flesh is obtained by cracking open a fresh coconut and scraping out the flesh using a coconut scraper. It isn't the easiest thing to do at home, but you can also buy frozen scraped coconut flesh from Asian grocery stores.

Coconut flour is made by dehydrating coconut meat, then grinding it into a flour. It can be used as a gluten-free substitute for wheat flour in baking and savoury dishes, but be mindful that coconut flour soaks up liquid like a sponge, so you may have to increase your liquid ingredients to accommodate for this.

Coconut milk is the liquid that comes from the second extraction from the grated meat of a fresh coconut. It has a far thinner consistency than coconut cream. The rich taste of coconut milk can be attributed to the high saturated fat and oil content, so for the best flavour, always choose the full-fat version. Coconut milk imparts distinct flavour to south Indian cooking. It is great added to curries, and makes a delicious dairy-free milk alternative. Drizzle it on porridge, or use it as a base for smoothies. When buying tinned coconut cream or milk, always choose unsweetened varieties.

Coconut oil Extracted from mature coconuts, coconut oil is used throughout the subcontinent. In Sri Lanka, we used to cook with heat-extracted coconut oil, which is certainly not good for you. I cook with coconut oil because it makes food taste good, but these days I only use organic, unrefined virgin coconut oil, because it hasn't been heat treated, and therefore is a bit better for you. Coconut oil has been used for centuries, but since the virgin coconut oil sensation hit the West, all sorts of statements have been made about its amazing health benefits — yet some say it is as bad, or worse, than animal fat. (Interestingly, in the Pacific region, virgin coconut oil is used as a beauty product, for rubbing on the skin only.) I know people who drink it, and use it in everything. I am no scientist, but I can't imagine that copious amounts of any oil — or any ingredient, for that matter — can be good for you, especially oils that solidify. But as with anything, moderation is the word. Look for balance, flavour and texture, and enjoy your food. Just use it sparingly and enjoy its beauty.

Coconut sugar is produced by making several slits into the bud of a coconut tree and collecting the sap. The sap is then boiled until it thickens and solidifies. Coconut sugar is nearly 50 per cent fructose.

Coconut water is the tasty, clear liquid inside young coconuts. It contains several key electrolytes — essential minerals such as potassium, sodium, calcium, chloride, magnesium and phosphate, which are lost when we sweat or exercise — making it useful for hydrating the body. It also contains B vitamins, and enzymes that help digestion. In Sri Lanka, the orange-shelled king coconut, or thambili, is highly prized, and in fact used only for its very tasty water. Coconut water also comes bottled or packaged for convenience, but beware of flavoured or sweetened products. It should contain only coconut water and nothing else.

Desiccated coconut is coconut meat that has been finely shredded, then dried. Shredded coconut is similar, but has a coarser texture.

CUMIN With its rich earthy flavour, cumin is often called 'the curry spice'. The seeds are from a small flowering plant, which is native to the eastern Mediterranean and south Asia and looks similar to fennel. *See also pages 20–23.*

CURD The Sri Lankan name for buffalo yoghurt.

CURRY LEAVES The aromatic leaves of a tree from the rue family, used in southern Indian, Sri Lankan and Malaysian cooking. Fresh curry leaves, also known as karapincha (in Sri Lanka) and kadi patta (Hindi), lend their resinous fragrance to dishes from chutneys to curries, and are usually fried before using. Curry leaves are at their aromatic best when fresh, rather than the dried or powdered form.

CURRY POWDER Countless combinations of spices are used to produce an array of flavours suited to particular curries. Curry powder gets its colour, aroma and distinctive flavour from the dark roasting of its spice components, including coriander seeds, cumin seeds, fennel seeds, fenugreek and cardamom. Curries are generally classified as white (mild and rich in coconut milk); red (rich in chilli powder or ground chillies); or black (where powdered spice mixtures are given a deeper, richer flavour by dry-roasting them in a pan). *See also page 25.*

FENUGREEK A member of the pea family, grown in semi-arid regions; also known as methi. Fenugreek leaves have a sweet smell and a flavour reminiscent of maple, and can be used fresh or dried. The small square brown fenugreek seeds, either whole, or dried and ground, are used in virtually all Sri Lankan curries to thicken sauces and instil a faintly bittersweet, musky flavour; use in small quantities and heat slowly to reduce bitterness. *See also pages 20–21.*

GHEE A clarified butter, widely used across the subcontinent. *See also pages 106–107.*

GINGER Practically every curry dish includes ginger root, the tuber of a perennial plant grown throughout Asia. Look for young, firm, smooth-skinned ginger with a fresh, spicy fragrance; it should feel heavy for its size. Wrinkled flesh is an indication of aged ginger past its prime; it will be hotter and more fibrous. Wherever possible, choose organic ginger, as it spends a year underground and absorbs all it has been given. Remove the skin before using.

GORAKA A souring and thickening agent unique to Sri Lanka, goraka is a fluted orange or yellow fruit (also called gambodge). The segments are dried, turning black. They can be soaked in hot water and ground to a paste, or added whole and removed after cooking. It is most commonly used in fish curries.

MALDIVE FISH Intensely flavoured dried, cured fish (usually tuna), used in tiny quantities for its umami flavour, Maldive fish is to Sri Lankan cooking what dried shrimp and shrimp paste are to South-East Asian cuisines. It is also a thickening agent.

MINT A perennial herb native to north-west India, mint is ubiquitous in chutneys, relishes and other condiments, and brings cooling refreshment to drinks such as lassis. Dried mint might be stirred through a range of dishes or yoghurt sauce, or sprinkled liberally over steamed dumplings and fried vegetables.

MORINGA A long, ridged, dark green, triangular pod, often referred to as drumsticks, with juicy flesh and a slightly bitter flavour. It is a popular ingredient in vegetable curries, particularly kiri hodi or white curry. After cooking, discard the outer skin, before scooping out the pulp in the soft centre. The leaves are used to add sourness, and are good in seafood curries.

MUSTARD An annual herb, used since earliest recorded history. Many spice blends would be incomplete without mustard seeds, which lend a nutty flavour and crunch when fried, and are used to finish soups, sauces and curries.

MUSTARD OIL Also known as sarson ka tel, this is a peppery oil widely used in northern India; it mellows as it heats.

NIGELLA SEEDS Commonly used on Turkish bread, these small, very black seeds have a slightly sharp, almost metallic taste, and no noticeable aroma.

NUTMEG This aromatic, woody spice comes from the kernel within a fleshy fruit that resembles a peach and grows on an evergreen tree. The nutmeg shell is dried until it rattles; the thin outer shell is then removed, leaving the inner nutmeg, which can be grated or ground into a powder. Whole nutmegs should be sound and unbroken, with little or no evidence of worm activity.

OKRA Known as ladies' fingers throughout the subcontinent, okra is a pod from the mallow family that lends thickness to vegetable stews, yet crisps up beautifully in dry stir-fries.

PALM SUGAR Also known as jaggery, gur or lump cane sugar, this dark, coarse, unrefined sugar is usually sold in large chunks or compressed into a cake. It is made from boiled-down sugar cane juice, and tastes like soft brown sugar, with a subtle maple flavour. It is a key sweetening agent in Indian cooking.

PANDAN LEAVES Most Sri Lankan households grow the pandanus plant, which is frequently referred to as the vanilla of Asia. The long green leaves are not eaten, but used to infuse aroma and colour into curry dishes and rice, or used as a garnish.

PANEER Soft and crumbly, this fresh cheese is made from compressed milk curds. *See pages 94–95, 106–107.*

PEPPERCORNS All true pepper, whether black, white or green, comes from the berries of a tropical evergreen vine. The enzymes in the outer husk of the peppercorns turn the green berries black as they dry and give the characteristic flavour. Green peppercorns are picked green to prevent the enzymes turning them black. White pepper is made by soaking the nearly ripe peppercorns in water, then rubbing them to remove the outer husk before drying and grinding them. White pepper is hotter than black, but lacks the 'oily', spiciness of black pepper. Use whole black peppercorns when cooking Sri Lankan dishes.

POMEGRANATE Native to Persia (Iran) and parts of the subcontinent, this exotic, tangy and vividly coloured fruit has been cultivated throughout the Mediterranean since antiquity. The jewel-like seeds can be used whole, and the juice enjoyed fresh as a nutritious drink, or boiled down into a syrup (known as pomegranate molasses). A dried and powdered form is also available nowadays.

POPPY SEEDS Unlike their dark European counterpart, Indian poppy seeds are cream or grey-hued. The cream variety is preferred in Indian dishes.

PULSES A general name for the dried seeds of plants from the legume family. High in protein, pulses are essential to the subcontinental diet. *See pages 60–61.*

RICE An absolutely essential grain, rice is fundamental to subcontinental cooking. Many varieties are used; *see pages 158–161.*

RICE BRAN OIL A healthy oil with a high smoke point, extracted from the bran and germ of husked rice. It tastes good and is great when you need to sauté ingredients at a high temperature.

RICE FLOUR Ground from broken white rice, Indian rice flour is gluten-free and available in varying degrees of fineness.

ROSEWATER Indian rosewater is extracted from deep-red roses grown for their fragrance. Small amounts flavour desserts as well as meat dishes.

SAFFRON The stigmas of crocus flowers, saffron threads, or kesar, lend a golden hue and earthy flavour to savoury dishes, rice dishes and desserts. The most prized variety is grown in Kashmir.

SALT Different types of salt vary in strength and flavour. Always use the same brand, so you'll always know how much to add to your cooking. Himalayan 'black salt', or kala namak, which is often pink or purplish in colour, adds a pleasing sulfurous note to condiments and drinks. Rock salt is usually added to water and used partially dissolved.

SEMOLINA A flour ground from durum wheat; *see pages 174–175.*

STAR ANISE The dried seed pod of a shrub native to south-west China, star anise is added whole to stews and curries to provide a subtle licorice hit.

SULTANAS Also called golden raisins, sultanas are a vital ingredient in everything from Delhi-style pilaus to kheer puddings and spicy snack mixes.

TAMARIND The edible pulp of a pod-like fruit, with a tangy sweet–sour flavour; *see pages 210–211.*

TURMERIC Used in almost every curry in small quantities, turmeric, a rhizome from the ginger family, adds a beautiful yellow colour and is a good substitute for saffron. Ground turmeric is mildly aromatic with a pungent, bitter flavour, and gives spice blends their signature golden hue. Turmeric can also be used fresh.

YOGHURT Thick natural yoghurt is used extensively in Afghan cuisine, and in many dishes across the subcontinent. Chakah (yoghurt drained until it becomes the texture of soft cream cheese) is the basis of sauces, dips and drinks, and is added to curries. Yoghurt is a cultured product, made by fermenting milk with beneficial bacteria.

Cooking with Spices

Spices are the crux of cooking across the subcontinent. For me, the intoxicating aroma of spices being ground or cooked is the scent of my childhood, my travels and my connection to place — there is nothing more beautiful than the smell of spices as they evolve and intensify.

Depending on how you handle spices, their flavour profile can change dramatically. From the blooming of spices in oil before building a curry, to sizzling onions and chilli in ghee to fold through dhal, understanding how to work with spices is key to releasing their full potential and intensifying their glorious spectrum of flavours.

When dry-roasted, a spice's flavour changes in fundamental ways: volatile aromatics begin to cook off, while compounds in the spice recombine to form new flavours that are often deeper, roasted and earthier.

Frying spices in oil gives a completely different flavour to dry-roasting. It tends to enhance the original flavours of a spice, making them bolder and more intense, almost as if they've become more sure of themselves. In short, oil-fried spices have a brighter, fresher aroma than dry-roasted spices.

Dry-roasting spices, on the other hand, will bring out volatile compounds and propel aromatics through the air, so be prepared to cough a bit, especially when roasting chilli. It is also good to dry-roast the spices whole — this really intensifies their flavour, especially with cumin seeds and coriander seeds. When you then grind these spices using a mortar and pestle, they release their magic, an intense and wonderful aroma and flavour that travels directly into your food.

Fenugreek seeds should always be dry-roasted. Whenever I buy them, I roast the whole packet to use over the following weeks. Never, ever, use burnt fenugreek — it will make your entire curry bitter.

When frying spices in oil, the flavours tend to open out rather than intensify. Spices such as mustard seeds pop like popcorn, releasing their flavours; while others intensify and flavour the ghee, spreading their taste through the entire mix.

TEMPERING

Frying spices in oil to release essential oils is known as tempering. The aromatics created are nothing short of phenomenal. There are three main ways to fry spices.

FRYING IN A SMALL QUANTITY OF OIL

1. Heat a small amount of vegetable oil, virgin coconut oil or ghee until hot. Add any tougher spices such as cinnamon sticks, black peppercorns or dried red chillies. Sometimes these spices are ground first, but not always.
2. Add any seeds next, in quick succession. It's not uncommon to also add some chopped onion or grated fresh coconut, to add flavour and body to the final dish. The onion and coconut also act as a buffer by introducing a small amount of water to the oil, lessening the risk of the smaller seeds and spices burning.
3. Once the spices have been fried and smell aromatic, grind the mixture to a paste with a spice grinder. This can be added to your ingredients, as you would paste from a jar (except it will taste amazing because it is free of preservatives and pH balancers, which always inhibit the real flavour of food).

FRYING SLOWLY WITH ONION

This is known as bhunooing, or slow-frying with onion. The purpose is to build flavour slowly.

Bhunooing results in creamy, rich flavours by the gentle extraction of oils from the spices and the slow cooking of onions until they are melting and sweet. This method does not require grinding, so to get the beautiful hues of a curry, powdered spices such as red chilli, turmeric and coriander are often added at the very end of the slow-frying process. Take special care: powdered spices are fragile and can scorch easily.

1. Add a large quantity of oil or ghee — up to 125 ml (4 fl oz/ ½ cup) for a biriyani, for example — to the pan and heat until smoking, then lower the heat.
2. Add any whole spices, such as cinnamon sticks, cardamom pods, cloves, cumin seeds, star anise and bay leaves, and fry gently, allowing them to change colour.
3. Add chopped onions, reduce the heat to low and cook, stirring, for about 3 minutes, until they're a lovely golden colour. Use as a garnish on rice, as a condiment, or to add deep flavour to your stir-fries.

FRYING QUICKLY IN HOT OIL

With this method the spices are usually ground with fresh garlic and ginger too, and they are added to the oil all at once. This is often done when the rest of the dish has been cooked. The heat is kept high and the spices are allowed to splatter and splutter, sizzle and pop as they release their aromas into the fat. The piping-hot oil is poured directly onto the waiting dish to liven it up and add aroma, as a finishing touch.

This is the key to dishes such as dhal and tamarind chutney: the hot tempered spices are quickly stirred in, then the dish is brought to the boil, turned off and left for a few minutes for the flavours to combine.

1. Add a tablespoon or two of oil or ghee to a pan over high heat and cook until smoking.
2. Add small quantities of whole spices such as cumin seeds, coriander seeds, black mustard seeds, cardamom pods, dried red chillies and cinnamon sticks.
3. Whole cinnamon sticks will start to unfurl, cumin and coriander seeds will turn a shade darker, cardamom pods will puff, mustard seeds will pop, and dried chillies will turn brown in patches — and all of this happens in just 30 seconds to a minute.

TEMPERING TIPS

Watch, watch, watch and smell! Spices can go from toasty and fragrant to burnt in seconds. Since you are adding spices within seconds of each other, it is handy to have them already measured out, so you're not fumbling around with a bunch of spice bottles.

Start by sizzling whole spices (they take longer to 'bloom' than ground). Keep stirring or shaking the pan so they cook evenly. Ground spices bloom in a few seconds, often after a quick stir, so add these last.

Use an appropriately sized saucepan. A limited surface area helps the spices fry more efficiently.

While you can get away with using only ground spices, fresh whole spices that are fried first and then ground lend dishes a robustness and an unmistakable silkiness and depth that's often unachievable with ground versions. When spices are at their freshest, they give out the best flavour possible, so buy in small quantities and store spices in airtight containers in a dark place, away from sunlight.

CURING PANS

The heat of the pan is crucial when cooking food of the subcontinent: you need the pan performing optimally, from delivering flash heat to high dry heat for cooking spices to release their flavours. Whenever you buy a new wok or pan, always 'cure' it before using, to make it non-stick.

1. Wash your cookware with hot water and soap, as a protective film is often applied by manufacturers.
2. Dry thoroughly and place on the stove. Turn the heat on and pour in a small amount of vegetable oil.
3. Using a clean tea towel or paper towel, carefully rub the oil over the surface to form a thin layer. Turn the heat up high until the oil just reaches smoke point. Remove from the heat.
4. Once the pan has cooled, repeat the process several times, until nothing sticks when cooked in it.

To care for your pan, wash it with warm soapy water while it is still hot, and never in the dishwasher.

Curing cast-iron frying pans regularly also helps to protect the surface of your favourite cookware. This process is simple.

1. Heat a good layer of salt in the pan until the pan gets very hot.
2. Using a soft, heat-resistant brush, gently rub the salt over the surface. Toss the salt away and use a clean tea towel to coat the pan's surface with a thin layer of oil.

Whole spices

Aromatic spices were once worth more than gold, used to flavour food and perfumes, and as medicines and currency. The subcontinent is blessed with an abundance of native spices, while others have found their way into its varied cuisines via ancient traders who crisscrossed the world.

1. **FENNEL SEEDS** have a mild sweet aniseed flavour. In Sri Lanka, roasted ground fennel seeds are a principal ingredient in curry powders.

2. **AJWAIN SEEDS** Also called carom or bishop's weed. They have a thyme-like aroma, and are often used in bean dishes for their gas-fighting properties.

3. **CORIANDER SEEDS** Sometimes called Chinese parsley, both the seeds and leaves of this fragrant herb are widely used in the subcontinent.

4. **DRIED CHILLIES** Choose ones that are soft, pliable, deeply coloured and fragrant, and feel firm but fleshy, like a raisin or prune.

5. **SWEET BASIL SEEDS** Also called tukmaria, sabja, kasa kasa and falooda seeds, these tiny black seeds feature in sweet Asian drinks.

6. **BLACK CARDAMOM** These smoky black pods add a camphor-like perfume to rice dishes and sweets.

7. **BLACK SESAME SEEDS** The unhulled seeds of the sesame plant impart a delicate, nutty flavour to dishes.

8. **KASHMIRI CHILLIES** Like a subcontinental paprika, and less spicy than Indian red chillies, they lend a smoky, earthy note to dishes.

9. **SICHUAN PEPPERCORNS** aren't a true pepper, as they come from the prickly ash shrub. They are famed for their mouth-numbing effect.

10. **BLACK MUSTARD SEEDS** Can be used whole or finely ground. Try frying them whole in oil with curry leaves and onion, or dry-roasting them in a pan.

11. **DILL SEEDS** look similar to cumin seeds, but have their own unique flavour, and are added whole to pickles, chutneys and vegetables during cooking.

12. **FENUGREEK SEEDS** are used in virtually all Sri Lankan curries to thicken sauces and instil a faintly bittersweet, musky flavour; use in small quantities and heat slowly to reduce bitterness.

13. **CARAWAY SEEDS** have a warm, slightly sweet anise flavour that works well in many Indian dishes.

14. **WHITE SESAME SEEDS** These are the hulled seeds of the sesame plant, and the type most widely used in cooking.

15. **YELLOW MUSTARD SEEDS** are larger and not as hot as black or brown mustard seeds, and in subcontinental cooking are the least preferred.

16. **CINNAMON STICKS** A significant spice in Sri Lankan cooking, used in sweet and savoury dishes. Whole sticks ground for the meal at hand are far superior to pre-ground cinnamon.

17. **CHILLI FLAKES** are better suited to some dishes than chilli powder. For the freshest flavour, choose one without dust in the bottom of the bag or bottle.

18. **PANCH PHORON** A Bengali spice mix, containing fennel, black mustard, nigella, fenugreek and cumin seeds. It is usually toasted or fried before using.

19. **CUMIN SEEDS** Dried or roasted cumin seeds, ground into a powder, are an essential element of most spice blends across the subcontinent. Black cumin seeds, called kala jeera, are slightly sweeter, with lemony caraway notes.

20. **BLACK PEPPERCORNS** The dried berries of a tropical evergreen vine.

21. **GREEN CARDAMOM** Related to ginger, the pods, seeds and ground seeds of this fragrant spice are used in sweets, curries, rice dishes and chai.

Dried spices

The colours of all the different spices just make me want to cook and experiment. I hope you enjoy navigating your own journey down the spice trail I have left for you, and make spices a part of your daily life.

1. AMCHUR POWDER is made from dried, unripe mangoes and imparts a sour, tangy flavour to soups, curries and vegetables.

2. GROUND CARDAMOM is often used in sweets, as an easy way to add a warm, exotic flavour.

3. ROAST CHILLI POWDER is made from whole chillies that have been toasted to intensify their flavour and colour, before being ground to a powder.

4. GROUND CUMIN With its rich earthy flavour, cumin is often called 'the curry spice'.

5. HIMALAYAN PINK SALT is sold ground or in rock form. It is also known as kala namak, and is sometimes heated until black in colour. It lends a pleasing sulfurous note to condiments and drinks.

6. GROUND CORIANDER is used in most masala spice blends, but loses flavour quite rapidly, so it's best to freshly grind the seeds as required.

7. DARK ROASTED CURRY POWDER has a deeper colour and more powerful flavour than raw curry powder; see spice blend recipe on page 25.

8. CHILLI POWDER is made from ground dried chillies. Stick to one brand, to be sure you're familiar with the intensity.

9. GARAM MASALA An Indian spice blend, used for warmth rather than heat; see recipe on page 24.

10. SMOKED PAPRIKA is made from pimiento peppers that have been smoked, then dried and ground. It adds flavour, colour and a light smokiness to dishes.

11. TURMERIC Used in almost every curry in small quantities, turmeric, a rhizome from the ginger family, adds a beautiful yellow colour and is a good substitute for saffron. Ground turmeric is mildly aromatic with a pungent, bitter flavour, and gives spice blends their signature golden hue.

12. GROUND CINNAMON is great in desserts, but make sure it is *real* cinnamon, not cassia.

13. GROUND CLOVES Cloves are the extremely aromatic dried flower buds of a variety of myrtle tree. Whether ground or left whole, cloves imbue dishes and curries with their pungent spice.

14. JAFFNA CURRY POWDER A hot spice blend from northern Sri Lanka and southern India; see recipe on page 25.

15. CHAAT MASALA A tangy, sour and salty spice mix that is widely used in Indian snacks and street foods, and is usually sprinkled over just before serving. See recipe on page 24.

16. GROUND NUTMEG This warmly aromatic, woody spice is commonly used in sweet dishes and complements vegetables such as pumpkin, carrot and spinach. For the freshest flavour, hole dried nutmeg kernels can be grated or ground into a powder.

17. ASAFOETIDA Named for its foetid aroma, and also known as hing, asafoetida is the dried resinous sap of a variety of giant fennel, and comes in powder or lump form. Cooked, it has an onion-like flavour, and is especially prized by those who refrain from eating onion or garlic, such as the Jains and Hare Krishnas.

18. RAW CURRY POWDER Raw or unroasted curry powder is the variety typically sold in supermarkets; in Sri Lankan cooking it is traditionally used in vegetarian curries. See recipe on page 25.

Spice blends

Spices are used to phenomenal effect across the subcontinent. Too often people associate spice with heat, but it is also used to create depth and zing and interest in a dish. It is well worth your time and effort to make these spice blends and store them in your cupboard — I promise they will take your cooking to the next level. Each of them will keep in a small airtight jar for up to 1 year.

Garam masala

Literally meaning 'warm spice', garam masala is an Indian staple. The exact blend of spices varies between households and regions, though it typically includes cinnamon, cardamom, cloves, cumin, coriander, nutmeg and black peppercorns. It adds warmth and depth of flavour, rather than heat.

MAKES 100 g (3½ oz)

2 cinnamon sticks (not cassia!)
10 green cardamom pods
8 black cardamom pods
15 cloves
1 tablespoon cumin seeds
1 tablespoon coriander seeds
1 tablespoon black peppercorns
½ teaspoon freshly grated nutmeg
2 dried red Kashmiri chillies

Place a dry heavy-based frying pan over medium–high heat until fully heated and slightly smoking. Add all the ingredients and shake and stir for about a minute, or until the spices smell toasted, are slightly darker, and give off just a slight bit of smoke. Tip into a bowl and leave to cool.

Grind to a fine powder, using a spice grinder or mortar and pestle, and store in an airtight container.

Chaat masala

A unique blend of spicy, salty and tart, this is the spice mix that lends instant zing to many Indian snacks and street foods, and is often added just before serving. I got sick of just about everything having this flavour, due to the asafoetida and black salt. The latter is quite sulfurous; the asafoetida needs to be used sparingly. While you will find slight variations all over India, Pakistan, Nepal and Bangladesh, this recipe has the tang and flavour that I like in small amounts.

MAKES 100 g (3½ oz)

3 tablespoons cumin seeds
1 tablespoon coriander seeds
1½ teaspoons fennel seeds
4 tablespoons amchur (dried mango powder)
3 tablespoons powdered black salt
1½ teaspoons freshly ground black pepper
¼ teaspoon asafoetida
1½ teaspoons ground ginger
1 teaspoon dried powdered mint
1½ teaspoons ajwain seeds
1 teaspoon citric acid, optional

In a dry heavy-based frying pan, toast the cumin, coriander and fennel seeds over low heat for about 3–5 minutes, stirring often, until dark brown. Remove from the pan and leave to cool.

Using a spice grinder or mortar and pestle, grind all the ingredients into a fine powder. Store in an airtight container.

Jaffna curry powder

Great with seafood, as well as vegetables, this bright red spice mix is used in northern Sri Lanka and southern India. It is quite hot, so adjust the quantity of dried chillies and black pepper to suit your taste.

MAKES 350 g (12 oz)

25 g (1 oz/¼ cup) cumin seeds
35 g (1¼ oz/⅓ cup) fennel seeds
2½ teaspoons fenugreek seeds
125 g (4½ oz) dried red chillies, with or
    without stalks
150 g (5½ oz/1⅔ cups) coriander seeds
3 tablespoons whole black peppercorns
2.5 cm (1 inch) knob of fresh turmeric, peeled
2 fresh curry leaf sprigs, leaves picked

In a dry heavy-based frying pan, over low heat, toast the cumin, fennel and fenugreek seeds for a minute or two, stirring often. When the fennel seeds are golden, tip the spices into a bowl and set aside.

In the same pan, dry-roast the remaining ingredients separately, stirring constantly to avoid burning or over-roasting any of the ingredients, adding them to the bowl to cool as each batch is done, but keeping the curry leaves separate.

Using a spice grinder, grind all the ingredients, except the curry leaves, to a fine powder. Add the curry leaves and allow to cool before storing.

Raw curry powder

This is great for vegetable curries, and is best cooked with the vegetables. Use it as you would a store-bought curry powder. It is perfect for curried egg sandwiches.

MAKES 100 g (3½ oz)

6 tablespoons coriander seeds
2 tablespoons cumin seeds
1 teaspoon fennel seeds
1 teaspoon brown mustard seeds
1 x 5 cm (2 inch) cinnamon stick, crumbled

4 cloves
4 green cardamom pods
5 dried curry leaves
1 teaspoon whole black peppercorns

Turn on your kitchen exhaust fan, so you don't have a houseful of coughing people.

Heat all the spices in a dry heavy-based frying pan over medium heat for a few minutes, stirring often, until aromatic and golden brown. Tip into a small bowl to cool.

Grind to a fine powder, using a spice grinder, and store in an airtight container.

Dark roasted curry powder

This powder looks good and tastes amazing, and is wonderful sprinkled over your finished curry, or even a salad. When cooking a meat-style curry, this is the one to use.

MAKES 250 g (9 oz)

90 g (3¼ oz/1 cup) coriander seeds
3 fresh curry leaf sprigs, leaves picked
2 teaspoons cloves
2 teaspoons green cardamom pods
2 cinnamon sticks, crushed
2 teaspoons raw rice
2 teaspoons fenugreek seeds
2 teaspoons brown mustard seeds
2 teaspoons fennel seeds
50 g (1¾ oz/½ cup) cumin seeds
5 dried red chillies, crumbled (including the seeds)

Toast the coriander seeds and curry leaves in a dry heavy-based frying pan over medium heat. After a couple of minutes, add the cloves, cardamom, cinnamon and rice and toast until golden brown.

Now add the fenugreek, mustard, fennel and cumin seeds and dry-roast for a few more minutes, or until fragrant, taking care not to burn them. Finally add the chilli pieces and toast for a minute or so.

Tip into a small bowl to cool. Grind to a powder, using a spice grinder or mortar and pestle, and store in an airtight container.

Chapter 1

Street Food

Nothing can hold a candle to the culinary pleasures of street food.

Often, when we travel, we want to discover the cultural traits of a country. What is it that makes this place and its people special? What are they all about? In my opinion, nothing will give you a more definitive glimpse into a community than its street food. And the subcontinent is home to some of the most vibrant and prolific street food cultures in the world.

Across the subcontinent, street food is the pride and joy of its people and something that immediately connects me to this special region.

I love the perfectionism, with each vendor specialising in one particular food so that they can give you their very best, be it a lassi, or a hot puri with a dollop of spiced chickpeas, tamarind chutney and yoghurt. Whatever the dish, it is immediate, vibrant and so damn tasty. Culinary traditions overlap and interact, often in very frenetic ways, to create some of the best foods I have ever tasted.

It is this pride in the cooking, and the personal interaction with each vendor, that gives street food its beating heart. I love how it blurs between the personal and the private: quality food in an intimate setting juxtaposed with an intense energy. The smell, the jostling of elbows, the vibrancy and the noise, the excitement and happiness that comes with food that you can tear and dredge and scoop and roll — all while trying not to spill it down your front.

I think this is why so many people shy away from making street food at home: they feel it's never quite the same as the real thing. But I encourage you to try. If anything, it will connect you to the experience you had, or you might get the chance to try new flavours, and that alone is well worth attempting. So much so that I've dedicated a chapter in this book to it.

I've spent longer living away from Sri Lanka than I have living there, yet it is still home for me. The food that lines its streets will forever be my language. For me, it is comfort, sadness, happiness, belonging, excitement and pure undiluted joy, and it defines me, whether I want it to or not. So, as you can imagine, it has been difficult for me to whittle down the amazing street foods of the subcontinent to one or two from each region, but I have selected recipes that are both close to my heart and show the vegetable as king. All of them give that instant satisfying hit that only the best street foods can bring.

Fried leek pastries

Afghanistan is a fascinating country in which to research vegetarian meals, because some believe it is their god-given right to eat meat, and vegetarians are often shunned. Traditionally these pastries, known as boolawnee, also contain chicken — but they are so stunningly tasty they need no meat at all. Serve with Mint chutney (page 219), Chutney for momos (page 221) or Tomato chilli jam (page 229).

REGION Afghanistan | **MAKES** about 30 | **PREPARATION** 1 hour + 30 minutes resting
COOKING 10 minutes + 3–5 minutes per batch | **DIFFICULTY** Medium

vegetable oil, for deep-frying

PASTRY
300 g (10½ oz/2 cups) plain (all-purpose) flour, plus extra for dusting
½ teaspoon salt
20 g (¾ oz) butter
170 ml (5½ fl oz/⅔ cup) iced water

LEEK FILLING
3 teaspoons rice bran oil
1 garlic clove, crushed
2 whole leeks, white part only, washed well and diced
2 teaspoons salt
¼ teaspoon hot chilli powder

For the pastry, sift the flour and salt into a bowl. Working quickly, rub in the butter until the mixture resembles breadcrumbs; having cool hands will really help here, as the butter may otherwise melt.

Make a well in the centre, pour in the water and mix to a firm dough. Turn out onto a lightly floured work surface and knead for 5 minutes, or until elastic, dusting with more flour if necessary. Wrap the dough in plastic wrap and leave to rest in the fridge for 30 minutes.

Meanwhile, get started on the filling. Heat the rice bran oil in a small frying pan over medium heat and cook the garlic for a minute or two, until lightly coloured. Tip the garlicky oil into a small bowl and leave to cool.

Measure out 3 cups of the leek and place in a bowl. Add the salt and chilli powder and knead with your hands, to soften the leek. Stir in the garlic oil. Place the mixture in a heavy-based frying pan and heat through for about 3–5 minutes, until the leek softens, then remove from the heat and leave to cool.

Roll pieces of the dough into balls the size of a large hazelnut, then roll each out thinly, into a 10 cm (4 inch) circle. (Alternatively, roll out the dough and cut into 10 cm/4 inch rounds using a cookie cutter.)

Place about 2 teaspoons of the leek filling in the centre of each circle. Moisten the pastry halfway round the edge of the circle, then fold the pastry over the filling. Press the edges together to seal well.

Using the edge of a thimble (the traditional method) or a teaspoon, make little crescent-shaped marks around the pastry edge, or decorate by pressing with the tines of a fork.

Pour about 10 cm (4 inches) of vegetable oil into a deep heavy-based saucepan and heat to 180°C (350°F), or until a cube of bread dropped into the oil turns brown in 15 seconds.

Fry three or four pastries at a time in the hot oil for about 3–5 minutes per batch, or until golden brown, turning with tongs to brown them evenly. Be careful, as the hot oil will spit! Drain on paper towel while cooking the remaining pastries.

Enjoy the pastries hot or warm, with your choice of chutney or relish.

Buckwheat & cabbage momos

Momos originated in Tibet — but with the movement of the Tibetan people around the world, every country in the mountainous areas of the subcontinent consider momos as their own. This cabbage and buckwheat momo, however, is uniquely Bhutanese. The great thing with these is that you can fry or steam them.

REGION Bhutan | **MAKES** about 30 | **PREPARATION** 1 hour
COOKING 15 minutes + 7–8 minutes per batch | **DIFFICULTY** Medium

To make the filling, put the cabbage in a covered steamer basket over a wok or saucepan of simmering water for 5 minutes. Drain well, leave to cool, then squeeze dry. Finely chop the cabbage, place in a large bowl and set aside.

Using a spice or coffee grinder, pulverise the poppy seeds and peppercorns to a fine powder. Add to the cabbage, along with the onion, garlic, ginger, feta, chilli powder and salt and mix until well combined.

Melt the butter in a frying pan and brown over medium–high heat, stirring often, for about 4 minutes; browning the butter will add a nutty flavour to the filling. Leave to cool, then strain through a sieve lined with muslin (cheesecloth).

Add the browned butter to the filling and mix well.

To make the dough, combine the flours and oil in a bowl, then work in 250 ml (9 fl oz/1 cup) water until the dough forms a ball, adding a little more water if necessary. Dust the ball with flour and knead for about 5 minutes, until the dough feels smooth and silky; it should not be sticky, nor should it be dry.

Cut the dough into eight equal portions. Dust them with flour, then wrap seven of the pieces in plastic wrap to stop them drying out.

Roll the rested dough into a long thick rope. Cut off finger-width pieces and roll each one into a 2.5 cm (1 inch) ball. Use a rolling pin to flatten a piece of dough, into a nice circle. Add a tablespoon of filling to the centre and pinch the edges shut, into the desired shape; most momos are crescent-shaped. Like all things this needs practice; you can also watch the technique demonstrated online if needed.

Repeat with the remaining dough and filling.

In a large saucepan of simmering water, cook the dumplings in batches for 7–8 minutes, or until the pastry is cooked through.

Serve hot, with the momo chutney.

TIP Instead of steaming the dumplings, you can fry them in hot unrefined peanut oil for 3–5 minutes on each side, over medium heat. Drain on paper towel and serve immediately.

Chutney for momos (page 221), to serve

CABBAGE FILLING
½ white cabbage, roughly chopped
3 tablespoons poppy seeds
¼ teaspoon sichuan peppercorns
1 small red onion, finely chopped
2 garlic cloves, finely chopped
1 teaspoon very finely chopped fresh ginger
65 g (2¼ oz/½ cup) crumbled feta cheese
1 teaspoon chilli powder
¼ teaspoon salt
120 g (4¼ oz) unsalted butter

BUCKWHEAT DOUGH
300 g (10½ oz/2 cups) plain (all-purpose) flour, plus extra for dusting
130 g (4½ oz/1 cup) buckwheat flour
60 ml (2 fl oz/¼ cup) vegetable oil

Aloo chop
Stuffed potato dumplings

I first discovered these seriously tasty vegetarian dumplings in Madras (now known as Chennai), when I was scared to eat anything containing meat through fear of food poisoning! Bright red inside, they look fantastic, and are adaptable to a range of meals. I serve these on one of my most popular curries, which happens to be a fish curry.

REGION India | **MAKES** about 30 | **PREPARATION** 1 hour
COOKING 45 minutes + 3–5 minutes per batch | **DIFFICULTY** Medium

300 g (10½ oz) beetroot (beet)
rock salt, for spreading
1 kg (2 lb 4 oz) good boiling potatoes, such as russet or sebago, peeled and cut into quarters
300 g (10½ oz) sweet potato, peeled
300 g (10½ oz) frozen peas (or fresh peas, if they are young and not too tough)
150 g (5½ oz) cauliflower, cut into florets
1 tablespoon virgin coconut oil
1 small brown onion, chopped
3 garlic cloves, crushed
1 small knob of fresh ginger, peeled and finely grated
½ teaspoon ground turmeric
2 teaspoons chilli powder
125 g (4½ oz/⅔ cup) raisins
3 Indian green chillies, chopped
2 tablespoons Garam masala (page 24)
Tomato chilli jam (page 229), to serve
chopped lettuce, to serve

FOR CRUMBING
150 g (5½ oz/1 cup) plain (all-purpose) flour
300 ml (10½ fl oz) milk
6 eggs
240 g (8½ oz/4 cups) panko breadcrumbs or fresh sourdough crumbs
500 ml (17 fl oz/2 cups) vegetable oil, for deep-frying

Preheat the oven to 180°C (350°F). Bake the beetroot on a bed of rock salt for 30–40 minutes, or until cooked through; the rock salt concentrates the heat from the oven and allows the beetroot to 'dry' cook, so it won't make your dumplings too wet. Allow to cool, then remove the skin.

Meanwhile, bring a large saucepan of water to the boil over high heat. Cook the potato and sweet potato for about 15–20 minutes, or until just cooked when tested with a skewer, but not falling apart. Remove using a slotted spoon and place in a covered bowl to sit and dry out.

Blanch the peas in the same water for about 2 minutes, then remove with a slotted spoon. Blanch the cauliflower for about 4 minutes, then remove. Drain all the vegetables thoroughly, then place in a large bowl. Add the beetroot and mash them all together using a large fork or potato masher; do not use a blender, or the potatoes will become starchy and mess up your mixture. Set aside.

Heat the coconut oil in a frying pan over medium heat. Add the onion and cook for about 5 minutes, or until browned, stirring often. Add the garlic and ginger and cook for another minute or two, until they just take on some colour. Stir in the turmeric and chilli powder and continue to cook for a few minutes.

Add the mashed vegetables and mix thoroughly. Stir in the raisins, green chilli and garam masala. Season to taste, then shape into balls the size of golf balls.

To prepare for crumbing, combine the flour, milk and eggs in a large bowl and mix into a smooth batter. Spread the breadcrumbs in a wide shallow bowl.

Dip the dumplings into the batter, then roll them in the crumbs, making sure they stick well. (You can chill them at this point, if making ahead; leave at room temperature for 15 minutes before cooking them, or they'll be cold in the middle.)

Heat the vegetable oil in a heavy-based saucepan to 180°C (350°F), or until a cube of bread dropped into the oil turns brown in 15 seconds. Working in batches, fry the dumplings for 3–5 minutes, or until golden and cooked through. Drain on paper towel and keep warm while cooking the remaining dumplings.

Serve hot, with the tomato chilli jam, on chopped lettuce.

Malpua
Fried pancakes

Enjoyed as a snack or dessert, malpua are famously prepared during the holy month of Ramadan by Muslim families across India, Pakistan and Bangladesh to break their fast. In some regions the batter is prepared by crushing ripe bananas (or in Bangladesh, coconut), adding flour, and water or milk, and perhaps a pinch of cardamom. It is deep-fried in oil and served hot. The Bihari version has sugar added to the batter prior to frying, while in nearby Odisha the fritters are dipped in syrup after they are fried.

In northern India, malpua don't contain fruit, but may contain maida (refined flour), semolina, milk and yoghurt. After resting for a few hours, the batter is spooned into hot oil to form a crisp-edged bubbling pancake, which is then immersed in a thick sugar syrup.

REGION India | **SERVES** 4 | **PREPARATION** 5 minutes + 6 hours resting
COOKING 15 minutes + 2–5 minutes per batch/pancake | **DIFFICULTY** Medium

---

To make the batter, combine the flour, palm sugar, baking powder, fennel seeds, poppy seeds, cardamom and a pinch of salt in a large bowl. Stir in the warm milk and whipped yoghurt. Add a bit more milk if needed to make the batter of pouring consistency. Cover with a tea towel or plastic wrap and leave to rest at room temperature for 5–6 hours.

Near serving time, prepare the syrup. Pour the water into a large saucepan and bring to the boil over high heat. Add the sugar. Allow the mixture to come up to a bubble without stirring, then reduce the heat to low and cook until the syrup reaches the 'soft ball stage', or 105–110°C (220–230°C) on a sugar thermometer. To test, dip a spatula in the liquid, then carefully place a drop of sugar syrup on your forefinger. Touch your finger to your thumb: the syrup is ready when it sticks onto your thumb, with just one thread. If the syrup is thicker, stir in a little more water, bring it back to the boil and turn off the heat. Stir in the cardamom pods, set aside and keep warm.

In a non-stick frying pan, heat about 2.5 cm (1 inch) oil over medium–high heat, to 170°C (325°F), or until a cube of bread dropped into the oil turns brown in 20 seconds.

Reduce the heat to low. Pour a ladleful of batter into the oil and fry for 1–2 minutes, until golden brown underneath, then turn and cook on the other side. Drain on paper towel, then immediately immerse in the warm sugar syrup.

Repeat with the remaining batter; depending on the size of your pan, you may be able to cook two or three at a time.

Garnish with the almonds and serve as soon as possible, while the malpua are warm and juicy.

TIP To keep the malpua perfectly round, use a steel egg ring in the pan when frying them.

rice bran or grapeseed oil, for shallow-frying
1 tablespoon chopped almonds

BATTER
150 g (5½ oz/1 cup) plain (all-purpose) flour
250 g (9 oz/2 cups, lightly packed) grated white palm sugar (jaggery)
¼ teaspoon baking powder
1 teaspoon fennel seeds
½ teaspoon poppy seeds
¼ teaspoon ground cardamom
a pinch of salt
125 ml (4 fl oz/½ cup) warm milk
70 g (2½ oz/¼ cup) Greek-style yoghurt or buffalo curd, whipped with a whisk until smooth

CARDAMOM SYRUP
750 ml (26 fl oz/3 cups) water
285 g (10 oz/1½ cups) rapadura sugar or grated palm sugar (jaggery)
6 green cardamom pods, cracked

Mumbai frankie

Originally a simple man's food to help get through the day, this quick and filling dish hails from Mumbai, as the name would suggest. It is an amazing snack for those on the run — spicy, tasty and so easy to make. The amchur adds a lovely sourness to this beautifully flavoursome, energy-dense vegetarian dish. If you don't have time to make your own roti, this dish also works really well with frozen roti parathas, from the freezer section of Asian grocery stores.

REGION India | **MAKES** 4 | **PREPARATION** 20 minutes
COOKING about 30 minutes | **DIFFICULTY** Medium

4 cooked roti, preferably roti canai
melted butter or ghee, for brushing
1 large onion, finely chopped
1 teaspoon frankie masala (a spice mix readily available in spice shops), or Chaat masala (page 24)

MASALA WATER
80 ml (2½ fl oz/⅓ cup) water
1½ teaspoons amchur (dried mango powder)
½ teaspoon chilli powder
¼ teaspoon Garam masala (page 24)
a pinch of salt

STUFFING
1½ tablespoons rice bran oil or butter
1 teaspoon Ginger garlic paste (page 241)
400 g (14 oz/1¾ cups) mashed potato
¾ teaspoon chilli powder
1 teaspoon Garam masala (page 24)
½ teaspoon Chaat masala (page 24; optional)
1 tablespoon finely chopped coriander (cilantro)
a generous pinch of salt, to taste

For the masala water, bring the water to the boil in a small saucepan, then remove from the heat. Stir in the remaining ingredients until well combined and allow to cool.

For the stuffing, heat the rice bran oil or butter in a heavy-based frying pan over medium heat and cook the ginger garlic paste for a few seconds. Add the mashed potato, ground spices, coriander and salt, mixing well. Stir for another minute, or until all the ingredients are combined well and the spices evenly mixed through. Set aside.

Heat a flat round grill (such as a tawa) or barbecue hotplate to medium.

Place a roti on the grill. Spread one-quarter of the stuffing around the middle of the roti and carefully roll it up. Brush the roti with melted butter or ghee and gently grill for a minute or two until golden underneath, then carefully flip it over and cook on the other side until the roti is golden and the filling is warmed through. Take care not to cook it too much, or the roti will become too crispy.

Remove from the grill and unroll the roti, filling side up. Top with a quarter of the chopped onion, then sprinkle evenly with ¼ teaspoon of the frankie masala and about 1½ teaspoons of masala water, before rolling it up tightly in foil or baking paper.

Repeat with the remaining ingredients to make three more frankies. Serve immediately, cut in half if desired.

VARIATIONS
Cheese frankie: For each frankie, sprinkle 4 tablespoons grated cheddar or haloumi over the stuffing before grilling.
Sichuan frankie: Smear 1½ tablespoons sichuan sauce evenly over each roti before stuffing and grilling.
Paneer frankie: In the stuffing, replace 175 g (6 oz/¾ cup) of the mashed potato with 115 g (4 oz/¾ cup) chopped paneer.
Jain frankie: In the stuffing, replace the mashed potato with the same amount of raw mashed banana, and replace the onion with the same amount of thinly sliced cabbage. You can also grate a little cheese over the stuffing for extra flavour.

Phulkopir singara
Cauliflower samosas

The humble samosa is enjoyed all over the subcontinent in many different forms, and loved by all, but what it says to me is how close all these cultures are. If you don't want to make the pastry, you can use 4 sheets of frozen shortcrust pastry and cut the preparation time at least by half.

REGION Bangladesh | **SERVES** 4 | **PREPARATION** 1 hour + 20 minutes resting
COOKING 15 minutes + 3–4 minutes per batch | **DIFFICULTY** Medium

For the pastry, place the flours, salt and baking powder in a large bowl and whisk to combine. Add the ghee or oil and mix in just enough water to make a smooth, soft dough. Cover the dough with plastic wrap and leave to rest at room temperature for 20 minutes.

For the filling, fry the peanuts in a small saucepan in a few drops of rice bran oil over medium heat until they turn a dark golden brown, stirring often. Tip into a bowl and set aside.

In a heavy-based saucepan, heat another 3–4 teaspoons of oil over medium heat. Add the panch phoron and toss for a few seconds. Add the ginger and green chilli and cook, stirring, for another 2–3 minutes. Now stir in the potato, cauliflower, peas and tomato and cook for 5 minutes.

Slowly stir in the ground spices, then season to taste with salt and sugar. Cover and cook over medium heat for about 3 minutes, stirring a few times to ensure the spices don't burn.

Combine the ingredients for the toasted spice mix. Add to the filling mixture with the fried peanuts and mix well. Remove from the heat and leave to cool.

Cut the dough into four equal portions. Roll each one out on a lightly floured work surface into a 14–15 cm (5½–6 inch) disc and cut it into quarters.

Spoon some filling inside each portion, brush the edges with water, then fold together to form a triangle, sealing the edges together.

Pour about 10 cm (4 inches) of vegetable oil into a heavy-based saucepan and heat to 180°C (350°F), or until a cube of bread dropped into the oil turns brown in 15 seconds.

Without overcrowding the pan, cook two or three samosas at a time, for 3–4 minutes each batch, until golden brown.

Drain on paper towel and serve hot or warm, with tamarind chutney.

vegetable oil, for deep-frying
Tamarind chutney (page 220), to serve

FOR THE PASTRY
150 g (5½ oz/1 cup) plain (all-purpose) flour
75 g (2½ oz/½ cup) atta flour (high-protein durum wheat flour)
a pinch of salt
½ teaspoon baking powder
3 teaspoons melted ghee or rice bran oil

FILLING
12–15 peanuts
rice bran oil, for pan-frying
a pinch of panch phoron
2.5 cm (1 inch) knob of fresh ginger, peeled and very finely chopped, or crushed and chopped in a blender
3–4 Indian green chillies, chopped
1 potato, peeled and finely diced
½ small cauliflower, chopped
a handful of frozen peas
1 tomato, chopped
½ teaspoon ground turmeric
½ teaspoon ground cumin
½ teaspoon ground coriander
½ teaspoon chilli powder
a pinch of salt, or to taste
a pinch of sugar, or to taste

TOASTED SPICE MIX
½ teaspoon cumin seeds, dry-roasted and ground
½ teaspoon coriander seeds, dry-roasted and ground
2–3 dried red chillies, dry-roasted and ground

Pani puri with aloo chaat masala & raita

Pani puri is straight street food, known by various other names throughout India. When you order it, the vendor will deep-fry three or four 'puri' (hollow, round pastry puffs) until crisp, fill or top them with a big dollop of spiced potato ('aloo') and serve them up with raita and a flavoured mint sauce known as 'pani'. Variations abound, but the taste explosion is always heavenly.

REGION India | **SERVES** 6 | **PREPARATION** 20 minutes + 2 hours soaking + 30 minutes resting
COOKING about 30 minutes | **DIFFICULTY** Medium

500 ml (17 fl oz/2 cups) vegetable oil, for deep-frying
Raita (page 45), to serve

PANI
100 g (3½ oz) tamarind pulp, soaked in 250 ml (9 fl oz/1 cup) water for 2 hours
250 g (9 oz) mint, leaves picked
1 teaspoon cumin seeds, dry-roasted and ground
2 teaspoons ground cumin
1 teaspoon rock salt
½ teaspoon freshly ground black pepper

PURI
2 tablespoons fine semolina
300 g (10½ oz/2 cups) atta flour (high-protein durum wheat flour)
½ teaspoon salt
45 ml (1½ fl oz) rice bran oil, plus extra for brushing

POTATO FILLING
4 boiling potatoes, such as russet or sebago, cooked and cooled
½ teaspoon salt
1 teaspoon chilli powder
2 tablespoons virgin coconut oil
½ teaspoon brown mustard seeds
½ small onion, diced
1 small dried red chilli, broken into pieces
a sprinkling of Chaat masala (page 24), to taste

To make the pani, mash the soaked tamarind pulp with your hands and remove the seeds. Strain the pulp into a bowl and set aside. Using a blender or mortar and pestle, grind the mint leaves to a smooth paste with 250 ml (9 fl oz/1 cup) water. Add to the strained tamarind pulp, along with the remaining pani ingredients, and stir to combine. Set aside.

For the puri, put the semolina in a mixing bowl, add 100 ml (3½ fl oz) water and soak for 10 minutes. Add the atta flour, salt and rice bran oil and mix together, then turn out onto a work surface and knead into a firm dough. This is a slightly tricky dough: it needs to just come together, but not be too wet either. (You'll know you've got it right when you cook them. If the puri float and puff, you have it! If they sink and don't puff, add a little more water.) Rub some extra oil on the dough, cover with a wet tea towel and rest at room temperature for 30 minutes.

Roll the rested dough into 20 balls about the size of golf balls, then roll each one out into a small chapatti using a rolling pin.

To cook the puri, heat the vegetable oil in a deep heavy-based saucepan to 180°C (350°F), or until a cube of bread dropped into the oil turns brown in 15 seconds.

Without overcrowding the pan, cook three or four puri at a time, for about 3 minutes, until they turn brown, gently pushing them under the oil with a slotted spoon until they puff and turn crisp. Drain on paper towel and keep warm. For the potato filling, peel the potatoes and place in a bowl. Add the salt and chilli powder and mash, then set aside.

Heat the coconut oil in a frying pan over medium heat and fry the mustard seeds for a minute or two, until they start to pop. Add the onion and dried chilli pieces and cook for 3 minutes, or until the onion is golden. Tip the mixture over the mashed potato and mix together well. Sprinkle with chaat masala and check the seasoning. Keep warm.

For each serving, take two or three puri and gently push them into each other, into a stack of crispy goodness. (This is how you'd get them in a street food stall — but if you want to show them off, just place them on a plate, side by side.) Dollop with the potato filling and raita. Serve with a small bowl of pani.

Zaw

Zaw is simply puffed rice; but it is unfair to just call it puffed rice, as it has to be one of the most famous and loved dishes in Bhutan.

People have their own way of eating zaw. The most common way is to top up butter tea (page 283) with a generous scoop or two of zaw — like a cappuccino, except the foam is zaw — so that while you sip your tea, you can also enjoy the still crispy zaw. After you finish your tea, the soft and soggy rice with a tender tea flavour remains at the bottom of your cup to be relished. Try topping your coffee or hot chocolate with it!

In India, puffed rice is mixed with spices and chaat masala and sold as snacks.

REGION Bhutan | **MAKES** 3 cups of rice | **PREPARATION** 20 minutes + 8 hours soaking + 40 minutes drying
COOKING 40 minutes | **DIFFICULTY** Easy

Put the rice in a large bowl and cover with plenty of cold water. Leave to soak for 8 hours, or overnight.

Next day, pour the rice into a large strainer. When all the water has drained, turn the rice out onto a clean tea towel. Spread out the grains in a thin, even layer and leave to air dry for 30–40 minutes. Transfer to a large bowl and set aside.

Heat a large heavy-based saucepan over medium heat. When hot, add just enough rice bran oil to cover the base and reduce the heat.

Add half the rice. Stir constantly for 9–10 minutes, then begin tasting the rice. Once it has a little crunch, continue stirring and tasting for another 10 minutes, or until the grains have begun to change colour and are crunchy almost all the way through. Be sure to turn the heat down if the rice begins to smoke or darken too quickly. When ready, pour the rice onto a large plate and set aside.

Cook the remaining rice in the same manner.

When all the rice is done but still quite warm, stir in the butter. There should be just enough to coat the grains. Sweeten with the sugar and season to taste with the salt.

The zaw is best enjoyed fresh, but can also be used the next day.

If you're going to store it, let the rice cool completely, and wait until the grains have absorbed the butter and no longer look oily, then transfer to an airtight container.

210 g (7½ oz/1 cup) Bhutanese red rice, white basmati or medium-grain sushi rice
2 tablespoons rice bran oil
40 g (1½ oz) butter
1 tablespoon rapadura sugar
a pinch or two of sea salt

Pakora
Vegetable & chickpea flour fritters

Across the subcontinent it is common to hear or smell something sizzling in oil by the side of the road, usually at a bus stop or somewhere busy, where the vendor will skilfully scoop up a little bit of batter, containing anything from onion to cauliflower or broccoli, and swirl it around in the hot oil. Their crispy pakoras hit the spot every time. Served with a dip of some sort, sometimes yoghurt or mint chutney, or a sambar, they are filling and delicious — and coming out of that hot oil they are generally safe, too.

Making them at home is easy. Just be sure to cut the vegetables to the same size, so they cook through evenly.

REGION Pakistan, India, Bangladesh, Nepal | **SERVES** 4 | **PREPARATION** 30 minutes
COOKING 5 minutes per batch | **DIFFICULTY** Easy

1 litre (35 fl oz/4 cups) rice bran oil or vegetable oil, for deep-frying
40 g (1½ oz/1 cup) chopped spinach or kale
125 g (4½ oz/1 cup) chopped cauliflower
60 g (2¼ oz/1 cup) chopped broccoli
1 onion, cut into rings
black sesame seeds, to garnish
coriander (cilantro) sprigs, to garnish
Tamarind chutney (page 220), Yoghurt pakora dipping sauce (page 252), or Velvet tomato catsup (page 248), to serve

PAKORA BATTER
100 g (3½ oz) chickpea flour (besan)
100 g (3½ oz) tempura flour
¼ teaspoon ground turmeric
1 teaspoon coriander seeds, dry-roasted and ground, or ¼ teaspoon ground coriander
½ teaspoon caraway seeds
a generous pinch of salt

For the batter, place all the ingredients in a bowl, add 200 ml (7 fl oz) water and whisk together until smooth. The mixture should be like a thick pancake batter.

Heat the rice bran oil in a sturdy wok or heavy-based saucepan to 180°C (375°F), or until a cube of bread dropped into the oil turns brown in 15 seconds.

To make the pakoras, take either individual pieces of your chosen vegetable, or a combination of them, and place into the batter to lightly coat.

Carefully add a few pakoras to the hot oil, allowing them to clump together. Don't put too many in at once, or the oil will cool, and the pakoras will be limp and soggy. Cook for 3–5 minutes, until they turn a light golden brown, then remove and drain on paper towel.

Serve warm, with a sprinkling of black sesame seeds, coriander sprigs and a dipping sauce of your choice.

Samoosi yirakot
Stuffed vegetable turnovers

Afghani cuisine uses many of the same spices as the Middle East and India, but is milder and lighter than its Indian cousin, as you'll see with these lovely turnovers.

If convenient, you can make the dough a few hours ahead, which will give a better result, as the matzoh meal will absorb all the liquid in the dough.

REGION Afghanistan | **SERVES** 6 (makes about 12) | **PREPARATION** 30 minutes
COOKING 20 minutes + 3 minutes per batch | **DIFFICULTY** Medium

1 litre (35 fl oz/4 cups) vegetable oil, for deep-frying
Green coconut chutney (page 208), to serve

DOUGH
115 g (4 oz/1 cup) fine matzoh meal
1 egg, beaten
¼ teaspoon salt
125 ml (4 fl oz/½ cup) chilled water, approximately

FILLING
1 potato, peeled and cut into small pieces
1 carrot, chopped
60 g (2¼ oz/½ cup) chopped cauliflower
75 g (2½ oz/½ cup) green peas, fresh or frozen
1 tablespoon rice bran oil
1 onion, chopped
1 garlic clove, chopped
½ teaspoon Garam masala (page 24)
½ teaspoon ground turmeric
a pinch of saffron threads
¼ teaspoon salt
¼ teaspoon freshly ground black pepper

To make the dough, mix the matzoh meal in a bowl with the egg and salt, adding just enough of the chilled water to make a moist dough that holds together. Set aside.

For the filling, bring a large saucepan of salted water to the boil. Add the potato and carrot and blanch for 3 minutes. Add the cauliflower to the pan; if using fresh peas, add them now as well. Blanch for another 2 minutes, or until all the vegetables are firm but cooked. (If using frozen peas, add them right near the end.)

Drain the vegetables and set aside.

Heat the rice bran oil in a heavy-based saucepan over medium heat. Add the onion and garlic and cook, stirring, for about 3 minutes, until the onion is lightly browned.

Stir in the garam masala and turmeric and cook for a further 2 minutes, or until the mixture becomes aromatic.

Gently stir in the cooked vegetables, saffron, salt and pepper. Set aside to cool.

Place a golf ball–sized piece of the dough on a lightly floured work surface and press it out into a 6 cm (2½ inch) square. Put 1 tablespoon of the vegetable mixture on the bottom half of the square, then fold it over into a triangle. Prepare all the turnovers this way.

Pour the vegetable oil into a wok or heavy-based saucepan and heat to 180°C (350°F), or until a cube of bread dropped into the oil turns brown in 15 seconds.

Working in batches, gently add the turnovers to the hot oil and cook for about 3 minutes, or until golden and cooked through. Drain on paper towel.

Serve warm, with green coconut chutney.

Sobjir
Vegetable cutlets

This tasty street food is from Bangladesh. It might be easier to crumb the cutlets if they are firm, so you could place the shaped cutlets in the freezer for 15 minutes prior to crumbing. You can also use panko crumbs, for a lovely crisp texture.

REGION Bangladesh | **SERVES** 6 | **PREPARATION** 30 minutes
COOKING 30 minutes + 6–8 minutes per batch | **DIFFICULTY** Medium

Add the whole potatoes to a saucepan of boiling water and cook for 15–20 minutes, or until tender. Drain and leave to cool, then grate and set aside.

Meanwhile, in another large saucepan, bring 750 ml (26 fl oz/3 cups) water to the boil. Add the mixed vegetables and a pinch of salt and boil for 4–5 minutes. Strain and set aside. Once cooled, squeeze the water from the vegetables, then coarsely mash them, without making a paste of them.

Heat the rice bran oil in a frying pan until it starts to smoke. Add the cumin seeds and crushed cashews and cook over medium heat for a few seconds. Stir in the chilli powder and garam masala, then add the onion and cook for about 3 minutes, or until the onion is soft.

Add the green chilli, ginger paste and garlic paste and cook for another few seconds. Now add the mashed vegetables (except the grated potato) and cook, stirring, for another minute or two, until the moisture evaporates.

Transfer the mixture to a bowl, add the grated potato and mix together. Stir in the lemon juice and chopped coriander and season to taste with salt, mixing well. If the mixture is still a bit wet, add some breadcrumbs to firm it up.

Spread the remaining breadcrumbs in a shallow bowl. Beat the egg with the flour and 2 teaspoons water.

Take a large tablespoonful of the vegetable mixture and press it together into a 'cutlet' of your desired shape. Dip the cutlet in the egg wash and immediately coat it with breadcrumbs. Continue in the same way until all the cutlets are crumbed; you may need a little more egg mixture and crumbs.

Pour about 2.5 cm (1 inch) of vegetable oil into a deep-sided frying pan and heat to 170°C (325°F), or until a cube of bread dropped into the oil turns brown in 20 seconds.

Carefully add a few cutlets to the hot oil and cook for 3–4 minutes on each side, or until golden brown. Drain on paper towel and keep warm while cooking the remaining cutlets.

If you have the taste for chaat masala, sprinkle some on before serving. The cutlets are best enjoyed hot, but are also delicious as a cold snack. Enjoy with a chutney or sambal of your choice.

2 russet or sebago potatoes, peeled
2 cups mixed chopped vegetables of your choice, including corn, broccoli, carrot, peas
a pinch of salt, plus extra for seasoning
1 tablespoon rice bran oil
½ teaspoon cumin seeds
2 tablespoons crushed cashews
½ teaspoon chilli powder
1 teaspoon Garam masala (page 24)
1 onion, chopped
3 Indian green chillies, chopped
2.5 cm (1 inch) knob of fresh ginger, peeled and crushed into a paste
4 garlic cloves, crushed to a paste with ¼ teaspoon salt
1 tablespoon lemon juice
¼ bunch coriander (cilantro), chopped
approximately 110 g (3¾ oz/1 cup) dry breadcrumbs, for crumbing
1 egg
35 g (1¼ oz/¼ cup) plain (all-purpose) flour
vegetable oil, for shallow-frying
a pinch of Chaat masala (page 24), for sprinkling (optional)
Tamarind chutney (page 220) or a sambal of your choice, to serve

Puri chana chaat masala
Spiced chickpeas with puffed roti

Chickpeas are the 'chana' element of this dish, flavoured with a spice mix known as 'chaat masala'; the 'puri' are a puffed fried roti that brings it all together. I used to live on this in Nepal — one of those flavours I can always remember.

You can enjoy this dish hot or cold. To serve it warm, follow the recipe below; alternatively, serve it at room temperature, more as a salad.

REGION Nepal | **SERVES** 4 | **PREPARATION** 25 minutes + overnight soaking if using dried chickpeas
COOKING 10 minutes | **DIFFICULTY** Medium

Combine all the chaat masala ingredients in a bowl and set aside.

For the chana masala, heat the coconut oil in a heavy-based saucepan over medium heat. Add the onion and ginger and cook, stirring, for 3–5 minutes, until the onion is translucent.

Stir in the chilli and tomato and cook for a further 2 minutes. Add the drained chickpeas and 2 teaspoons of the chaat masala; store the remaining spice mix in a small airtight jar for next time. Mix well and cook for about 3 minutes, or until the chickpeas are heated through. Taste and season with more salt if necessary.

Place all the raita ingredients in a bowl and mix together. Check the seasoning and season again to taste.

To serve, stack three puri on each plate, or on banana leaves if you want to be authentic. Spoon a dollop of the chana masala on top. Add a spoonful of tamarind chutney and a teaspoon of raita. Sprinkle with an extra pinch of the chaat masala, garnish with coriander sprigs and serve.

TIP If using dried chickpeas, soak 500 g (1 lb 2 oz) chickpeas in plenty of cold water overnight. Next day, rinse them and cook in boiling water for about 20 minutes, until soft but not mushy, then use as directed.

12 Puri, prepared and deep-fried
    according to the recipe on page 38
Tamarind chutney (page 220), to serve
coriander (cilantro) sprigs, to garnish

CHAAT MASALA
2 teaspoons ground coriander
½ teaspoon chilli powder
½ teaspoon ground turmeric
½ teaspoon Garam masala (page 24)
1 teaspoon amchur (dried mango powder)
½ teaspoon cumin seeds, dry-roasted
    and ground
½ teaspoon black salt, or plain salt

CHANA MASALA
2½ tablespoons virgin coconut oil
1 onion, finely diced
a thumb-sized knob of fresh ginger,
    peeled and cut into thin strips
1 Indian green chilli, chopped
1 ripe but firm tomato, diced
400 g (14 oz) tin chickpeas (see tip),
    rinsed and drained

RAITA
500 g (1 lb 2 oz) plain yoghurt
2 Lebanese (short) cucumbers, halved,
    seeded and very finely chopped
juice of 1 lemon
1 small red onion, very finely diced
1 teaspoon cumin seeds,
    dry-roasted and ground
½ teaspoon diced green chilli
½ teaspoon sea salt

Vada pav
Mumbai burgers

My first experience of these yummy burgers was on the train from Mumbai to Hyderabad, around 1983. This vegetarian delicacy originated around 1960, and combines a wonderful local deep-fried spiced potato ball with a touch of the colonial influence in the form of a burger bun. As with most things, this iconic Mumbai street food is evolving and finding its way all over India.

REGION India | **SERVES** 4 | **PREPARATION** 15 minutes + 10 minutes resting
COOKING 25 minutes | **DIFFICULTY** Medium

vegetable oil, for deep-frying
4 small white burger buns
butter, for spreading
Green coconut chutney (page 208),
    to serve
Tamarind chutney (page 220), to serve
chopped coriander (cilantro), to serve
deep-fried green chillies, to serve
    (optional)

POTATO MASALA
500 g (1 lb 2 oz) potatoes, peeled and
    cut into 2 cm (¾ inch) cubes
2 teaspoons virgin coconut oil
½ teaspoon brown mustard seeds
a few fresh curry leaves
¼ teaspoon ground turmeric
3 green chillies, finely chopped
2.5 cm (1 inch) knob of fresh ginger,
    peeled and finely chopped
5 large garlic cloves, finely chopped
a pinch of salt, or to taste
a few coriander (cilantro) sprigs,
    finely chopped

CHICKPEA BATTER
200 g (7 oz/1⅔ cups) chickpea flour
    (besan), sifted
½ teaspoon chilli powder
¼ teaspoon ground cumin
a pinch of bicarbonate of soda
    (baking soda)
a pinch of salt, or to taste

For the potato masala, cook the potatoes in a large saucepan of salted boiling water for 5 minutes, or until tender. Drain the potatoes, then place back in the saucepan and put the lid on top; this will make the potatoes go fluffy. Set aside.

Heat the coconut oil in a heavy-based saucepan over medium heat until it starts to lightly smoke. Add the mustard seeds and, when they start to pop, add the curry leaves. When they stop popping, add the remaining masala ingredients, except the coriander, and cook together for 2–3 minutes, or until the mixture becomes fragrant.

Now add the potatoes and mix well, with enough force to break the potatoes but not mash them. Check for seasoning and leave to cool, then add the coriander.

In a bowl, mix together all the chickpea batter ingredients, adding enough water to give you a batter that resembles a pancake mix. Set aside to rest for 10 minutes.

Shape the potato masala into balls the size of golf balls. (This can be done a few hours ahead if needed.)

When you're ready to cook, pour about 20 cm (8 inches) of vegetable oil into a heavy-based saucepan and heat to 190°C (375°F), or until a cube of bread dropped into the oil turns brown in 10 seconds.

Dip the potato masala balls into the chickpea batter, then cook two to three at a time for 3–4 minutes, until golden. Drain on paper towel.

To assemble, cut the buns in half and lightly toast them, then butter them. Smear one half with tamarind chutney, and the other half with green coconut chutney. Place a few potato masala balls inside each bun and gently crush them, then sprinkle with chopped coriander.

Close up the buns and serve immediately, with deep-fried green chillies if desired.

Sel roti

I love this roti. It is very famous in Nepalese cuisine — a sweet rice bread, distinct from any other breads of the world. Sel roti resembles a large, thin, puffed-up doughnut, with a crispy texture and a reddish brown colour. As well as being a street food, you will also see this bread in religious ceremonies.

The rice takes some time to soak, but you can do this overnight, while you sleep. I have had this bread in the morning, and with the ripe banana it was delicious. Make sure you have a chopstick on hand during the frying process, to help shape the roti.

REGION Nepal | **SERVES** 4 | **PREPARATION** 6 hours + 12 hours soaking + 1 hour resting
COOKING 3–5 minutes per roti | **DIFFICULTY** Medium

---

600 g (1 lb 5 oz/3 cups) long-grain
   white rice
1 very ripe banana, peeled and mashed
220 g (7¾ oz/1 cup) sugar, or to taste
½ teaspoon ground cardamom
185 g (6½ oz) butter or ghee, melted
80 g (2¾ oz/½ cup) rice flour, as needed
1–1.25 litres (35–44 fl oz/4–5 cups)
   vegetable oil, for deep-frying
cinnamon sugar, for sprinkling

Soak the rice in plenty of water in the fridge overnight.

Next day, drain the rice and place in a blender or food processor. Add the banana, sugar, cardamom and butter and blend to a semi-thick purée, by adding 250–375 ml (9–13 fl oz/1–1½ cups) water; depending on the size of your machine, you may need to do this in two batches.

Cover and set aside to rest at room temperature for 20–30 minutes.

Transfer the batter to a mixing bowl and beat vigorously to make a smooth, fluffy, semi-thick batter. Cover and rest for another 30 minutes.

Mix the batter again with your hand, until all the ingredients are fully recombined. The consistency should be similar to a thick but pourable cream. If the batter is too runny, add an extra 1–2 tablespoons of rice flour and mix well. If it seems too thick, gradually stir in 1–2 tablespoons water, mixing well.

Pour the vegetable oil into a heavy-based saucepan and heat over medium–high heat to about 170–180°C (325–350°F). Test the readiness by placing a small drop of batter into the hot oil. If it bubbles and rises to the surface immediately, the oil is ready.

Slowly pour about 60 ml (2 fl oz/¼ cup) of the batter into the oil, making a large circle. You can pour it in by hand, or using a squeezable paper or plastic cup, or a pastry bag with a medium-size opening.

Stretch and move the batter, using chopsticks to create a round shape. As the roti puffs and rises, use your chopstick to gently spin it from the centre, so it looks like a bagel or large doughnut, pushing it down into the oil until it is light golden brown. Flip and fry the second side until brown.

Remove with a slotted spoon and drain on paper towel. Repeat with the remaining batter. Drain on paper towel.

Sprinkle the roti with some sugar mixed with ground cinnamon and serve warm, with a cup of chai.

Kara boondi chaat
Crispy chickpea flour snacks

Kara boondi are crisp little pearls of spiced chickpea batter, enjoyed as a snack; I also use them as a garnish in our restaurant. They are tasty enough on their own, but when you mix them with the chaat they become deliciously reminiscent of the snacks on the beach in Sri Lanka.

Some people want perfectly shaped balls of kara boondi, which takes a bit more practice. I prefer them all the size of puffed rice.

REGION India, Pakistan, Bangladesh | **SERVES** 6–8 as a snack | **PREPARATION** 20 minutes
COOKING 5–10 minutes | **DIFFICULTY** Medium

For the kara boondi, mix the chickpea flour, rice flour, 1 teaspoon of the chilli powder and a pinch of salt together in a bowl. Mix in a little water to make a thick paste. Add more water, little by little, to form a mixture the consistency of a thick pancake batter. Add the rice bran oil and mix well.

In a large heavy-based saucepan, heat the vegetable oil over medium–high heat to 180°C (350°F). To test, carefully place a little bit of the batter into the oil; it should immediately come to the top of the oil and sizzle.

To cook the batter, place a pasta strainer, or a steamer tray with holes, over the top of the saucepan. Pour a ladleful of the batter into the strainer and quickly push the batter through the holes so it flows into the hot oil. This will give you lots of crispy pearls of kara boondi. Cook each batch for 20–30 seconds, until golden and crisp, then drain on paper towel and set aside to cool completely.

Once all the batter has been cooked, fry the peanuts, cashews and curry leaves in the same oil until crisp, then remove from the oil, drain and leave to cool completely.

Place the kara boondi in a bowl. Add the fried peanuts, cashews and curry leaves. Sprinkle with the remaining 1 teaspoon chilli powder, and a pinch more salt if needed, and toss to combine.

The kara boondi can be enjoyed as is, and will keep in an airtight container in the pantry for up to 2 days.

If using the chaat, place the onion in a bowl, along with the tomato, cucumber, chilli, coriander and peanuts. Sprinkle with the chaat masala and mix together.

Add the kara boondi and tamarind chutney and mix well. Add the lemon juice and mix thoroughly.

Serve immediately.

KARA BOONDI
120 g (4¼ oz/1 cup) chickpea flour (besan)
2 tablespoons rice flour
2 teaspoons chilli powder
a pinch of salt, to taste
2 teaspoons rice bran oil
approximately 1 litre (35 fl oz/4 cups) vegetable oil, for deep-frying
4 tablespoons raw peanuts
1 tablespoon broken cashews
1 fresh curry leaf sprig, leaves picked

CHAAT
40 g (1½ oz/¼ cup) finely chopped onion
60 g (2¼ oz/¼ cup) seeded chopped tomatoes
45 g (1½ oz/¼ cup) diced cucumber (peeled and seeded)
1 Indian green chilli, finely chopped
¼ bunch coriander (cilantro), leaves chopped
2 tablespoons chopped roasted peanuts
1–2 tablespoons Chaat masala (page 24)
4 tablespoons Tamarind chutney (page 220)
2 tablespoons lemon juice

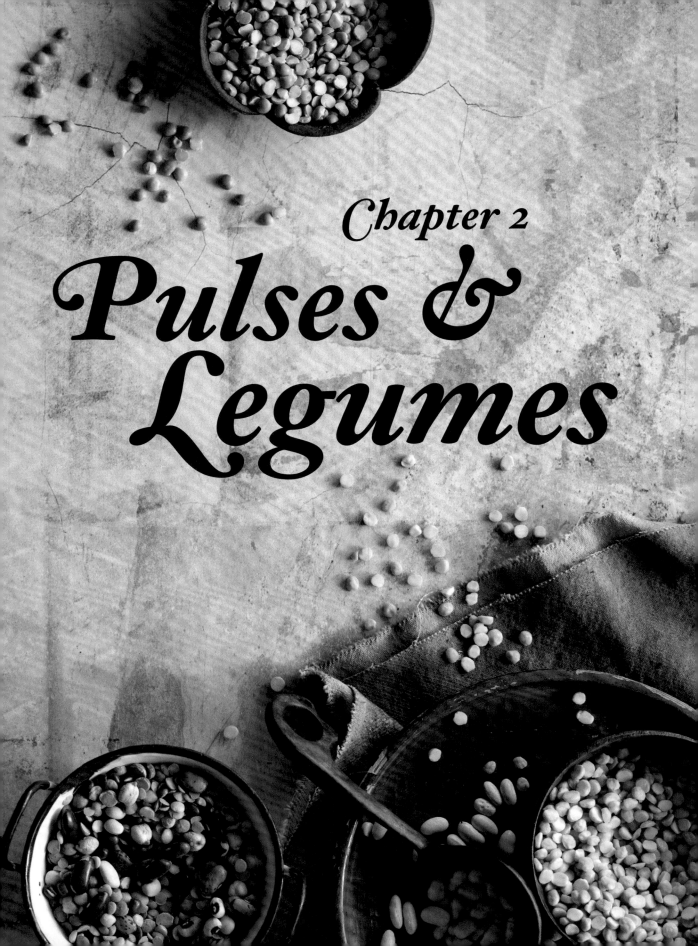

Chapter 2
Pulses & Legumes

One of the reasons the varied cuisines of the subcontinent are considered so healthy is the inclusion of whole grains in so many of their dishes.

While the subcontinent is often referred to as the spice centre of the world, I think it should equally be known for the phenomenal integration of pulses and legumes into the diet.

You could map the subcontinent by its variations on dhal, from rich and creamy in the north to the soupy sambars of southern India, while the preparation of rice and beans unites and divides from Afghanistan to Nepal. The preparation of lentils, chickpeas, beans, and grains such as rice and wheat, is at the heart of cooking across the subcontinent, and a great source of pride and the soul of many a culinary conversation. They're staple ingredients with a phenomenally long history behind them, all of which we're fortunate enough to inherit in our multicultural society.

Archaeological remains found in Turkey date chickpea and lentil production back to 7000–8000 BCE. Pharaohs were buried with lentils, Esau sold his birthright for a bowlful of the stuff in the Old Testament, and legend tells us that Cicero, the famed orator of ancient Rome, was so named because one of his forebears had a nose like a chickpea ('cicer' in Latin).

Essentially peasant fare, highly economical while providing the nutrients needed in a diet often low in animal protein, these humble foods are now being looked on with awe as we try to improve our diets and the wellbeing of our planet. The answer to many of our global crises could be held in these little dried orbs: they're sustainable, profitable for farmers, highly nutritious, an important source of protein, and a critical part of the world's food basket, especially for developing countries. Many claim increasing our consumption of pulses and legumes can help fight obesity, cancer and even premature death from lifestyle diseases, all while saving the planet and tackling world poverty and hunger.

But more than anything, pulses and legumes are spectacularly tasty. In this chapter I have included a range of dishes that showcase these humble foodstuffs and ultimately speak of home for me.

Medu vada
Deep-fried black lentil patties

I know these very tasty savoury doughnuts as ulundu vadai. They are slightly fermented and spiced, and served in tea shops around Sri Lanka. Some people also make these with yellow lentils, but this classic recipe uses unskinned black ones (urad dhal).

Although they can be a bit heavy, these patties are a wonderful hot snack. The secret to the perfect patty comes down to the amount of liquid. Too wet and it will fall apart in the fryer, and not moist enough means it will be dry.

REGION India | **MAKES** about 18 doughnuts; serves 4 | **PREPARATION** 20 minutes + overnight soaking
COOKING 3–5 minutes per batch | **DIFFICULTY** Medium

200 g (7 oz/1 cup) dried black lentils (urad dhal)
2 teaspoons crushed garlic, fried in virgin coconut oil until golden brown
1 tablespoon fresh Ginger paste (page 241) or ginger juice
1 Indian green chilli, chopped very finely with the seeds
2 tablespoons chopped coriander (cilantro) leaves
1 curry leaf sprig, leaves finely chopped
½ teaspoon black peppercorns, crushed
¼ teaspoon bicarbonate of soda (baking soda)
approximately 1 litre (35 fl oz/4 cups) vegetable oil, for deep-frying
Green coconut chutney (page 208), Nepalese tomato achar (page 213) or Aam kasundi (page 253), to serve

Soak the lentils in water overnight, or until the black coating is easily removed.

Remove the black coating by rinsing the lentils thoroughly with water.

Using a blender, and the minimum amount of water needed to make a pliable mixture, grind the lentils into a paste that can be formed into a ball, without being too crumbly or too wet. You may need to stop every now and then, to ensure the machine does not get too hot.

Add the garlic, ginger, chilli, coriander, curry leaves, pepper and bicarbonate of soda. Season with salt and mix well.

Pour about 10 cm (4 inches) of oil into a sturdy wok or heavy-based saucepan and heat to 180°C (350°F), or until a cube of bread dropped into the oil turns brown in 15 seconds.

Wet your hands, take a large tablespoonful of the lentil mixture and make a patty in the palm of your hand. Poke a hole in the middle of the patty with your finger, to give you a doughnut.

Carefully place into the hot oil, adding a few more doughnuts, but not enough to crowd the pan. Cook for 3–5 minutes, turning over halfway through, until golden brown on both sides.

Remove the first doughnut from the oil and carefully break it in half, to check it is cooked through, so you can adjust the cooking time as needed. Drain on paper towel while cooking the remaining doughnuts.

Serve hot, with your choice of chutney or sambal.

Piaju
Crisp black lentil & onion fritters

Popular during Ramadan, these fritters are similar to others enjoyed across the subcontinent, but are made using hulled black lentils. These delicious snacks are very easy to make — the only trick is to keep the lentil paste coarse, rather than smooth.

REGION Bangladesh | **MAKES** 15 | **PREPARATION** 15 minutes + 2 hours soaking
COOKING 6–8 minutes per batch | **DIFFICULTY** Easy

200 g (7 oz/1 cup) dried black lentils (urad dhal)
3 garlic cloves, chopped
1 teaspoon salt
½ teaspoon ground turmeric
½ teaspoon cumin seeds
2 tablespoons chickpea flour (besan)
2 Indian green chillies, very finely chopped
1 red onion, thinly sliced
1 tablespoon fresh thyme leaves
1 tablespoon finely chopped coriander (cilantro)
300 ml (10½ fl oz) rice bran oil
100 g (3½ oz) chopped baby spinach, to garnish

Wash the lentils well and soak them in a bowl of water for at least 2 hours.

Drain and rinse the lentils, then place in a blender with 125 ml (4 fl oz/½ cup) water.

Add the garlic, salt, turmeric and cumin seeds and grind until smooth; the consistency should be of a somewhat wet paste, rather than a batter.

Scrape the mixture into a bowl and add the chickpea flour, chilli, onion, thyme and coriander and mix well.

Heat the rice bran oil in a heavy-based frying pan for about 2–3 minutes over medium heat. Test the temperature with a small drop of the mixture; it should sizzle to the top.

For each fritter, carefully add about 2 tablespoons of the lentil mixture to the hot oil, leaving enough space in between so they can cook without overcrowding each other.

Cook for about 3–4 minutes on each side, until nicely golden. Drain on paper towel and keep warm while cooking the remaining fritters.

Arrange on a serving plate, toss with the spinach leaves and serve.

Dhal bhat tarkari
Lentil, rice & vegetable curry

While trekking in the Himalayas, this was our staple meal: tasty, filling and full of carbs to fuel the ascent. The individual words simply translate as 'lentil', 'rice' and 'vegetable curry', but dhal bhat tarkari is a foundation of Nepalese cuisine — a basic combination that takes on innumerable configurations based on season, region and household preferences, and is a great framework for healthy, well-balanced vegetarian meals. Feel free to experiment with the vegetables, lentils, spices and flavourings.

REGION Nepal | **SERVES** 4–6 | **PREPARATION** 25 minutes
COOKING 40 minutes | **DIFFICULTY** Medium

For the dhal, heat the ghee or coconut oil in a heavy-based saucepan over medium heat. Add the mustard seeds. When they start to splutter, add the curry leaves. Next, add the ground spices and stir for about 30 seconds to lightly toast them.

Immediately stir in the onion and chilli and cook, stirring, for 3–4 minutes, or until the onion is cooked through and translucent. Add the tomatoes and allow to cook down for a minute or two.

Stir in the lentils and 1 litre (35 fl oz/4 cups) water. Bring to the boil, then reduce the heat to medium–low and simmer for about 15 minutes, or until the lentils break down. Season to taste with salt and freshly ground black pepper.

Meanwhile, prepare the rice, using a rice cooker or the absorption method (page 159).

For the tarkari, heat the ghee or coconut oil in a wok or large heavy-based saucepan over medium heat. Add the curry leaves. When they stop popping, add the coriander, cumin and turmeric and stir for about 30 seconds to lightly toast the spices. Stir in the onion, garlic and ginger and cook for 4–5 minutes, or until the onion is translucent. Add the tomatoes and allow to cook down for a minute or two.

Add the potato and cauliflower and stir to heat them through. Stir in 250 ml (9 fl oz/1 cup) water and season with salt and pepper.

Bring to the boil, then reduce the heat to medium–low and simmer for 8–10 minutes, or until the vegetables are cooked through and tender. Adjust the seasoning if needed. Just before serving, stir in the chopped coriander.

Dhal bhat tarkari is typically served on a metal serving platter known as a thali, with a bowl of dhal, a bowl of vegetable curry and a scoop of rice in the middle.

Serve with lemon or lime wedges, and condiments such as the Fruit chaat on page 230.

DHAL (LENTIL SOUP)
3 tablespoons ghee or virgin coconut oil
1 teaspoon brown mustard seeds
1 fresh curry leaf sprig, leaves picked
1 teaspoon ground coriander
2 teaspoons ground cumin
1 teaspoon ground turmeric
1 brown onion, finely chopped
1 Indian green chilli, finely chopped
250 g (9 oz/1 cup) chopped tomatoes
200 g (7 oz/1 cup) red lentils, washed
    twice and drained
½ bunch coriander (cilantro), chopped

BHAT (RICE)
400 g (14 oz/2 cups) basmati rice,
    red rice, organic brown rice, or other
    rice of your choice
1 litre (35 fl oz/4 cups) water
a pinch of salt

TARKARI (VEGETABLE CURRY)
3 tablespoons ghee or virgin coconut oil
1 fresh curry leaf sprig, leaves picked
1 tablespoon ground coriander
2 teaspoons ground cumin
1 teaspoon ground turmeric
1 onion, finely chopped
3–4 garlic cloves, finely chopped
2.5 cm (1 inch) knob of fresh ginger,
    peeled and finely grated
2 tomatoes, seeded and chopped
2 small potatoes, cut into cubes
½ head cauliflower, cut into florets
½ bunch coriander (cilantro), chopped
2 lemons or limes, cut into wedges

Cheela
Sprouted mung bean pancakes

My mum became a vegetarian for almost 10 years, and during that time was constantly sprouting some sort of bean or pea. There was always a jar of something sprouting away in the fridge, years before it became popular. She had a very healthy diet and I can remember the flavour of the sprouts and the salads she made with them.

Sprouted mung beans add an intense flavour to these beautiful pancakes. If you don't have time to sprout your own, you can buy sprouted mung beans from health food stores and greengrocers.

Serve with Green coconut chutney (page 208), use them to roll up some leftover curry, or have them with eggs for breakfast.

REGION India | **SERVES** 6–8 | **PREPARATION** 15 minutes + 3 days sprouting
COOKING 4–6 minutes per batch | **DIFFICULTY** Easy

Using a high-speed blender (see tip), grind the sprouted mung beans and chilli, adding a little water as needed, until you have a smooth paste. You may need to stop every now and then, to ensure the machine does not get too hot.

Scrape the mixture into a bowl. Add the chickpea flour, onion, spring onion, coriander and all the spices, including the salt and mix them through. Gradually stir in about 375 ml (13 fl oz/1½ cups) water to get a smooth, pancake-like batter.

Heat a non-stick tawa or heavy-based frying pan over medium heat. Using a paper towel, smear the pan with rice bran oil.

For each pancake, pour in a spoonful of the batter, spreading it evenly in the pan; you should be able to cook two or three at a time. Cover the pan and leave to cook for 2–3 minutes over medium heat, until bubbles form.

Open the lid, drizzle the pancake with some oil and turn it over. Cook for a further 2–3 minutes, then remove from the pan and keep warm.

Repeat with the remaining batter. Serve hot.

TIP Dried pulses can destroy a blender, so it is important to soften them with a long soaking before trying to blitz them into a paste. If the seeds are hard, they will need much longer to blend. A bar blender is best for this recipe; a bowl blender will not work.

200 g (7 oz/1 cup) dried mung beans (moong dhal), sprouted for 3 days (see page 64)
1 teaspoon chopped Indian green chilli
2 tablespoons chickpea flour (besan)
1 onion, finely chopped
1 teaspoon chopped spring onions (scallions)
½ cup chopped coriander (cilantro)
1 teaspoon ajwain seeds or caraway seeds
½ teaspoon chilli powder
1 teaspoon Chaat masala (page 24)
1 teaspoon ground coriander
1 teaspoon freshly ground black pepper
a pinch of salt
rice bran oil, for pan-frying

Ful medames
Broad bean dip

This dip is a favourite dip all through the Arab world. I tasted the best on a recent trip to Kuwait, served in a Sri Lankan tea shop and cooked by a Persian (Iranian) chef. Here is the Afghan version, which is wonderful served with fresh tamiz — a thick Afghan bread that is very popular in Saudi Arabia as well.

REGION Afghanistan | **SERVES** 6 | **PREPARATION** 10 minutes + overnight soaking (optional)
COOKING 15 minutes (+ 3 hours cooking if using dried beans) | **DIFFICULTY** Easy

200 g (7 oz/1 cup) dried broad beans (fava beans), or a 540 g (1 lb 3 oz) tin of fava beans
1 tablespoon olive oil, plus extra for drizzling
1 yellow onion, chopped
2 garlic cloves, crushed
1½ teaspoons ground cumin
1 teaspoon ground coriander
½ teaspoon cayenne pepper
½ teaspoon chilli powder (optional)
2 tablespoons tahini, or to taste (optional)
1 tablespoon chopped flat-leaf (Italian) parsley
1 large tomato, chopped
½ red onion, finely chopped
lemon quarters, to serve
Obi non (page 171) or Afghan bread, to serve

If using dried beans, soak them overnight in plenty of cold water. Next day, drain the beans and place in a saucepan with 1 litre (35 fl oz/4 cups) water. Bring to the boil, then reduce the heat, cover and simmer for 2–3 hours, or until the beans are very tender. Drain, reserving 100 ml (3½ fl oz) of the cooking water, and set aside.

If using tinned beans, drain half and reserve 100 ml (3½ fl oz) of the liquid from the tin.

Heat the olive oil in a frying pan and cook the onion and garlic over medium heat for about 3 minutes, or until the onion starts to brown. Add the ground spices, stirring well.

Add the beans and reserved cooking water or brine. Season to taste with salt and freshly ground black pepper and simmer for 5–10 minutes over low heat, stirring occasionally.

Remove from the heat and stir in the tahini, if using.

Transfer to a serving bowl, drizzle generously with olive oil and sprinkle with the parsley, chopped tomato and onion.

Serve as a dip, with lemon quarters and bread. The dip can be served hot or cold, although my preference is hot.

TIP A great way to add more flavour to the beans is to give them a quick smoking. When you've finished cooking the bean mixture, place it in a serving dish that has a lid, and arrange the garnishes on top. Get a piece of charcoal very hot, then carefully place it in a small aluminium foil boat. Add some extra chopped onion and a bit of oil to the foil, then rest the open parcel of foil on top of the dip. Cover the dish and leave for 5 minutes. Carefully remove the lid — the dish will be very smoky! Remove the foil boat before serving.

Falafel

Originating in Egypt, the fabulous falafel has been claimed by many countries, including India, and to my surprise Israel, where it is considered a national dish. The name is either Arabic or Sanskrit, depending on which strain of history you wish to follow; to me it is the quintessential Arabic dish, so I am going to hand it to Afghanistan via Iran for this book.

We all know them in some form or another, mostly green inside and very tasty! Falafels have always been a go-to vegetarian protein, ensuring that after a night on the town a vegetarian can go to a kebab store with their carnivorous friends to get a vegie shawarma.

I have been looking for a falafel recipe to call my own; I have tasted a few beauties, but no one has shared their recipe. This one comes from Sri Lanka via Doha, the capital of Qatar! Many Sri Lankan chefs work overseas, especially in the Middle East and Maldives, and I tried this version while consulting on some menus for a resort in the south of Sri Lanka. I managed to get this recipe by swapping it for one of my own. Hope you enjoy it as much as I do.

REGION Afghanistan | **MAKES** about 50 | **PREPARATION** 30 minutes + overnight soaking + 1 hour chilling | **COOKING** 5–7 minutes per batch | **DIFFICULTY** Easy

Soak the chickpeas in plenty of water overnight.

Next day, drain the chickpeas and place in a bowl blender with the parsley and garlic. Blend the mixture until well chopped.

Add the cumin and baking powder, season generously with salt and freshly ground black pepper, and blend again until thoroughly combined.

Scrape the mixture into a bowl, cover with plastic wrap and chill in the fridge for at least 1 hour.

Roll the mixture into balls, about the size of golf balls.

Heat about 10 cm (4 inches) of vegetable oil in a heavy-based saucepan over medium heat.

When the oil is hot, add the falafels in batches, taking care not to crowd the pan, and cook for 5–7 minutes, turning halfway through, until the falafels are a lovely golden colour and cooked all the way through.

The falafels are much tastier while they are hot, but you can refrigerate any leftovers and simply warm them back up for serving, by gently pressing them in a hot pan or microwaving for 20 seconds.

500 g (1 lb 2 oz/2½ cups) dried chickpeas
½ cup roughly chopped flat-leaf (Italian) parsley
1 garlic clove, roughly chopped
1 teaspoon ground cumin
2 teaspoons baking powder
2 teaspoons salt, or to taste
vegetable oil, for deep-frying

Pulses

Pulses, commonly referred to as dhal (or dal), are an essential ingredient of subcontinental cuisine. In Sri Lanka, with its partially vegetarian population, pulses are a key element in the diet, and dhal is eaten with curry and rice at most meals, particularly breakfast.

Dried beans, whole peas and chickpeas need to be soaked before cooking, whereas lentils and split peas do not. Before soaking, discard any broken or shrivelled seeds, or any foreign matter such as pebbles, then place in a sieve and rinse under cold running water. Place in a deep container, cover with plenty of cold water and leave to soak for 8–10 hours. Discard the soaking water, and rinse the pulses well under cold running water, to remove any carbohydrates responsible for wind. The pulses can be cooked on the stovetop, in a slow cooker, and for certain recipes, in the oven.

---

1. RED KIDNEY BEANS These beans are named for their resemblance to a kidney, both in colour and shape. They are a star ingredient in Rajma chawal (page 69).

2. PULSES A pulse is the dried seed of plants from the legume family, and includes the dried seeds of legumes such as beans, peas (including chickpeas) and lentils. Inexpensive and highly nutritious, pulses are rich in protein, vitamins, minerals and fibre, and feature prominently in subcontinental cuisine.

3. URAD DHAL These small black oval-shaped beans, split or whole, are the base of the famous idlis, vadas and dosas of southern Indian cooking. Their dark skin hides a pale yellow interior, and their texture becomes slightly glutinous with cooking. Urad dhal are available in various forms. You can buy the black beans with their outer skin intact, either as whole beans, or split in half. White urad dhal are simply hulled beans, with the black outer skin removed; these are pale or white in colour, and are available whole or split in half. Black urad dhal have a deeper flavour and contribute a darker colour to finished dishes.

4. BLACK-EYED PEAS Also known as cow peas or lobia, these nutritious peas are boiled and often eaten for breakfast across the subcontinent.

5. RED LENTILS are the most common pulses for dhal dishes as they need no soaking and cook quickly. Highly nutritious, they form the base of many meals.

6. CHANA DHAL Often cooked on its own, and also called Bengal gram, this small, split yellow pulse is used to add body to dishes and crunch to tarkas. 'Chana' is a small Indian chickpea, and 'dhal' is the Indian term for dried, split and hulled pulses, which include peas, beans and lentils. Sweet, nutty chana dhal is an excellent source of protein and a favourite in soups, stews and curries. Rinse and soak before cooking.

7. MOONG DHAL Also called green gram, these mint-green pulses are yellow underneath. Unlike many dhals, green moong dhal are left whole when cooked.

8. WHITE URAD DHAL These tiny pulses are hulled black urad dhal; the ones in the photo have been split in half, but are also available whole.

Kala chana
Bengal gram curry

Also known as Bengal gram, kala chana is a type of chickpea, but dark brown in colour and smaller in size than the common chickpea. This is a mildly spiced black chickpea curry, made in a Punjabi style.

REGION Bangladesh | **SERVES** 3–4 | **PREPARATION** 25 minutes + 9 hours soaking
COOKING 30–45 minutes | **DIFFICULTY** Easy

200 g (7 oz/1 cup) dried black chickpeas
   (kala chana)
2 tablespoons ghee or rice bran oil
1 teaspoon cumin seeds
1 onion, finely chopped
4–5 garlic cloves, finely chopped
1–2 Indian green chillies, finely chopped
1 fresh curry leaf sprig, leaves picked
1 large tomato, finely chopped
¼ teaspoon ground turmeric
1 teaspoon ground coriander
½ teaspoon Kashmiri red chilli powder
a pinch of asafoetida (optional)
2 dried red chillies, cut in half
1 teaspoon salt, or to taste
½ teaspoon Garam masala (page 24)
coriander (cilantro) leaves, to garnish

Put the chickpeas in a bowl, add 750 ml (26 fl oz/3 cups) water and leave to soak overnight, or for at least 8–9 hours.

Next day, drain the chickpeas, rinse well and set aside.

Heat the ghee or oil in a pressure cooker or heavy-based saucepan. Add the cumin seeds. When they start to pop, add the onion and cook, stirring, for 3 minutes, or until the onion is translucent and lightly golden. Add the garlic, green chilli and curry leaves and cook for 15–20 seconds.

Now add the tomato and cook it down for 5–7 minutes, stirring lightly now and then, until the oil starts to separate from the mixture.

Add the turmeric, ground coriander, chilli powder and asafoetida, if using. Stir for 2–3 seconds, then add the chickpeas, along with all their soaking water. Add the dried chillies and salt, stirring well.

Pressure-cook over medium to high pressure for 10–15 minutes, or if using a saucepan, cover and simmer for 30 minutes, until the chickpeas are well cooked and softened.

Lastly, sprinkle with the garam masala and stir it in.

Garnish with coriander and serve with steamed rice, rotis or chapatti.

TIP Some recipes suggest adding bicarbonate of soda (baking soda) to the cooking water when cooking pulses. I don't generally recommend this, as it can make the pulses too soft.

A quick guide to pulses, legumes and sprouting

While sprouting of pulses and legumes has become quite popular of late, across the subcontinent sprouting has been done for hundreds of years, both as a way of maximising the nutritional benefits of these humble foods, as well as providing different textural profiles to a dish.

Pulses — chickpeas, lentils, dried peas and beans — are the dried edible seeds of legume plants. The terms 'pulse' and 'legume' are sometimes used interchangeably, but legume is a much broader category, applying to plants that enclose their fruit in pods, including all pulses, as well as fresh beans and peas, and surprising additions like peanuts and Australian native wattleseed.

These days you'll find a wide variety of sprouted legumes readily available in health food stores and greengrocers, but making them yourself using certified organic seeds has to be better for you, and much more satisfying.

The first step is to fill your cupboards with a stockpile of dried and tinned pulses. Cost effective and shelf stable, they're perfect for keeping in your pantry for those dreaded empty-fridge scenarios. While pre-soaking helps to reduce the cooking time of dried pulses by up to a quarter, and also helps with digestion, don't forget that tinned pulses are an equally great alternative for all kinds of dishes when you are time poor. Dried lentils and split peas cook quickly, making them ideal for weeknight dinners, whereas dried beans and chickpeas will take much longer, and will require more planning.

Nutritionally there is little difference between the tinned and dried variety, other than the sodium that is added to the tinned version. Try to select tinned varieties with little or no added salt, and always rinse the contents thoroughly before using.

HOW TO SPROUT DRIED BEANS OR PEAS

Begin by placing them in a colander and washing them thoroughly in a few changes of water. Place the pulses in a container large enough to hold them all, and twice their volume in water. Pour in enough room-temperature water to completely cover the pulses by about 5 cm (2 inches), then let them sit overnight, or for at least 8 hours. By this time, they will have soaked up a lot of water and will have almost doubled in volume.

Soak some paper towel in water, then squeeze out any excess water. Drain the soaked legumes in a colander and cover them with the damp paper towel. Place the colander out of direct sunlight and let them sprout. All you need to do every 12 hours or so, for the next 3–4 days, is shake them around in the colander — hands-free if possible, or delicately so as to not break any tender sprouts — then gently rinse them off, and cover again with a damp paper towel before setting aside.

Once sprouted, they will continue to grow in sunlight. My mum always kept them in a jar in the fridge with some fresh tissue, to slow their growth, keep them crunchy and stop any bad odours.

Goen hogay
Sprouts & cucumber with onion & cheese

Rice forms the main body of most Bhutanese meals, accompanied by one or two side dishes consisting of meat or vegetables. Pork, beef and chicken are the meats most often eaten, while commonly eaten vegetables include cucumber, spinach, pumpkin (winter squash), turnip, radish, tomato, river weed, onion and green beans. I have added sprouted beans to this refreshing salad because we are not living high in the mountains and can have a bit more variety. Feel free to add whatever greens you like.

The Bhutanese serve soothing side dishes like this to temper their chilli-laden mains. They would use a local farmer's cheese in this dish, but as it is only available in Bhutan, we'll improvise with feta, which makes an acceptable substitute.

REGION Bhutan | **SERVES** 4 | **PREPARATION** 15 minutes | **DIFFICULTY** Easy

Put the cucumber in a food processor and give the machine four or five pulses, to chop the cucumber coarsely. Add the onion and give the machine another four or five pulses, to chop the onion finely.

(Alternatively, you could finely chop the cucumber and onion with a knife, but the blender makes it all nice and juicy.)

Combine in a bowl with the remaining ingredients, season to taste with salt and freshly ground black pepper, and serve.

½ telegraph (long) cucumber

1 red onion, quartered

1 cup sprouted mung beans (see opposite page)

85 g (½ cup) crumbled Danish feta cheese

1 medium-hot green chilli, seeded and diced

1 large vine-ripened tomato, finely diced

½ teaspoon ground sichuan peppercorns

Kitchari

Kitchari (pronounced kitch-a-ree) is a staple comfort food of India, also known as khichari, khitchari and kitchiri, and also sometimes referred to as kedgeree (though incorrectly, as that is an English dish). The word 'kitchari' means 'mixture' or 'mess', as in 'mess of pottage' or 'mess of stew' or porridge mixture, usually of two grains.

Traditionally made of basmati rice and yellow dried split mung beans (moong dhal), along with digestive spices and ghee, kitchari is used as a cleansing and detoxifying food in Ayurveda. This is one kitchari recipe that is particularly nourishing and easy to digest — as long as you avoid using vegetables from the nightshade family, which are considered to have an inflammatory effect.

REGION India | **SERVES** 6 | **PREPARATION** 15 minutes
COOKING 1¼ hours | **DIFFICULTY** Easy

400 g (14 oz/2 cups) dried split yellow
   mung beans (moong dhal)
2 tablespoons ghee or organic
   sesame oil
2 teaspoons black mustard seeds
2 teaspoons cumin seeds
1 teaspoon fennel seeds
1 teaspoon fenugreek seeds
1 fresh curry leaf sprig, leaves picked
2 teaspoons ground turmeric
1 teaspoon ground cumin
1 teaspoon ground coriander
1 teaspoon ground cinnamon (optional
   in winter)
2 teaspoons freshly ground black pepper
200 g (7 oz/1 cup) white basmati rice
2 cloves
2 fresh bay leaves
3 green cardamom pods
2–5 cups chopped organic, seasonal
   vegetables, such as spinach, carrots,
   celery, bok choy (pak choy) and kale
   (avoid nightshades)
chopped coriander (cilantro), to serve
   (optional)

Rinse and strain the mung beans five times, or until the water runs clear. Set aside.

Heat the ghee or sesame oil in a large saucepan over medium heat. Add the mustard, cumin, fennel and fenugreek seeds and toast until the mustard seeds pop.

Add the curry leaves and ground spices, stirring well, then stir in the rice and beans.

Pour in 2 litres (70 fl oz/8 cups) water, and add the cloves, bay leaves, cardamom pods and vegetables.

Bring to the boil, then reduce the heat and simmer for at least 1 hour, until the beans and rice are soft, and the kitchari has a porridge-like consistency.

Serve warm, garnished with chopped coriander if desired.

Lobia masala
Black-eyed pea curry

Also known as cow peas, and in Sri Lanka as kaupi, and India as lobia, black-eyed peas are easy to grow, can tolerate the dry, and are an easy form of protein and calories across the subcontinent. When the peas sprout, farmers plough them into the soil, to regenerate it for the next crop.

Black-eyed peas are often ground into a flour and pastes for use in different recipes; the starch is said to digest quite slowly this way. (I remember my grandmother telling me this was good for maintaining healthy cholesterol and blood sugar levels. When I was growing up, Ayurveda was part of everyday life in Sri Lanka and India, as it still is today.) The peas also make a delicious curry, such as this one.

REGION India | **SERVES** 4 | **PREPARATION** 30 minutes + 4–5 hours soaking
COOKING about 1 hour | **DIFFICULTY** Easy

Wash the peas and leave to soak in plenty of lukewarm water for 4–5 hours.

Drain the peas and place in a pressure cooker or heavy-based saucepan with a pinch of salt and enough water to cover. Pressure cook the peas for 10 minutes, or boil them for about 25 minutes, or until tender. Drain and set aside.

Heat 2 tablespoons of the rice bran oil in a heavy-based saucepan. Add the onion, green chilli and ginger garlic paste and cook over medium heat for 3 minutes, or until the onion is soft and translucent. Add the tomato and cook, stirring now and then, for about 5 minutes, until the tomato turns pulpy and is thoroughly cooked. Set aside.

In a large heavy-based saucepan, heat the remaining 1 tablespoon of oil over medium heat. Add the bay leaf, cloves, cinnamon stick and cumin seeds. When the cumin seeds start to splutter, stir in the tomato mixture, along with the pepper, ground spices, salt and 1 litre (35 fl oz/4 cups) water.

Cook, uncovered, over medium–low heat for at least 15 minutes, or until the gravy is dry and a little dark in colour.

Add the boiled peas, along with 125 ml (4 fl oz/½ cup) of water, mix all the ingredients well. Stir in the crushed potatoes and leave to cook for about 10 minutes, or until the gravy thickens.

Garnish with coriander leaves and a sprinkling of garam masala. Serve hot, with chapatti.

185 g (6½ oz/1 cup) dried black-eyed peas
60 ml (2 fl oz/¼ cup) rice bran oil
2 onions, chopped
1 Indian green chilli, chopped
1 tablespoon Ginger garlic paste (page 241)
2 tomatoes, chopped
1 fresh bay leaf
2 cloves
1 cinnamon stick, broken in half
½ teaspoon cumin seeds
½ teaspoon freshly ground black pepper
2 teaspoons ground coriander
½ teaspoon ground turmeric
¼ teaspoon chilli powder
1 teaspoon salt, or to taste
2 potatoes, boiled in their skins, then peeled and crushed
2 teaspoons finely chopped coriander (cilantro) leaves
¼ teaspoon Garam masala (page 24)
chapatti, to serve

Pindi chole
Chickpea curry

High in protein, the seeds of the legume **Cicer arietinum** *are variously known as kabuli chana (particularly in northern India), gram, Egyptian pea and garbanzo bean — and to many in the West as the chickpea.*

Here they star in pindi chole, a very popular main-course Punjabi dish made with chickpeas cooked in various spices. It is a fairly dry curry, but full of goodness and flavour. The dish has many preparations, and many will disagree with this version. The tea leaves add a lovely amber colour to the curry. Serve with Puri (page 38) or roti.

REGION Pakistan | **SERVES** 4 | **PREPARATION** 30 minutes + overnight soaking
COOKING about 1¼ hours | **DIFFICULTY** Medium

250 g (9 oz) dried chickpeas
1 tablespoon best-quality black tea leaves, such as Dilmah Brilliant Breakfast
1 cinnamon stick, broken into 3–4 pieces
1 tablespoon cloves
5–6 green cardamom pods
5–6 black cardamom pods
2–3 fresh bay leaves
1 teaspoon regular salt, plus more to taste
1 teaspoon ground turmeric
1 teaspoon ground coriander
1 teaspoon ground cumin
1 teaspoon chilli powder
1 teaspoon dried fenugreek leaves (kasuri methi)
1 teaspoon pomegranate powder
1 teaspoon amchur (dried mango powder)
2 tablespoons rice bran oil
2 tablespoons ajwain seeds or caraway seeds
4–5 garlic cloves, chopped
1 teaspoon fresh Ginger paste (page 241)
2–3 Indian green chillies, chopped
1 tablespoon tamarind water (see page 211)
a pinch of black salt

TO GARNISH
chopped coriander (cilantro)
chopped green chillies
lemon wedges

Soak the chickpeas overnight in plenty of cold water.

Next day, drain the chickpeas and rinse them well, then place in a heavy-based saucepan.

Take a small clean piece of muslin (cheesecloth) and prepare a bouquet garni with the tea leaves, cinnamon, cloves, green and black cardamom pods and bay leaves. Add the bundled spices to the chickpeas, along with the regular salt and 1 litre (35 fl oz/4 cups) water, or enough to cover the chickpeas. Bring to the boil and allow to boil, uncovered, for at least 1 hour. The water should be nearly evaporated.

Remove and discard the bouquet garni. Strain the chickpeas, reserving the liquid. To the chickpeas add all the ground spices, pomegranate powder and amchur and mix gently. Set aside.

Heat the rice bran oil in a frying pan over medium heat. Add the ajwain seeds, garlic, ginger paste and green chilli and fry for a minute or two, until fragrant. Pour the mixture over the chickpeas and stir it in.

Return the reserved chickpea cooking liquid to the chickpeas and stir in the tamarind water, a pinch of black salt, and regular salt to taste. Cook over low heat for 5–7 minutes, or until the liquid has nearly evaporated, gently stirring a few times, taking care not to break up the chickpeas. The chickpeas should be nicely coated with spices and almost dry.

Turn into a bowl and garnish with coriander and green chillies. Serve with lemon wedges and puri or roti.

Rajma chawal
Red kidney bean curry with rice

Originally a staple of the village kitchen, this rustic, traditional meal is cooked in households all over India. Simple and nutritious, it is naturally gluten free, vegan and suited to people with allergies.

Using tinned beans and tomatoes significantly cuts down preparation time and makes this dish suitable for a quick weeknight meal. Just remember to read the tin label, as preservatives, sodium and sugar may be present from the canning process.

You can also make the rajma (bean curry) ahead of time, and reheat for serving. If making ahead, stir the coriander through just before serving.

REGION India | **SERVES** 4 | **PREPARATION** 25 minutes
COOKING 30 minutes | **DIFFICULTY** Easy

Heat the rice bran oil in a heavy-based saucepan over medium–high heat. Fry the onion for 7–8 minutes, until the onion is soft and golden around the edges.

Add the garlic, ginger and chilli and fry together for about 1 minute, or until fragrant.

Add the tomatoes, ground spices and amchur, if using. Season with salt and freshly ground black pepper.

Turn down the heat and cook, stirring every so often, for 7–10 minutes, or until the masala starts reducing and comes together in a sticky mass, and the oil starts separating from it. (At this point, if you prefer a smooth sauce, you can blend the mixture to a fine paste and return it to the saucepan; I like a bit of texture in my rajma, so I usually leave it as is.)

Stir in the kidney beans and coconut water. Simmer for a few more minutes, until the beans are heated through. Add a little more hot water if the sauce is too thick.

Just before serving, stir in some chopped fresh coriander. Taste, and adjust the seasoning with salt and pepper if needed. Sprinkle with extra garam masala and top with more coriander and the ginger strips, if using. Serve with steamed rice.

TIPS You can use fresh tomato purée for this recipe. Blanch two large ripe tomatoes in boiling water for 15 seconds, refresh in iced water, then peel off the skin and discard the seeds. Blend to a fine purée and use as directed.

You can also cook this dish in a pressure cooker, to really seal in all the flavours and speed up the cooking process.

2–3 tablespoons rice bran oil
1 onion, finely diced
3 garlic cloves, crushed
2.5 cm (1 inch) knob of fresh ginger, peeled and grated
1–2 green bird's eye chillies, finely chopped
375 g (13 oz/1½ cups) crushed tomatoes and their juices, or tomato passata (see tip)
1 tablespoon ground coriander
1 tablespoon ground cumin
1½ teaspoons Garam masala (page 24), plus extra to garnish
½ teaspoon amchur (dried mango powder); optional
2 x 540 g (1 lb 3 oz) tins red kidney beans, rinsed and drained
125 ml (4 fl oz/½ cup) coconut water; use water if you do not want the sweetness
chopped coriander (cilantro), to serve and to garnish
julienned strips of fresh ginger, to garnish (optional)

Subz khichda
Vegetable haleem

In the traditional haleem, the primary ingredient along with ground wheat is mutton. However, in a vegetarian haleem, you can replace the meat component with tempeh or soya nuggets and extra vegetables.

REGION Afghanistan | **SERVES** 4 | **PREPARATION** 15 minutes + 1 hour soaking
COOKING 20 minutes | **DIFFICULTY** Medium

Soak the cracked wheat and barley in a bowl of water for 1 hour.

If using soya nuggets, soak them in a bowl of water for 20 minutes, until they expand. Drain them, then place in a blender and grind into large crumbs. Set aside.

Heat the rice bran oil and ghee in a large heavy-based saucepan. Add the onion and garlic and cook over medium heat for a few minutes, or until the onion is translucent.

Stir in the turmeric, chilli powder, ground coriander, cumin and cinnamon, mixing well.

Drain the cracked wheat and barley and add them to the pan, along with the ground soya nuggets or the tempeh. Stir well and cook for a further 5 minutes, or until the protein is thoroughly coated in the spices. Add the dried figs and apricots.

Pour in enough water to cover the mixture and bring to the boil. Reduce the heat to low, then cover and simmer for 8–10 minutes, or until the grains are tender.

Remove the lid and add the yoghurt, almond meal, cloves, Kashmiri chilli powder, mint, coriander and lemon juice, mixing well.

Bring back to the boil and season to taste. Garnish with fried onion and coriander sprigs and serve with rice or a bread of your choice.

TIP Tempeh is notorious for not being able to absorb any kind of marinade because it is so dense. The secret is to freeze it first. When you thaw it, the cell walls of the soy break down and allow the marinade or sauce to penetrate the tempeh. It won't affect the quality, but will sure make it taste better!

2½ tablespoons cracked wheat
100 g (3½ oz/½ cup) pearl barley
100 g (3½ oz) soya nuggets, or 100 g (3½ oz) frozen tempeh (see tip), thawed and chopped into 2 cm (¾ inch) cubes
2 tablespoons rice bran oil
2 tablespoons ghee
2 onions, finely chopped
1 tablespoon finely chopped garlic
1 teaspoon ground turmeric
½ teaspoon chilli powder
1 teaspoon ground coriander
1 teaspoon ground cumin
½ teaspoon ground cinnamon
3 dried figs, diced
2 dried apricots, diced
260 g (9¼ oz/1 cup) Greek-style yoghurt
3 tablespoons almond meal
a pinch of ground cloves
2 teaspoons Kashmiri chilli powder
2 tablespoons finely chopped mint
2 tablespoons finely chopped coriander (cilantro)
juice of 1 lemon

TO GARNISH
2 tablespoons fried onion
coriander (cilantro) sprigs

Curd vadai
Lentil patties with coconut curd

Another great street-food snack, these delicious lentil patties, or vadai, also look great served up at home as a starter, or even piled on a platter for everyone to share.

REGION Sri Lanka | **MAKES** ABOUT 24 | **PREPARATION** 20 minutes + 2 hours soaking
COOKING 5 minutes + 8–10 minutes per batch | **DIFFICULTY** Medium

---

vegetable oil, for deep-frying
coriander (cilantro) leaves, to garnish

VADAI (LENTIL PATTIES)
250 g (9 oz) white urad dhal (hulled dried
    black lentils)
5 Indian green chillies, chopped
1 small knob of fresh ginger, peeled
    and chopped
½ pinch of asafoetida
iced water (optional)
¼ bunch coriander (cilantro), leaves
    chopped

COCONUT CURD
250 g (9 oz) Greek-style yoghurt
150 ml (5 fl oz) milk
50 g (1¾ oz/⅔ cup) fresh grated coconut

FOR TEMPERING
1 tablespoon ghee
2 teaspoons brown mustard seeds
1 teaspoon cumin seeds
½ teaspoon asafoetida
2 dried red chillies, broken in half
10 fresh curry leaves, chopped

For the vadai, soak the lentils in 500 ml (17 fl oz/2 cups) water for 2 hours.

Drain and place in a blender, then grind until the lentils form a thick paste, like a very thick fritter mixture that is quite wet, but pliable enough to form a shape.

Just before you stop grinding, add the chilli, ginger and asafoetida. If you need to add a bit of water, make sure it is iced water. Stir in the coriander and set aside.

In a bowl, combine all the coconut curd ingredients.

For tempering, heat the ghee in a frying pan over medium heat. Add the spices, chillies and curry leaves and cook for a minute or two, until the mustard seeds start to pop and the mixture is aromatic.

Stir the tempered spices through the yoghurt curd mixture and set aside.

To cook the lentil patties, pour about 10 cm (4 inches) of vegetable oil into a heavy-based saucepan. Heat over medium-high heat to to 180°C (350°F), or until a small bit of batter sizzles when added to the oil.

Wet your hands, take some batter and shape it into a small doughnut, about 3 cm (1¼ inches) wide.

In batches, carefully add the patties to the oil, making sure not to overcrowd the pan. Cook for about 2–3 minutes, then scoop them out of the oil. Leave to rest for 3–4 minutes to allow the heat to penetrate, then add them back into the oil and cook for another 2–3 minutes, or until cooked through and golden all over. Drain on paper towel and keep warm while cooking the remaining patties.

Arrange on a serving platter, garnish with coriander and serve hot, with the spiced yoghurt.

Chapter 3
Salads

The salads of the subcontinent are a painter's palette of food, with incredible colour and diversity. They are also edible medicine.

What defines these salads is their attention to detail. They can bring comfort or vitality, and serve as a brisk pick-me-up or a textural masterstroke to an accompanying curry. They cool, cut through richness, deliver funk with fermentation, or themselves add a mouth-punching kick of heat. Cooks across the subcontinent macerate and marinate to stellar effect. They know how to assault the senses in the very best of ways, all with colour, variety, nutrition and taste.

Do people in the subcontinent eat just a salad? Generally, no. Across the region, a salad is considered an accompaniment, rather than the main event we often treat it as these days. But don't think this means it is an afterthought. It is equally considered for the flavour, health, colour and the complexity it can bring to the table as the other dishes it is served with. Salads are considered a vital element of the cuisine.

The food of the subcontinent is rich in tradition, full of marvellous and diverse dishes, with a blend of cooking techniques to create a distinctive mix of complex flavours. And I think salads showcase this to perfection.

When preparing salads, here are a few general tips. Always start with the best ingredients, choosing organic whenever possible. Give your fresh produce the squeeze test: soft and soggy vegetables will not yield a mouthwatering salad. Fresh vegetables and leaves really do look more bright, lively and light than their aged counterparts. Wash them first, or in the case of more fragile greens, you can refresh them in iced water; make sure they are dry before using them in a salad. Always dress your salads just before serving, garnishing right at the end with any herbs. And remember that most salads are best prepared as close to serving as possible.

I chose the salads in this chapter for their colour, variety, freshness and taste, and the myriad ways in which they can potentially be enjoyed, whether as a meal on their own, or as a side to a spread of dishes. I strongly encourage you to build on them and create your own salads — something uniquely yours, and part of your own family story.

Gotu kola sambal
Pennywort salad

Pennywort is being labelled as a 'superfood' nowadays, but in Sri Lanka, where it is known as gotu kola, it has always been considered a healthy and delicious condiment for a curry. As I am no doctor, I won't enter into the many things it is touted to cure — but it tastes damn good, so do try to get hold of some, or buy some from a nursery and grow your own; it makes a beautiful ground cover.

If you can't get hold of a fresh coconut and grate it, use frozen grated coconut from an Asian supermarket — or as a last resort, rehydrate some desiccated coconut.

REGION Sri Lanka | **SERVES** 4 as a condiment | **PREPARATION** 10 minutes | **DIFFICULTY** Easy

1 large handful pennywort, including
    the stems
½ small onion, finely chopped
1 small Indian green chilli, finely chopped
50 g (1¾ oz/⅔ cup) freshly grated
    coconut
½ teaspoon ground turmeric
juice of ½ lime

Very finely shred the pennywort, including the stems. (We've left the leaves whole in the photo.) Place in a bowl with all the remaining ingredients and mix together.

Season to taste with salt and freshly cracked black pepper, and a little more lime juice if needed; the salad should taste tangy.

Serve immediately with curries, or use instead of tabouleh in a salad or wrap.

TIP Instead of pennywort, you can use the finely shredded leaves from a bunch of flat-leaf (Italian) parsley. You could also use baby nasturtium leaves, or try other green vegetables such as bok choy (pak choy), choy sum, or a combination of your favourite green herbs, but parsley is the best.

Borani kachalu
Afghan spiced potato salad with minted yoghurt

Recipes like this one are hard to come by, and I have to credit this recipe to writer and cook Shayma Saadat, who has wonderful stories and memories of her father and the beauty of Afghan food.

REGION Afghanistan | **SERVES** 6 | **PREPARATION** 15 minutes
COOKING 30 minutes | **DIFFICULTY** Easy

1–2 tablespoons olive oil
½ onion, chopped
½ teaspoon crushed garlic
½ teaspoon finely grated fresh ginger
125 g (4½ oz/½ cup) crushed tinned tomatoes
⅛ teaspoon ground turmeric
½ teaspoon ground coriander
⅛–¼ teaspoon cayenne pepper, to taste
2 Indian green chillies, chopped
500 g (1 lb 2 oz) kipfler (fingerling) potatoes, peeled and sliced into discs 3 cm (1¼ inches) thick
mint leaves, to garnish
1 tablespoon virgin coconut oil

MINTED YOGHURT
200 g (7 oz/¾ cup) plain yoghurt
1 teaspoon chopped mint
a pinch of salt, or to taste

Heat the olive oil in a large heavy-based frying pan; choose one that has a lid. Add the onion and cook over medium heat for 2 minutes, then add the garlic and ginger and stir for 30 seconds, or until fragrant.

Add the tomatoes, ground spices and chilli and cook, stirring, for 1 minute. Now add the potato discs and gently stir for 2–3 minutes, ensuring that each disc is thoroughly coated with the sauce.

Pour 60 ml (2 fl oz/¼ cup) water over the potatoes, cover the pan and turn the heat down to low. Cook the potatoes in their own steam for 15 minutes, or until a knife slides through one freely; the tomato sauce should look thick, coating the potato discs. Remove from the heat and leave to cool to room temperature.

Meanwhile, prepare the minted yoghurt. Put the yoghurt in a small bowl and whisk in 2 tablespoons water. Stir in the mint and salt.

Arrange the potato discs in a serving dish and drizzle with the minted yoghurt. Garnish with extra mint.

For a final hit of flavour, heat the coconut oil in a small pan until it starts to smoke, then spoon it over the finished dish. Serve warm.

Karavila sambal
Bitter melon sambal

The reported health benefits of the bitter melon, also known as bitter gourd, have finally made it to the West, where it is now being sold in tablets to assist with all kinds of ailments. In Sri Lanka we used to eat it regularly.

My dad loved bitter melon this way, fried crisp with dried fish, but remember the greener it stays during its preparation, the better the melon is for you.

Salting the melon removes some of the bitterness, but it is called bitter melon for a reason! Do not combine the salad until ready to serve.

REGION Sri Lanka | **SERVES** 6 as a condiment | **PREPARATION** 20 minutes
COOKING 10–12 minutes | **DIFFICULTY** Easy

Cut each melon half into 4 mm (³⁄₁₆ inch) slices, sprinkle with salt and leave to sit for 5 minutes.

Wash the melon slices under fresh running water and pat dry with paper towel or a clean tea towel.

Pour the vegetable oil into a deep heavy-based saucepan and heat to 180°C (350°F), or until a cube of bread dropped into the oil turns brown in 15 seconds.

Working in batches, carefully add the melon slices to the hot oil and cook for 2–3 minutes, until they turn a light golden brown. Drain on paper towel and keep warm while cooking the remaining melon.

When all the slices are cooked, quickly fry the curry leaves in the hot oil for about 1 minute, until crisp.

Combine all the ingredients in a bowl, season with salt and freshly cracked black pepper and mix well. Serve immediately.

TIP Preparing the bitter melon using the method in the Ridged gourd curry recipe on page 120 will also retain the melon's colour. If you're really keen to get the maximum health benefits, juice the melon and have it as a quick shot, followed by lots of water.

5 bitter melons, cut in half lengthways, seeds removed
salt, for sprinkling, plus extra for seasoning
1 litre (35 fl oz/4 cups) vegetable oil or rice bran oil, for deep-frying
1 fresh curry leaf sprig, leaves picked
80 g (2¾ oz/1 cup) freshly grated coconut
2 Indian green chillies, chopped
1 onion, sliced
2 vine-ripened tomatoes, seeded and sliced
lime juice, to taste

Begun bhaja
Crispy eggplant with Bengali salad

Begun bhaja is a traditional Bengali dish in which delicately spiced slices of eggplant are fried until crisp, and usually served as a side dish with a simple, homely meal. Here it is served with a lovely fresh salad.

REGION Bangladesh | **SERVES** 5 | **PREPARATION** 50 minutes + 30 minutes chilling
COOKING 15 minutes | **DIFFICULTY** Medium

Start by making the salad. Place the cucumber, carrot, radish, tomatoes, onion and chilli in a large bowl.

Sprinkle with the sugar, pepper and salt and gently toss the salad until all the ingredients are uniformly mixed. Sprinkle with the lime juice and mustard oil, and crushed peanuts if using.

Cover and chill for 30 minutes, tossing the coriander through just before serving.

Meanwhile, put the spices for the begun bhaja in a small bowl. Add the salt, lemon juice and 2 tablespoons water, mixing well. Rub the spice mix over both sides of each eggplant disc until evenly coated, then set aside to absorb for at least 5 minutes.

Just before serving, place a large heavy-based frying pan over high heat and pour in about 1 cm (½ inch) of rice bran oil. Heat until smoking, then reduce the heat to its lowest setting.

Add the eggplant slices, in a single layer. Cook for 3–4 minutes, or until golden underneath, then flip and cook on the other side for a further 3–4 minutes. During this time you may need to add more oil to the pan, as the eggplant will soak it up — hence the need to use a healthy oil.

Serve immediately, while still hot, with the Bengali salad.

TIP When frying the eggplant, be sure to keep the oil temperature constant, because if it cools down, the eggplant will absorb all the oil and won't brown properly. The hot oil will cool down as soon as you add the eggplant (or any other ingredient), so you will need to turn up the temperature until it heats through again, and then turn it down when the oil is the right temperature. In short, you always need to adjust the temperature of your oil when shallow-frying.

BEGUN BHAJA
½ teaspoon chilli powder
1 teaspoon ground turmeric
1 teaspoon Garam masala (page 24)
a pinch of salt, or to taste
juice of 1 lemon
1 large eggplant (aubergine), sliced into discs 2 cm (¾ inch) thick
rice bran oil, for shallow-frying

BENGALI SALAD
½ telegraph (long) cucumber, peeled, seeded and finely chopped
1 carrot, shredded
50 g (1¾ oz/½ cup) finely chopped red radish
2 small–medium vine-ripened tomatoes
1 red onion, finely chopped
2 Indian green chillies, finely chopped
1 tablespoon sugar
¼ teaspoon freshly cracked black pepper
a pinch of salt, or to taste
juice of ½ large lime
a few drops of mustard oil
1 teaspoon crushed peanuts (optional)
½ cup chopped coriander (cilantro) leaves

Bhutanese cucumber salad

When I look at this recipe I see a Bhutanese Greek salad. It is light and tasty, yet has that typical Bhutanese heat — but you can omit the bird's eye chilli if you prefer, and just use the two long red chillies. This salad also offers a degree of stress relief, in the very satisfying act of smashing the cucumber.

REGION Bhutan | **SERVES** 4 as a side dish, or 2 as a starter
PREPARATION 15 minutes + 15 minutes resting | **DIFFICULTY** Easy

1 telegraph (long) cucumber
2 vine-ripened tomatoes, diced
½ red onion, thinly sliced
2 long red chillies, sliced, with the seeds
1 small red bird's eye chilli, seeded and finely chopped
a handful of fresh coriander (cilantro), finely chopped
2 spring onions (scallions), finely chopped
100 g (3½ oz) Danish feta cheese
1 teaspoon ground sichuan pepper

Cover the cucumber with plastic wrap and gently smash it up a bit using a rolling pin. Chop into 2 cm (¾ inch) cubes and place in a serving bowl.

Add the tomato, onion, chillies, coriander and spring onion. Crumble the feta into the salad, sprinkle with the sichuan pepper, season with salt and mix together well.

Before serving, leave to sit for 15 minutes or so, to allow the flavours to mingle and the salt to draw out some of the vegetable juices.

Cabbage salad

Tasty, crunchy and tangy, this salad, known in Pakistan as patta ghobi, is basically a Pakistani coleslaw, which we often serve at home as a simple side dish. If you don't like red cabbage, just use white cabbage. If there is a peanut allergy in the family, leave out the peanuts, and use olive oil instead of peanut oil.

REGION Pakistan | **SERVES** 4 | **PREPARATION** 15 minutes | **DIFFICULTY** Easy

250 g (9 oz) cabbage, a mixture of red and white, thinly shredded
2 large carrots, shredded
1 Indian green chilli, finely chopped
½ cup coriander (cilantro) leaves, chopped
½ teaspoon sugar
70 g (2½ oz/½ cup) roasted peanuts, crushed (optional)
60 ml (2 fl oz/¼ cup) unrefined peanut oil
lemon juice, to taste

Combine the cabbage, carrot, chilli, coriander and sugar in a large bowl. Add the peanuts, if using, and the peanut oil and mix thoroughly.

Add lemon juice and salt to taste, then serve.

TIP I use unrefined peanut oil in my recipes, as it has much more flavour than regular peanut oil. You'll find it in Chinese grocery stores.

Shredded carrot & spiced cashew salad

In the cool hills of Sri Lanka, where its most famous product, tea, is grown, sweet crunchy carrots are also cultivated. Easy to prepare, this is a tasty salad, with lots of texture. The devilled cashews tossed through also make a great snack to enjoy with a cool drink, and will keep in an airtight container in the pantry for several days.

REGION Sri Lanka | **SERVES** 2–4 | **PREPARATION** 10 minutes
COOKING 10 minutes | **DIFFICULTY** Easy

For the devilled cashews, heat the coconut oil in a heavy-based frying pan or wok over high heat until a light smoke haze appears. Add the cashews and fry for about 1 minute, or until golden brown. Add the curry leaves, then strain the mixture out of the hot oil, into a bowl. Toss with the chilli powder, pepper and salt and set aside.

For the salad, place the radish, coconut and carrot in a clean tea towel and squeeze out all the liquid. Place the shredded vegetables in a large bowl. Add the onion and coriander, if using, and 155 g (5½ oz/1 cup) of the devilled cashews. Set aside.

Heat the coconut oil in a frying pan over medium heat. Add the celery, fennel and cumin seeds and gently cook for a minute or two, until golden brown.

Drizzle the warm spiced coconut oil over the salad, along with the lime juice, and toss together. Serve immediately.

150 g (5½ oz/1¼ cups) shredded
   red radish
50 g (1¾ oz/⅔ cup) shredded
   fresh coconut
450 g (1 lb/3 cups) finely grated carrot
40 g (1½ oz/¼ cup) thinly sliced
   red onion
½ cup chopped coriander (cilantro)
   leaves (optional)
2 tablespoons virgin coconut oil
¼ teaspoon celery seeds
¼ teaspoon fennel seeds, crushed
¼ teaspoon cumin seeds
155 g (5½ oz/1 cup) Devilled cashews
   (see below)
2 teaspoons lime juice

**DEVILLED CASHEWS
   (MAKES 10 PORTIONS)**
100 ml (3½ fl oz) virgin coconut oil
500 g (1 lb 2 oz/3¼ cups) raw unsalted
   cashews
4 fresh curry leaf sprigs, leaves picked
2 teaspoons chilli powder
2 teaspoons freshly ground black pepper
2 teaspoons salt

Vaghareli makai
Spiced corn salad

The beautiful Mexican street snack, elotes, are grilled corn cobs, spiced with chilli and smeared with mayonnaise. Here is the Indian version, turned into a salad — so simple and tasty, not to mention healthy. Serve it as a side, pack it for a picnic, or serve it in a cup during kids' parties.

REGION India | **SERVES** 4 | **PREPARATION** 40 minutes
COOKING 20 minutes | **DIFFICULTY** Easy

2 fresh corn cobs
2 cm (¾ inch) knob of fresh turmeric, peeled and grated, or ½ teaspoon ground turmeric
1 onion, finely diced
2 Indian green chillies, finely chopped
¼ bunch coriander (cilantro), leaves picked and roughly chopped
¼ bunch mint, leaves removed and torn
½ teaspoon Chaat masala (page 24)
½ teaspoon Kashmiri chilli powder
juice and zest of 1 lemon
½ cup Kara boondi (page 49; optional)

SMASHED CORN
3 fresh corn cobs
1 tablespoon virgin coconut oil
2 French or red Asian shallots, thinly sliced
1 garlic clove, sliced
150 ml (5 fl oz) coconut water
1 tablespoon sugar, or to taste

For the smashed corn, cut the kernels from the three cobs of corn using a sharp knife. Put half the kernels through a juicer.

Heat the coconut oil in a frying pan over medium heat. Add the shallot and garlic and cook, stirring, for 2–5 minutes, or until translucent; you don't want them to colour.

Stir in the corn juice, remaining corn kernels and the coconut water, ensuring the kernels are covered in liquid. Cover and cook for 5–7 minutes, until the corn is tender. Taste the corn and season with a little sugar, depending on the sweetness of the corn.

Transfer to a blender and briefly blitz so that some corn kernels are broken, and others remain whole.

To make the salad, cut the kernels from the remaining two cobs of corn and place in a saucepan. Add the turmeric, a pinch of salt, and enough water to just cover the corn. Cook over medium heat for about 10 minutes, or until tender.

Drain the corn, leave to cool, then place in a bowl. Add the smashed corn, onion, chilli, herbs, spices and lemon juice and zest. Season to taste with salt and mix well.

Just before serving, add the kara boondi for extra texture and crunch, if using.

Sabzi pulao
Curried rice salad

Coriander, raisins and apple are key to this dish, with sesame oil adding a nice touch. The flavours get better on standing, as the rice and other ingredients really soak up the curried oil — so it's a good idea to make a big batch of this salad, because the leftovers will only get better.

REGION Pakistan | **SERVES** 4 | **PREPARATION** 30 minutes
COOKING 40 minutes | **DIFFICULTY** Easy

Cook the rice using the absorption method (see page 159) or a rice cooker.

In a large saucepan, heat 60 ml (2 fl oz/¼ cup) of the olive oil over medium–high heat. Stir in the curry paste or powder, chilli powder, turmeric, lime pickle, cumin seeds and sesame oil. Let the mixture simmer for a minute. Add the onion and cook, stirring, for about 3 minutes, until translucent.

Transfer the onion mixture to a large heatproof bowl. Add the rice and the remaining olive oil and mix thoroughly using a strong wooden spoon. Taste the rice at this point: if it needs more curry flavour, fry some more curry paste or powder, chilli powder and cumin seeds in more olive oil for a few minutes, then stir them through the rice until you've reached the desired spiciness.

Add the remaining ingredients and season with salt to taste. Cover and chill until ready to serve.

300 g (10½ oz/1⅓ cups) organic
  short-grain brown rice
100 ml (3½ fl oz) olive oil
2 tablespoons curry paste, or
  1–2 tablespoons mild curry powder
½ teaspoon chilli powder
½ teaspoon ground turmeric
½ teaspoon Chilli lime pickle
  (page 233), or Indian lime pickle
1 teaspoon cumin seeds
1 tablespoon sesame oil
1 large brown onion, chopped
1 bunch coriander (cilantro), leaves
  chopped
170 g (5¾ oz/1 cup) raisins
1 granny smith apple, cored and chopped
1 celery stalk, chopped
10 snow peas (mangetout), topped and
  tailed, each cut into 5 pieces
½ red capsicum (pepper), diced
4–6 spring onions (scallions), chopped
1 generous tablespoon untreated honey

Vellarikka kosumalli
Fresh cucumber & sprouted mung bean salad

Kosumalli is a traditional southern Indian salad prepared with fresh vegetables and sprouted and soaked mung beans. Follow the basic recipe here, then add whatever vegetables you like to your sprouted salad.

Sprouts are living, life-giving foods, and mung beans are loaded with amino acids. They have a great texture, are delicious, and are a great seed to start your home sprouting practice with, as they're easy to work with and very inexpensive.

REGION India | **SERVES** 2 | **PREPARATION** 10 minutes + 15 minutes salting + 3 days sprouting
COOKING 5 minutes | **DIFFICULTY** Easy

200 g (7 oz) telegraph (long) cucumber, grated or finely chopped
salt, for sprinkling
250 g (9 oz) sprouted mung beans (moong dhal; see page 64)
150 g (5½ oz) fresh grated coconut; alternatively you can use frozen grated coconut, or rehydrated desiccated coconut
lemon juice, to taste

FOR TEMPERING
1 teaspoon virgin coconut oil
½ teaspoon brown mustard seeds
2 Indian green chillies, split in half
1 fresh curry leaf sprig, leaves torn
a small pinch of asafoetida (optional)

Grate or finely chop the cucumber, then place in a bowl. Sprinkle generously with salt and set aside for 15 minutes.

For the tempering, heat the coconut oil in a frying pan over high heat, until it starts smoking. Add the mustard seeds. When they splutter, add the chillies, curry leaves and asafoetida, if using. Add the drained mung beans and stir for 2–3 seconds, then switch off the flame.

Squeeze out all the water from the cucumber, then place the cucumber in a serving bowl with the coconut. Pour the spiced mung bean mixture over and toss until well combined.

Add lemon juice and salt to taste, then serve.

Bonjan salat
Spicy eggplant salad

When most people think of Afghanistan, good food may not be the first thing that comes to mind. But there is plenty to be found, including this beautiful dish, which can be enjoyed cold or hot, just simply with bread.

This salad will also keep well in the fridge for a few days — if it makes it to the fridge!

REGION Afghanistan | **SERVES** 8 | **PREPARATION** 15 minutes + 15 minutes infusing
COOKING 30 minutes | **DIFFICULTY** Medium

Slice the eggplants crossways into pieces about 4 cm (1½ inches) thick. Sprinkle with the sea salt flakes and let stand for 15 minutes.

Rinse the eggplant slices under cold water, then pat dry with a clean tea towel.

Heat the rice bran oil in a large frying pan over medium heat. Working in batches, lightly brown the eggplant slices for 3 minutes on each side, or until soft and golden brown. Transfer to a serving bowl and set aside to cool.

Combine the remaining ingredients in a small saucepan, mixing well, and simmer over low heat for 10 minutes, to integrate the flavours. Pour the dressing over the eggplant.

Serve at room temperature, or cover and refrigerate until ready to use. This salad will keep in the fridge for several days.

3 eggplants (aubergines)
2½ teaspoons sea salt flakes
60 ml (2 fl oz/¼ cup) rice bran oil
375 ml (13 fl oz/1½ cups) Velvet tomato catsup (page 248)
¼ teaspoon freshly ground black pepper
½ teaspoon salt
1 teaspoon chilli flakes or finely chopped fresh red chilli
2 teaspoons ground cinnamon
1 tablespoon dried mint

Bhutanese red rice, goji berry & hazelnut salad

It is hard to find salads from regions that are high, cold and remote, and in Bhutan red rice is eaten for breakfast, lunch and dinner in many guises. This salad includes hazelnuts, which thrive in Bhutan and are being planted there in huge numbers, helping local people earn a living.

The goji berry vine has flourished in the valleys of the Himalayas for thousands of years, and its nutritious berries are reputed to have many healing powers. Unverified accounts claim goji berries were introduced to the West by a tourist who was astounded by the longevity of locals in a remote village in Tibet, ascribing their good health to all the goji berries they consumed.

Whatever the truth of this story, there is no doubting this salad is good for you.

REGION Bhutan | **SERVES** 4 | **PREPARATION** 15 minutes + 30 minutes chilling
COOKING 30 minutes | **DIFFICULTY** Easy

---

250 g (9 oz) Bhutanese red rice, or medium-grain brown rice if unavailable

4 spring onions (scallions), finely chopped

1 red capsicum (pepper), finely chopped

180 g (6 oz/1½ cups) dried goji berries, or other dried fruit such as mango, roughly chopped

180 g (6 oz/1⅓ cups) toasted hazelnuts, roughly chopped

DRESSING

60 ml (2 fl oz/¼ cup) olive oil

1 tablespoon mirin

80 ml (2½ fl oz/⅓ cup) rice vinegar

1 garlic clove, finely chopped

2 tablespoons lemon juice

1 teaspoon grated fresh ginger

1 tablespoon sugar

Cook the rice in a rice cooker with 350 ml (12 fl oz) water and a pinch of salt. Alternatively, bring the rice and 350 ml (12 fl oz) water to the boil in a heavy-based saucepan, then cover and simmer over low heat for about 20 minutes; turn off the heat, leave to stand with the lid on for 4 minutes, then fluff the rice grains with a fork. Set aside to cool.

Meanwhile, in a small bowl, whisk together all the dressing ingredients. Set aside for 20–30 minutes to allow the flavours to infuse.

When the rice is cool, place it in a large bowl and toss the remaining salad ingredients through. Add the dressing, to suit your taste.

Cover and refrigerate for 30 minutes before serving, to let the rice soak up the dressing.

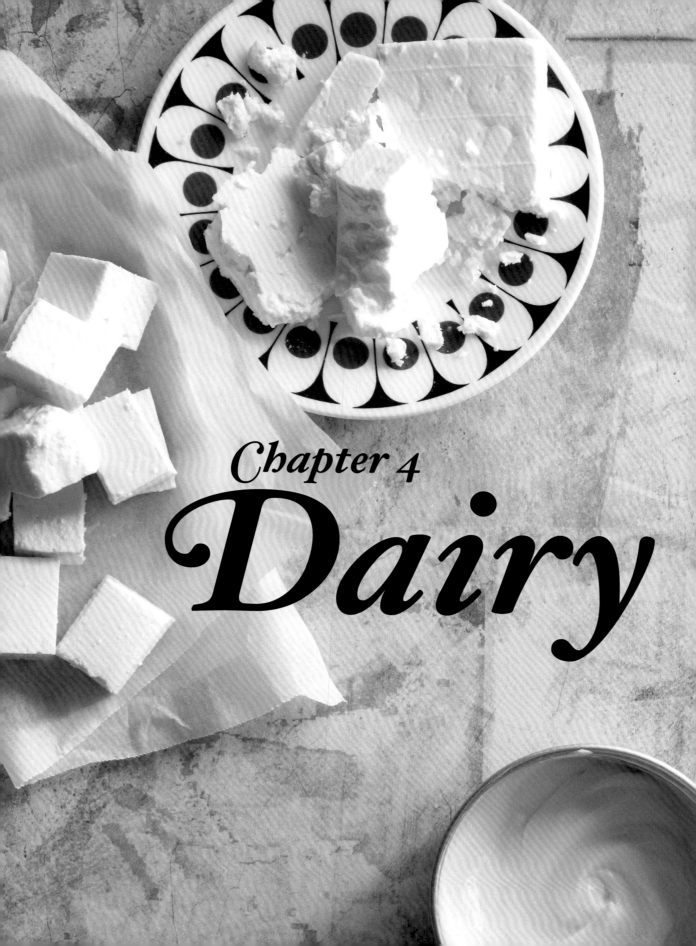

Chapter 4
Dairy

The first thing I go for whenever I am on the subcontinent is the curd.

Mostly made from rich and tangy buffalo milk, it is thick, rich and completely delicious. When I'm travelling through these countries I always seek out the street vendor with a giant wok full of boiling buffalo milk and have a glass. It is nourishing and most of all safe, as long as you can see the milk boiling.

Dairy is key to so many dishes across the subcontinent, most commonly in the form of cheese, milk, yoghurt and ghee. They add richness, moistness and an additional layer of flavour.

I'll never forget my mum just letting milk go 'off' in the Sri Lankan heat. It would curdle and separate, and then form a very rough kind of yoghurt, which was then hung in muslin (cheesecloth) and drained, to make a very basic cheese. Once it was mixed in with other flavours it tasted okay.

My mum always told me the mould that always formed on her yoghurt was just penicillin and good for you, except when it went red... Mostly it developed soft white and black mould on it (what is known as fermentative lactic acid bacteria), which made a seal of sorts on top of the milk, and then it would set. It was very tasty, especially with some precious sugar. Back in 1969, in our household sugar was rationed, and we were each given one jar a month to do with as we pleased; it was more precious than gold! It had to be cared for like a silk worm, as sugar ants were tiny and very crafty, going to great lengths to get to our precious stash. The jar was always kept in a saucer of water to prevent the little buggers getting to it, but if you left it for more than a day they would sacrifice themselves and form a bridge out of their bodies so the rest of the clan could get to the sugar. If this did happen and the jar was full of ants, it did not bother me — I'd brush away what I could and then just kept eating the sugar; little did I know it then, but I was eating a great deal of protein with my food! So between the yoghurt mould and the sugar ants, my fearless eating obviously started at a very early age.

Milk plays a large role in the food of the subcontinent, from classic chais to cooling lassis — the latter comprising milk or water-thinned yoghurt mixed with fruit or other flavourings. Similarly, yoghurt is used to create phenomenal curds, raitas and other cooling condiments, or as a softening and braising agent for meat dishes. Paneer, a homemade cheese very similar to cottage cheese, is used extensively in everything from curries to stand-alone dishes, because it not only tastes amazing, but holds its shape beautifully through the cooking process.

You can buy paneer from Indian grocers, but I recommend you try making your own (see page 94). It is a wonderful adventure in texture and flavour, and after a few goes you will wonder why you ever went out and bought it. Making paneer is a simple art that is well worth mastering.

Paneer
Fresh cheese

Paneer is a fresh, non-melting farmer-style cheese enjoyed throughout southern Asia. It is made by heating milk, curdling it by adding an acidic ingredient such as lemon juice or vinegar, then draining or pressing out the liquid whey. The cheese is so easy to make, and I am sure that once you do, you will use it in so many ways, such as the Paneer butter masala on page 96, Shashi paneer (page 97), Mughlai paneer (page 100), or simply served with an Indian flat bread, parathas or rice.

REGION India, Pakistan, Bangladesh, Nepal, Afghanistan | **SERVES** 10
PREPARATION 10 minutes + overnight pressing | **COOKING** 25–30 minutes | **DIFFICULTY** Easy

2 litres (70 fl oz/8 cups) full-cream milk
1 teaspoon salt
125 ml (4 fl oz/½ cup) lemon juice

TIP You can also make a round paneer. Cut a piece of muslin (cheesecloth) to fit a colander, large enough to overhang on all sides. If the muslin isn't very fine, use 2–3 layers. Set the colander in the sink. When the milk comes to the boil, add the salt and lemon juice and stir for 1 minute. Slowly pour the mixture into the colander, ensuring the muslin stays in place. The milk will curdle and the liquid will drip out of the colander; scrape the side of the muslin to speed up the drainage. The contents will reduce slowly. Grab the edges of the cloth into a bundle and secure with a rubber band. Continue squeezing the muslin until there is barely any water escaping. The cheese should be the size of a large softball, and should still feel moist, or it will be too dry. Place the muslin-wrapped cheese in a bowl lined with two layers of paper towel. Refrigerate for 2–3 hours, or until solid. To serve, unwrap and slice into 5 mm (¼ inch) discs.

Bring the milk and salt to the boil in a large heavy-based saucepan, stirring constantly. Remove from the heat and slowly stir in the lemon juice and 1 tablespoon water. Leave to sit for 20 minutes; the whey will develop a greenish hue.

Line a strainer with muslin (cheesecloth); if the mesh on the muslin is not very fine, line the strainer with several layers.

Strain the mixture through the muslin, into a clean bowl. Gently rinse under water for a few seconds to cool. Discard the whey, or use it in baking; traditionally whey is also fed to pigs and other livestock, rather than being wasted, as it is highly nutritious.

Line a slotted tray with more damp muslin and place on another tray to catch any drips. Pour the paneer into the tray. Depending on how thick you want it, bring up the sides of the cloth, ensuring all the cheese is well covered with the cloth. (The cheese needs to be really well covered at this point, otherwise it will take on other odours in the fridge.)

Place another tray on top and gently press the paneer down. Place some weights, such as tins of food, on the top tray; the heavier the weight, the firmer the cheese will be. Leave to sit in the refrigerator overnight before using.

The paneer can be refrigerated for up to 4 days, or tightly wrapped in plastic and frozen for up to a fortnight.

Paneer butter masala

Butter masala has to be one of the best-known and beloved Indian sauces — and to have it with your own homemade paneer cheese makes it even better. You can make a no-onion, no-garlic version by skipping the garlic and onion.

Onions, cashews and tomatoes naturally lend a sweet flavour to the gravy, so use sugar only if needed to suit your taste.

REGION India | **SERVES** 4 | **PREPARATION** 20 minutes
COOKING 35 minutes | **DIFFICULTY** Medium

1 tablespoon virgin coconut oil
1 large onion (250 g/9 oz), diced
3 large tomatoes (450 g/1 lb),
   finely chopped
a pinch of salt, to taste
½–¾ teaspoon Garam masala (page 24)
1 teaspoon ground coriander
10–12 cashews
½–¾ teaspoon Kashmiri red chilli
   powder (adjust for the best colour)
¼–½ teaspoon sugar (optional, to taste)
30 g (1 oz) butter
1 fresh bay leaf
3 green cardamom pods
1 small cinnamon stick
2–3 cloves
1½ teaspoons Ginger garlic paste
   (page 241), or ¾ teaspoon
   fresh Ginger paste (page 241)
250 g (9 oz) Paneer (page 94),
   cut into cubes
½ teaspoon dried fenugreek leaves
   (kasuri methi); see tip
60 ml (2 fl oz/¼ cup) thin (pouring)
   cream, plus extra to serve
crushed black pepper (optional),
   to garnish
coriander (cilantro) leaves (optional),
   to garnish

Heat the coconut oil in a frying pan over medium heat. Add the onion and cook, stirring now and then, for 3–5 minutes, unti translucent.

Stir in the tomatoes and salt and cook for 3 minutes, then cover and cook for a further 5 minutes, or until the mixture turns soft and mushy.

Add the garam masala, ground coriander, cashews, chilli powder and sugar, if using. Cook, stirring lightly every now and then, for another 5 minutes, or until the mixture starts to separate from the oil and begins to leave the side of the pan.

Remove the pan from the heat and leave to cool.

When the mixture has cooled, transfer it to a blender, keeping the pan handy. Add 250 ml (9 fl oz/1 cup) water to the blender and whiz until the sauce is very smooth.

Melt the butter in the same pan over medium heat, then add the bay leaf, cardamom pods, cinnamon stick and cloves. Fry for 1–2 minutes, or until fragrant. Add the ginger garlic paste and cook, stirring, until the raw smell disappears.

Pour the blended purée back into the pan. Add more Kashmiri chilli powder if the mixture is not red enough, and if it is too thick, stir in 60–125 ml (2–4 fl oz/¼–½ cup) water. Cook, stirring for 4 minutes, or until the gravy thickens and reaches the consistency of a thick sauce.

Add the paneer and fenugreek, stir well and cook for about 3 minutes.

To enrich the sauce and impart that classic texture, stir in the cream just before serving.

Transfer the paneer butter masala to a serving bowl. Garnish with a little more cream, and crushed black pepper or coriander leaves, and serve.

TIP Instead of dried fenugreek leaves, you can use fresh leaves if available — or use 1 tablespoon of chopped fresh celery leaves per teaspoon of dried fenugreek leaves.

Shashi paneer
Cashew, onion & paneer curry

The literal translation of shahi paneer is 'royal paneer', which is a very appropriate name for this dish, fit for a king. Paneer, a homemade cheese, is accompanied with a rich and creamy sauce made from cashews.

Paneer is very delicate, so take care to handle it gently or it will break up very easily. If you like a thicker or thinner gravy, just adjust the amount of water.

REGION India | **SERVES** 6 | **PREPARATION** 25 minutes + 15 minutes soaking
COOKING 30 minutes | **DIFFICULTY** Medium

Soak the cashews in the milk for 15 minutes.

Heat 2 tablespoons of the coconut oil in a non-stick wok or frying pan over medium–high heat. Add the onion and cook, stirring now and then, for 3 minutes, until it starts to turn brown. Add the ginger, garlic and chilli and cook for 2–3 minutes.

Stir in the tomato sauce, mixing well, and cook for 5 minutes, or until the oil separates from the mixture.

While the sauce is cooking, put the soaked cashews and milk in a blender and whiz until smooth.

When the oil has separated from the onion mixture, add the ground spices and mix well. Add the cashew mixture and stir until the gravy is smooth.

Stir in the sugar, 375 ml (13 fl oz/1½ cups) water, and salt to taste. Bring to the boil.

While waiting for the gravy to boil, heat the remaining 1 tablespoon coconut oil in a non-stick frying pan over medium–high heat and fry the paneer cubes until light golden brown all over, turning the cheese gently. Drain on paper towel.

Once the gravy comes to the boil, add the paneer and gently stir it through.

Serve immediately, garnished with fresh coriander and additional broken cashews.

125 g (4½ oz/¾ cup) cashews, chopped, plus extra to garnish
250 ml (9 fl oz/1 cup) milk
3 tablespoons virgin coconut oil
2 small onions, finely chopped
1 tablespoon grated fresh ginger
3 garlic cloves, finely chopped
1 Indian green chilli, or to taste, finely chopped
250 ml (9 fl oz/1 cup) tomato sauce, such as the Velvet tomato catsup on page 248
2 teaspoons ground cumin
2 teaspoons ground coriander
2 teaspoons Garam masala (page 24)
1 tablespoon sugar
a pinch of salt, or to taste
400 g (14 oz) Paneer (page 94), cut into cubes
5 coriander (cilantro) sprigs, finely chopped, to garnish

Spinach & cheese momos

Momos are believed to have originated in Tibet, and then spread via traders throughout the subcontinent. The name has stayed the same, even though the fillings vary widely these days, giving you creative licence to put anything you like into these delicious little parcels. The perfect momo has a shell that's delicate, yet firm enough to hold in the juices. One bite and the juice will squirt out if you're not careful. The difficulties come with making the traditional dumpling shape, and for this I would suggest you go online and learn how to wrap them.

REGION Nepal | **SERVES** 4; makes about 20 | **PREPARATION** 30 minutes + 10 minutes resting
COOKING 15 minutes per batch | **DIFFICULTY** Medium

In a bowl, mix all the filling ingredients together and season to taste. Set aside.

For the dough, mix the sifted flour and baking powder together in a bowl, then slowly stir in the water, so the mixture gathers together into a ball, like a bread dough, but not sticky; add a tiny bit more water only if necessary.

Turn the dough out onto a floured work surface and knead for 3 minutes, then cover with a tea towel and allow to rest for 10 minutes.

Roll the rested dough into a long thick rope. Cut off finger-width pieces and roll each one into a 2.5 cm (1 inch) ball.

Use a rolling pin to flatten a piece of dough, into a nice circle. Add a tablespoon of filling to the centre of the circle and pinch the edges shut, into the desired shape. Most momos are crescent shaped.

Repeat with the remaining dough and filling; the momos are best cooked straight away.

Bring about 5 cm (2 inches) of water to the boil in a saucepan or sturdy wok. Line a metal or bamboo steamer with baking paper to prevent sticking. Arrange a batch of momos in the steamer, in a single layer, leaving space in between. Cover with a tight-fitting lid and steam for 15 minutes, or until cooked through.

Remove from the steamer and keep warm while cooking the remaining momos.

Serve warm, with your choice of condiment, such as the Chilli sesame momo dipping sauce on page 252, or the Chutney for momos on page 221.

TIP You can also use silverbeet (Swiss chard) in the momos, instead of spinach, and tofu instead of paneer.

DOUGH
- 500 g (1 lb 2 oz/3⅓ cups) plain (all-purpose) flour, sifted, plus extra for dusting
- 2 teaspoons baking powder
- 350 ml (12 fl oz) water, at room temperature

SPINACH CHEESE FILLING
- 250 g (9 oz) English spinach, washed well, patted dry and finely chopped
- 3 tablespoons chopped Paneer (page 94)
- 1 red onion, finely chopped
- 1 tablespoon crushed garlic
- 1 tablespoon finely chopped coriander (cilantro)
- 1 tablespoon finely chopped spring onion (scallion)
- 2 tablespoons rice bran oil
- ½ teaspoon salt

Mughlai paneer kofta curry

*There is a bit of preparation to this rich and tasty dish, but it is well worth the effort.
Serve these golden homemade cheese, potato and nut dumplings with roti, parathas
or rice, to soak up all that creamy almond and cashew curry sauce.*

REGION India | **SERVES** 6; makes 20–24 dumplings | **PREPARATION** 15 minutes + 15 minutes soaking
COOKING 40–50 minutes | **DIFFICULTY** Medium

2 tablespoons virgin coconut oil
1½ teaspoons Ginger garlic paste
    (page 241)
1 teaspoon sugar
¼ teaspoon ground turmeric
1 teaspoon Garam masala (page 24)
2 teaspoons dried fenugreek leaves
    (kasuri methi), crushed
a pinch of salt, or to taste
250–310 ml (9–10¾ fl oz/1–1¼ cups)
    thick (double) cream
coriander (cilantro) leaves, to garnish

PANEER KOFTA DUMPLINGS
350 g (12 oz) crumbled Paneer (page 94)
230 g (8 oz/1 cup) boiled and mashed
    potato, such as russet
½ cup mixed chopped cashews,
    almonds, pistachios and sultanas
    (golden raisins)
2 Indian green chillies, finely chopped
3 cm (1¼ inch) knob of fresh ginger,
    peeled and grated
¼ teaspoon ground turmeric
½ teaspoon Garam masala (page 24)
a pinch of salt, or to taste
1 litre (35 fl oz/4 cups) vegetable or
    rice bran oil, for deep-frying

ONION PASTE
40 g (1½ oz/¼ cup) blanched almonds
40 g (1½ oz/¼ cup) cashews
3 large onions, quartered
3 Indian green chillies, roughly chopped
1 cinnamon stick, broken
3 cloves
4 green cardamom pods
2 teaspoons cumin seeds, dry-roasted
    and ground
1 tablespoon coriander seeds

To make the dumplings, put the paneer and mashed potato
in a large bowl. Add the mixed nuts and fruit, chilli, ginger,
turmeric and garam masala. Season with salt and mix together
well. Shape the mixture into balls a bit smaller than a golf ball,
pressing together tightly. Set aside.

Heat the vegetable oil in a heavy-based saucepan over
medium heat. Add the dumplings in batches, taking care not
to overcrowd the pan, and cook for about 5 minutes, until
golden brown. Set aside on paper towel while cooking the
remaining dumplings.

To make the onion paste, soak the almonds and cashews
in warm water for 15 minutes, then drain and place in a food
processor. Add the onion, chilli, cinnamon, cloves, cardamom
pods and cumin and coriander seeds. Grind the mixture into
a smooth paste and set aside.

Heat the coconut oil in a heavy-based saucepan over
medium heat. Add the onion paste, ginger garlic paste and
sugar. Cook, stirring lightly, for 5–7 minutes, or until the oil
starts to split from the onion paste.

Add the turmeric, garam masala and fenugreek leaves
and cook for a further 2–3 minutes.

Stir in 500 ml (17 fl oz/2 cups) water (I much prefer a runny
gravy), and salt to taste. Cook for 7–10 minutes, or until the
sauce comes up to a rapid boil.

Stir in the cream, mixing well, then leave to cook for
about 2 minutes.

Just before serving, reheat the dumplings in a warm oven.

Arrange the kofta on top of the sauce and garnish with
coriander. Serve hot.

Kimish panare
Fresh Afghan cheese with raisins, olives & grapes

My wife, Karen, has been making this for years. We often serve it when guests come around, as it is so easy and people love it. We serve it with warm pitta bread.

REGION Afghanistan | **SERVES** 6 | **PREPARATION** 15 minutes
COOKING 15 minutes | **DIFFICULTY** Easy

Preheat the oven to 180°C (350°F).

If using paneer, cut it into wedges, or tear it into chunks. Randomly layer the cheese, olives, raisins and grapes in a lined baking tin or ovenproof pan, then douse with the olive oil.

Transfer to the oven and bake for 12 minutes, or until warmed through.

Serve immediately, sprinkled with the chilli flakes, parsley and a little salt and freshly ground black pepper.

300 g (10½ oz) Paneer (page 94) or cottage cheese
100 g (3½ oz) pitted black olives, halved lengthways
100 g (3½ oz) raisins
150 g (5½ oz) seedless red grapes, halved lengthways
2½ tablespoons olive oil
½ teaspoon chilli flakes
chopped flat-leaf (Italian) parsley, to garnish

Mor kuzhambu
Buttermilk curry

This delicious curry, in which yoghurt is thinned out and simmered with a spice paste, is from Dakshin *by Chandra Padmanabhan, which has been one of my go-to books for over 20 years. I still treasure my copy, all stained and torn from so much use.*

Serve with rice and poppadoms and the Fried potato curry on page 125.

REGION India | **SERVES** 4 | **PREPARATION** 25 minutes
COOKING about 20 minutes | **DIFFICULTY** Medium

---

520 g (1 lb 2½ oz/2 cups) curd, whisked,
   or Greek-style yoghurt if unavailable
¼ teaspoon ground turmeric
a pinch of salt, or to taste
¾ cup chopped vegetables, such
   as winter melon, okra, eggplant
   (aubergine), green capsicum
   (pepper), green peas and diced
   peeled potatoes

SPICE PASTE
1 tablespoon virgin coconut oil or ghee
1½ tablespoons chana dhal
1¼ tablespoons white urad dhal
   (hulled dried black lentils)
1¼ tablespoons fenugreek seeds
1 teaspoon coriander seeds
6 dried red chillies, halved
3 tablespoons grated fresh coconut
1 cm (½ inch) knob of fresh ginger,
   peeled and grated

FOR TEMPERING
1 teaspoon brown mustard seeds
1 teaspoon cumin seeds
½ teaspoon fenugreek seeds
1 dried red chilli, halved
8–10 fresh curry leaves

For the spice paste, heat 2 teaspoons of the coconut oil in a frying pan over medium heat. Cook the chana dhal, urad dhal, fenugreek seeds, coriander seeds and red chillies for 3–5 minutes, until fragrant and toasted. Tip into a bowl and leave to cool. Using a mortar and pestle or a blender, grind the mixture, together with the coconut and ginger, into a smooth paste, adding a little water to loosen the ingredients if necessary.

To the ground spice paste add the whisked yoghurt, turmeric, and salt to taste. Beat until the mixture is smooth, then set aside.

Heat the remaining 2 teaspoons of oil in a heavy-based saucepan over high heat and add the tempering ingredients. Once the mustard seeds start to splutter, add the chopped vegetables and cook, stirring, for 3 minutes. Pour in enough water to cover the vegetables, then bring to the boil, cover the pan and simmer over low heat until tender; the time will vary depending on the vegetables.

When the vegetables are tender, stir in the spiced yoghurt mixture over low heat. Remove from the heat when the sauce just begins to boil, taking care not to let it curdle.

Serve immediately, with your choice of accompaniments.

Cheese kottu

In Sri Lanka, the sound of kottu paddles beating on a steel griddle is like bird song or the sound of the ocean: it is always around. And once you try this dish, whenever you are in Sri Lanka, you will follow the sounds to track down the nation's favourite street snack.

This is another one I would suggest you look up on the internet, because the technique is part of the show. This dish needs to be made in front of your guests, and your neighbours need to wonder what you are up to!

REGION Sri Lanka | **SERVES** 2 | **PREPARATION** 15 minutes
COOKING 5–10 minutes | **DIFFICULTY** Medium

Heat a flat barbecue plate on low heat. Add the coconut oil and heat until smoking.

Add the onion, ginger and garlic and, using your kottu paddles or two barbecue scrapers, stir-fry the mixture for 2 minutes, until fragrant.

Add the carrot, leek, fresh chillies and cabbage, if using. Stir-fry the mixture for a further 2 minutes.

Add the beaten eggs and mix them in, ensuring you scrape the bottom of the barbecue clean so nothing sticks.

Add the shredded roti or tortillas and mix well.

Pour the kiri hodi over. Now commence your rhythmic chopping of the roti, and keep going until it is well chopped and all combined. Sprinkle with the chilli flakes, salt and freshly ground black pepper.

To serve, place on a plate lined with a banana leaf, or even into a banana leaf cone. Garnish with the shredded cheese so it slightly melts on the kottu, and serve hot.

2½ tablespoons virgin coconut oil
1 small red onion, thinly sliced
1 teaspoon chopped fresh ginger
1 teaspoon chopped garlic
2 carrots, julienned
1 leek, including the green part of the stem, washed well and sliced
3 banana chillies, julienned
1–2 Indian green chillies, chopped
40 g (1½ oz/½ cup) shredded cabbage (optional)
2 eggs, beaten
2 Gothamba roti (page 185), or 3 wheat tortillas, shredded
100 ml (3½ fl oz) Kiri hodi (page 247)
1 teaspoon chilli flakes, or to taste
50 g (1¾ oz/½ cup) shredded cheddar cheese

Dairy & soy

Dairy and soy products are two opposites, really, but both play an important part in the subcontinental diet. Paneer cheese and ghee are among the most popular dairy products, along with buffalo milk. We have slipped coconut oil into this little collection too. I know it doesn't fit the category, but it is such a beautiful cooking oil, like a dairy-free ghee.

---

1. SEASONED TOFU is available in many flavours and is great for adding texture to dishes. Tofu is also known as bean curd, and is made by coagulating soy milk. Unseasoned tofu has a bland flavour, which makes it very versatile, as it takes on the aromatics of other ingredients it is cooked with. It is high in protein, and low in fat.

2. TEMPEH Like tofu, tempeh is a vegetarian soy food that has been enjoyed throughout Asia for centuries. It is made from cooked and slightly fermented soy beans, pressed together into a patty, like a very firm vegie burger. Many commercial varieties also contain grains such as barley. Tempeh is rich in protein and calcium, as well as beneficial isoflavones. Unlike tofu, it has a nutty flavour and firm texture, and doesn't easily crumble, as tofu does.

3. GHEE A clarified butter, ghee can be heated to much higher temperatures than regular butter without burning. It is made by simmering butter to remove the milk solids and has a distinctive flavour. It also keeps for extended periods unrefrigerated.

4. UNSALTED BUTTER is preferable to salted butter in general cooking and when making pastry dishes and baked goods, as it will not alter their flavour.

5. VIRGIN COCONUT OIL is healthier than coconut oil processed through the traditional methods of heat extraction. It adds such a great flavour, and can also be used as a massage oil or beauty product.

6. CREAM CHEESE is a soft, mild-tasting fresh cheese made from milk and cream. It has a fat content of around 35 per cent.

7. PANEER A staple across the subcontinent, paneer is a simple homemade cottage cheese set in muslin (cheesecloth). See recipe on page 94.

8. QUARK An acid-set cheese, quark is basically a European version of paneer.

9. FETA is a brined sheep's milk or goat's milk curd cheese, originating in Greece, but used worldwide. It can stand in for Bhutanese cheese in recipes in this book.

10. MASCARPONE Produced from cream and citric acid, mascarpone is easy to make at home and has many uses. It is prized for its creamy texture.

11. CHEDDAR is the single most popular cheese in the Western world, but is also increasingly used on the subcontinent. Originating in the British town of Cheddar, it comes in many guises, from the standard supermarket version to aged cloth-wrapped artisan cheeses that are served in the finest restaurants and hotels globally.

Kadhi
Dumplings in yoghurt sauce

These spiced chickpea-flour dumplings are cooked in kadhi, a rich yoghurt curry, and make a warming winter meal. They are often eaten with meats, but you could also offer them as part of a larger banquet. Serve hot, with plain rice or roti.

REGION Pakistan and India | **SERVES** 6–8 | **PREPARATION** 1 hour + 30 minutes resting
COOKING about 1 hour | **DIFFICULTY** Medium

1 litre (35 fl oz/4 cups) vegetable oil,
    for deep-frying
coriander (cilantro) leaves, to garnish
a pinch of Garam masala (page 24),
    to serve

DUMPLINGS
1 small red onion, finely chopped
120 g (4¼ oz/1 cup) chickpea flour
    (besan)
¼ teaspoon baking powder
1 teaspoon chilli powder
1 teaspoon salt
1 tablespoon chopped Indian green chilli
1 tablespoon chopped coriander
    (cilantro)
1 tablespoon chopped mint

KADHI (YOGHURT SAUCE)
3 tablespoons virgin coconut oil
1 onion, thinly sliced
1 tablespoon crushed garlic
2 teaspoons finely grated fresh ginger
1 tablespoon chopped Indian green chilli
½ teaspoon ground cumin
½ teaspoon ground coriander
1 teaspoon Garam masala (page 24)
½ teaspoon ground turmeric
1 fresh curry leaf sprig, leaves picked
a pinch of salt, or to taste
30 g (1 oz/¼ cup) chickpea flour (besan)
350 g (12 oz) plain yoghurt

For the dumplings, put the onion and chickpea flour in a bowl and mix in enough water to make a smooth paste. In a small bowl, mix together the remaining ingredients, then mix them into the chickpea flour until well combined. Cover and set aside to rest at room temperature for 30 minutes.

Meanwhile, make a start on the kadhi. Heat the coconut oil in a saucepan over medium heat, add the onion and fry for about 3 minutes, or until golden.

Make a paste of the garlic, ginger and chilli by grinding them together using a mortar and pestle, or crushing them with the back of a knife, then add to the onion. Stir in the cumin and coriander and cook, stirring, for 3 minutes, or until fragrant.

Now add the garam masala, turmeric, curry leaves and salt. Cook, stirring often, for another 5–10 minutes.

Meanwhile, mix the chickpea flour and yoghurt in a bowl until you get a smooth paste, adding small amounts of water as necessary.

Add the yoghurt mixture to the onion and cook, stirring constantly, until the mixture starts to come to the boil. Turn the heat down to low and leave to cook gently for about 20 minutes, or until the sauce thickens.

Shape the rested dumpling mixture into balls. The batter should be held together with the onion; it is quite wet and will not form uniform balls — more like pakoras.

To cook the dumplings, heat the vegetable oil in a deep heavy-based saucepan to 180°C (350°F), or until a cube of bread dropped into the oil turns brown in 15 seconds.

Working in batches, cook the dumplings for about 5 minutes, or until golden, then remove using a slotted spoon and drain on paper towel.

When the yoghurt sauce becomes thick, stir in 250 ml (9 fl oz/1 cup) boiling water and let it come to the boil.

Now add the dumplings and simmer over low heat for a final 10 minutes, or until the dumplings are heated through.

Serve immediately, garnished with coriander leaves and a sprinkling of garam masala.

Masala dahi
Spiced curd

Tangy, tasty and tempered with Indian spices, this is a beautiful condiment, generally served as a side dish. I don't mind eating it as a dip, with some roti.

REGION India | **SERVES** 6 | **PREPARATION** 10 minutes
COOKING 5 minutes | **DIFFICULTY** Easy

In a heatproof serving dish, mix together the yoghurt, fennel seeds, salt and sugar. Cover and refrigerate until you are nearly ready to serve.

Heat the ghee in a frying pan over medium heat. Add the dried chilli, mustard seeds, cumin seeds, curry leaves nd turmeric. Cook, stirring, for a minute or two, until the chilli turns dark, then stir in the chilli flakes.

Pour the spiced oil mixture over the yoghurt.

At the table, just before serving, fold the spices through the yoghurt.

- 450 g (1 lb) full-fat plain yoghurt
- ½ teaspoon ground fennel seeds
- a pinch of rock salt, or to taste
- ½ teaspoon sugar
- 4 tablespoons ghee
- 1 dried red chilli, halved
- ½ teaspoon brown mustard seeds
- ¼ teaspoon cumin seeds
- 4–6 fresh curry leaves
- a pinch of ground turmeric
- ½ teaspoon chilli flakes

Smoked yoghurt

There are several ways to prepare this. You can simply buy some good-quality liquid smoke and add it to your yoghurt. If you have a smoker, follow the manufacturer's instructions for cold smoking. Or you can use a smoking gun, available online — a fun tool with no mess and great results, again following the manufacturer's instructions.

SERVES 6 | **PREPARATION** 20 minutes
COOKING 40 minutes | **DIFFICULTY** Medium

Line the bottom of a roasting tin with ice cubes. Spread the yoghurt in a 20 cm (8 inch) square baking dish and nestle the dish into the ice.

Place half the wood chips in a small metal bowl. Using a blowtorch, light the chips, stirring as needed, until all the chips are charred. Blow out any embers that remain, and nestle the bowl into the ice. Cover the roasting tin with foil and leave to sit for 20 minutes.

Discard the wood chips and repeat the smoking process with the remaining wood chips.

Stir the lemon juice into the yoghurt and season to taste with salt and freshly ground black pepper. Cover and refrigerate until required; the yoghurt will keep for up to 1 week.

- ice cubes
- 260 g (9¼ oz/1 cup) full-fat plain yoghurt
- 1 cup fine-grained oak or hickory wood chips
- ½ teaspoon lemon juice

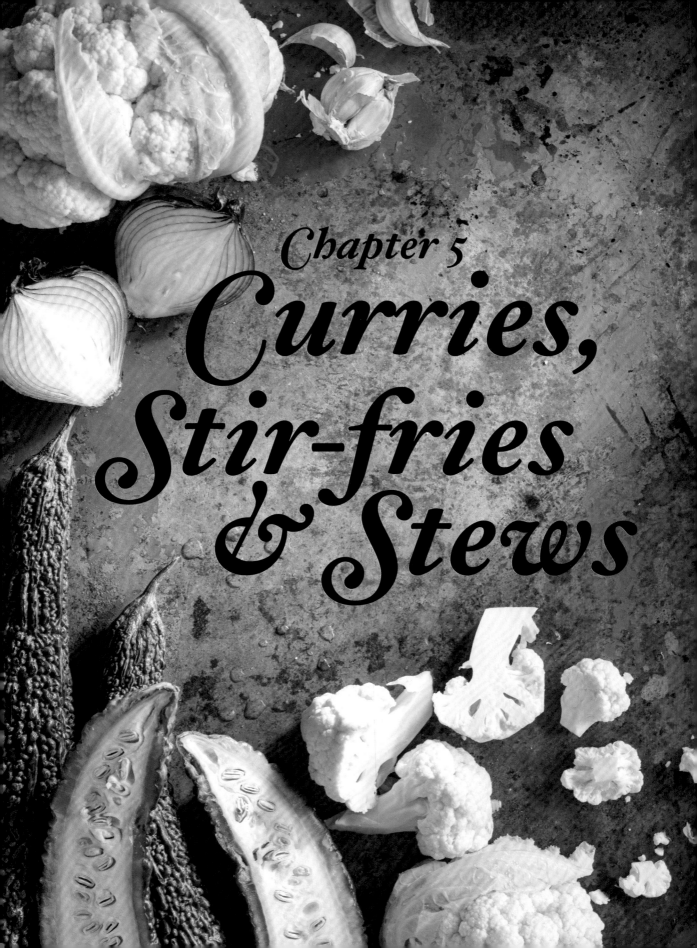

Chapter 5

Curries, Stir-fries & Stews

*In the 21st century vegetables
have gained new-found respect as
fundamental to our health, and also
the health of the planet.*

Slowly, around the world, there has been a reversal of the ingredient
hierarchy, with meat-free menus becoming the new normal, alongside
a genuine celebration of all things vegetable and what these dishes can
bring to the table.

As someone who has grown up with vegetables, deeply ingrained in both the
dishes I ate as a small boy and that I now cook as a chef, I find it interesting to
watch this cultural shift. I am excited by it and also fascinated. Vegetables have
always been a dietary mainstay across the subcontinent, out of both necessity and
choice. They demonstrate the diversity of this region's cuisine, as well as the amazing
range of vegetables available, and prove beyond doubt that flesh need not always be
the main event.

The people of the hill country throughout India, Nepal and Bhutan are, through
necessity and availability, nearly purely vegetarian; in fact Bhutan's national dish,
ema datshi (chillies and cheese) is vegetarian. To the south of India, the Hindus are
purely vegan, as are the Jains and some Buddhists — so vegetarian dishes abound
across this swathe of the subcontinent.

In Afghanistan, Pakistan and Bangladesh, on the other hand, there are very
few vegetarian restaurants, and being a vegetarian in these countries puts you in a
distinct minority. Yet all these countries have seriously amazing vegetarian dishes.
You might have to scratch a little harder to find them but, when you do, they are
worthy of a space on your table.

I have gathered together a broad range of vegetable dishes for this chapter.
It is, after all, the crux of my wants for this book — for you to discover interesting
and exciting ways to cook with the vegetable as star.

Masaura & potato tarkari

Enjoyed throughout Nepal, masaura are sun-dried vegetable nuggets made from black lentil paste and minced vegetables, often used in soupy curries. If you can't find masaura, you can use your favourite dried soy protein in this curry.

REGION Nepal | **SERVES** 2 | **PREPARATION** 25 minutes
COOKING 30 minutes | **DIFFICULTY** Easy

500 ml (17 fl oz/2 cups) vegetable oil, for deep-frying
1½ cups masaura, or diced tempeh or plain soy protein
2½ tablespoons virgin coconut oil
a pinch of cumin seeds
½ teaspoon fenugreek seeds
2 potatoes, peeled and cut into 5 cm (2 inch) cubes
1–2 Indian green chillies, finely chopped
½ teaspoon ground turmeric
a generous pinch of salt
3 tomatoes, finely chopped
½ teaspoon ground cumin
½ teaspoon ground coriander
½ tablespoon chilli powder
½ teaspoon Garam masala (page 24)
½ tablespoon Ginger garlic paste (page 241)
2 tablespoons chopped coriander (cilantro) leaves
2 teaspoons ground sichuan pepper, to garnish (optional)

Heat the vegetable oil in a heavy-based saucepan over high heat. Add your chosen vegetable protein and fry for 3–5 minutes, or until crispy, stirring frequently, as it tends to burn pretty quickly. Remove with a slotted spoon, drain on paper towel and set aside.

In a separate heavy-based saucepan, heat the coconut oil over medium heat, then gently fry the cumin and fenugreek seeds for about 1 minute, or until fragrant. Add the diced potato and green chilli and fry for about 5 minutes, stirring often, until the potato is golden brown.

Stir in the fried vegetable protein, ground turmeric and a good pinch of salt until well combined. Cover and cook over medium–low heat for 5 minutes.

Add the tomatoes, remaining ground spices and the ginger garlic paste, stirring well. Cover and simmer for a further 5 minutes.

Stir in 750 ml (26 fl oz/3 cups) water until well combined. Bring back to the boil and cook, uncovered, over medium heat for about 10 minutes, until the potato is tender and the sauce has reduced to a lovely gravy consistency.

Serve garnished with the chopped coriander, and sprinkled with the sichuan pepper if desired.

Palong shaak
Stir-fried Bangladeshi-style spinach

This simple, elegant and healthy spinach dish is spiced with panch phoran, which you will find in good spice shops — a mixture of fenugreek seeds, nigella seeds, cumin seeds, brown mustard seeds and fennel seeds in equal proportions. The flavour it adds to vegetables is amazing.

I also love to cook this dish with Chinese cabbage (wong bok), or even just regular cabbage.

REGION Bangladesh | **SERVES** 2 | **PREPARATION** 5 minutes
COOKING 10 minutes | **DIFFICULTY** Easy

Heat the coconut oil in a large heavy-based frying pan over medium heat. Add the onion, garlic and chilli pieces and cook, stirring, for about 4 minutes, until the onion is translucent.

Stir in the panch phoran and turmeric and fry for 2 minutes.

Add the spinach and season with a pinch of salt, mixing well. Cover and cook for about 3 minutes; the spinach will release plenty of water. (If you are using cabbage or wong bok instead of spinach, as suggested in the recipe introduction, you will need to cook it for at least 5–8 minutes at this point.)

Stir again, garnish with peanuts and serve.

2 tablespoons virgin coconut oil
1 small onion, chopped
2 garlic cloves, crushed
2 dried red chillies, broken
½ teaspoon panch phoran
¼ teaspoon ground turmeric
250 g (9 oz) English spinach, washed, picked and torn, including the stems
chopped roasted peanuts, to garnish

Shukto
Mixed vegetable curry with plantain & bitter melon

*I am treading cautiously and respectfully around this dish, which is revered
by Bangladeshi people. It is beautiful, and shows how countries renowned for
their fish and meat dishes can have stunning vegetarian dishes too.*

*Plantain and bitter melon, also known as bitter gourd, really are a great pair,
complementing each other both texturally and in flavour. Bitter melon is now
being made into tablets and sold in the West as a medicinal food, while we in the
subcontinent have known of its healing benefits for years, and understood how its
bitterness can be subdued by cooking it with plantain.*

REGION Bangladesh | **SERVES** 4 | **PREPARATION** 20 minutes
COOKING 20 minutes | **DIFFICULTY** Medium

---

2 marunga (drumsticks), or 1 white
   cucumber
5–6 green beans
1 eggplant (aubergine)
2 medium-sized bitter melons
1 ridged gourd
100 g (3½ oz) pumpkin (winter squash),
   peeled
2 potatoes, peeled
4 small or 2 large plantains, peeled and
   chopped into 1 cm (½ inch) discs
80 ml (2½ fl oz/⅓ cup) mustard oil
1 tablespoon brown mustard seeds
2 tablespoons raw white rice, coarsely
   made into paste by blitzing it in a
   blender with a little water
1 teaspoon fresh Ginger paste (page 241)
2 tablespoons mustard paste (see tip)
½ teaspoon ground turmeric

Cut the marunga and beans into 4 cm (1½ inch) lengths,
and dice the eggplant, bitter melons, gourds, pumpkin and
potatoes into evenly sized cubes.

Heat 60 ml (2 fl oz/¼ cup) of the mustard oil in a wok over
medium heat. Add the mustard seeds and ground rice paste.
As the mustard seeds start popping, add all the vegetables,
including the plantain, mixing the oil through them until the
vegetables are well coated. Cover and cook over low heat
for about 10 minutes, until the vegetables are half cooked.

Remove the lid and pour in about 125 ml (4 fl oz/½ cup)
water. Stir in the ginger paste, mustard paste and turmeric,
mixing well. Cook, uncovered, for about 5 minutes, or until the
vegetables are tender.

Stir in the remaining mustard oil and remove from the heat.
Serve warm, with white rice.

TIP You can buy jars of mustard paste at some Asian grocery
stores, or for this recipe grind 2 tablespoons brown mustard
seeds with ½ teaspoon sugar and a splash of water.

Qorma-e-shast-e-arus
Afghan okra stew

The Egyptians, as far back as the 12th century BCE, were the first to cultivate okra, a flowering plant that grew wild along the alluvial banks of the Nile River. It was propagated then through North Africa to the Mediterranean, the Balkans and India. There is so much history here; I love to imagine all the ways people through the centuries prepared this humble vegetable.

Okra has a reputation for being slimy, but it won't be if you choose the young tender vegetables. It's easy to check — just break the tip off one, and if it snaps off you know it is fresh; if it just bends, wait for a better batch.

Enjoy this lovely stew with an Afghan bread of your choice.

REGION Afghanistan | **SERVES** 4 | **PREPARATION** 15 minutes
COOKING 50 minutes | **DIFFICULTY** Easy

Heat the rice bran oil in a large frying pan over medium–high heat. Add the onion and cook for about 2 minutes, until golden.

Add the okra and turmeric and stir very gently, to avoid releasing the okra's thickening agent, until the okra is well coated with oil. Add the split peas and tomatoes, and season with salt and freshly ground black pepper. Mix well, stirring gently, and cook over medium heat for just a few minutes.

Pour in enough water to just cover the okra. Add the dill. Bring to the boil, then reduce the heat and simmer for 30–45 minutes, or until the oil has separated and risen to the surface of the sauce.

Serve warm, garnished with extra dill.

2½ tablespoons rice bran oil
1 onion, chopped
450 g (1 lb) okra
1 teaspoon ground turmeric
2 tablespoons dried green split peas
2 tomatoes, chopped
¼ bunch fresh dill, chopped, plus extra to garnish

Pipinna vyanjana
Cucumber curry

Toasted coconut gives this quick, fragrant curry a wonderful 'cooked on the open fire' taste, and also acts as a thickening agent.

REGION Sri Lanka | **SERVES** 6 | **PREPARATION** 15 minutes
COOKING 20 minutes | **DIFFICULTY** Easy

---

3 large telegraph (long) cucumbers,
　　or 2 white cucumbers
2 tablespoons grated fresh coconut
3 green cardamom pods
1 teaspoon chilli powder
1 teaspoon ground coriander
½ teaspoon ground cumin
½ onion, finely chopped
1 fresh curry leaf sprig, leaves picked
½ teaspoon fennel seeds
2 cm (¾ inch) piece of cinnamon stick
¼ teaspoon ground turmeric
2 small Indian green chillies,
　　finely chopped
150 ml (5 fl oz) coconut milk

Peel the cucumbers and cut them in half lengthways. Remove the seeds, then cut on the diagonal into slices about 2 cm (¾ inch) thick. Set aside.

Place the coconut, cardamom pods, chilli powder, coriander and cumin in a small heavy-based frying pan and shake over low heat for 8–10 minutes, or until the coconut is dark golden.

Transfer the mixture to a saucepan, along with the cucumber. Stir in the remaining ingredients and simmer over medium heat for 7 minutes, or until the cucumber is tender and the sauce has thickened.

Serve immediately.

Bomya or Qorma-e-shast-e-arus
Okra stew with lentils & smoked yoghurt

Okra is such a beautiful vegetable, when it is handled well. If you worry about it living up to its unfortunate reputation of being a little slimy, this recipe will ease your concerns. Remember to always choose small and straight okra, as the larger ones may be a bit tough.

This is a really rich and tasty stew, which you can serve as is, or with rice or chapatti. If you like a bit more fire, use a small green chilli in the stew, otherwise opt for a long green one, which will give you the same flavour without the heat.

REGION Afghanistan | **SERVES** 6 | **PREPARATION** 20 minutes + 30 minutes soaking
COOKING 50 minutes | **DIFFICULTY** Easy

Rinse the lentils and leave to soak in a bowl of water for 30 minutes.

In a heavy-based saucepan, heat the olive oil over high heat until smoking. Add the onion and fry for about 3 minutes, or until golden.

Drain the lentils and add them to the pan, along with the chilli and tomatoes. Cook, stirring often, for 5 minutes.

Add the okra and stock and bring to the boil. Reduce the heat and simmer for 30–35 minutes, or until the stew thickens and the lentils are soft. Season to taste with salt and freshly ground black pepper.

Serve with dollops of the smoked yoghurt, and sprinkled with the dill.

- 50 g (1¾ oz) puy lentils
- 100 ml (3½ fl oz) olive oil
- 2 onions, finely chopped
- 1 Indian green chilli, chopped
- 450 g (1 lb) very ripe tomatoes, diced
- 600 g (1 lb 5 oz) okra, washed, topped and tailed
- 1 litre (35 fl oz/4 cups) vegetable stock or water
- Smoked yoghurt (page 109), to serve
- 1 teaspoon chopped dill

Watakolu vanjanaya
Ridged gourd curry

This is a beautiful and unique curry, using an equally unique vegetable that is surprisingly easy to grow. In Sri Lanka, this is one of the curries you would have in your rice and curry selection. On a recent trip there I tasted this curry after many years, and it took me straight back to my grandmother's smoky black kitchen, where one of the house girls would meticulously clean the gourd, ensuring that the skin on the hard outer ridges was removed, but the skin within the concave dips retained.

If the gourd is in perfect condition, the seeds will still be white and edible; otherwise, it's best to remove the seeds if the gourd is a bit old. There is no real replacement for ridged gourd in terms of flavour and texture, but any member of the gourd family will work in this curry.

Vegans and pure vegetarians can omit the Maldive fish.

REGION Sri Lanka | **SERVES** 6 | **PREPARATION** 25 minutes
COOKING 20 minutes | **DIFFICULTY** Easy

---

2 ridged gourds
1 onion, diced
2 Indian green chillies, halved
    lengthways
½ teaspoon fenugreek seeds
1 fresh curry leaf sprig, leaves picked
1 teaspoon Maldive fish (optional), finely
    pounded using a mortar and pestle
1 teaspoon ground turmeric
2 teaspoons Raw curry powder (page 25)
½ teaspoon chilli powder
salt, to taste
300 ml (10½ fl oz) coconut milk
200 ml (7 fl oz) coconut cream
juice of ½ lime
a pinch of Dark roasted curry powder
    (page 25)

Take the gourds and peel the skin from the ridges, leaving the skin on the concave inner dips of the gourds. Cut each gourd in half, and then on an angle into 4 cm (1½ inch) pieces.

Place all the ingredients, except the coconut cream, lime juice and roasted curry powder, in a heavy-based saucepan, stirring until well combined.

Bring to the boil over medium–high heat and cook for about 10 minutes, or until the skin of the gourd is tender.

Stir in the coconut cream and bring to the boil, then immediately turn off the heat.

Stir in the lime juice and serve garnished with a sprinkling of roasted curry powder.

Peter Kuruvita's pumpkin curry

My dad's favourite curry, this dish is so tasty and easy to prepare. Serve it with roti and coconut sambal, or with another curry; the Ridged gourd curry on page 120 is ideal as they are different colours.

The coconut rice powder can be used in any curry, to thicken it and enrich the flavour.

REGION Sri Lanka | **SERVES** 6 | **PREPARATION** 20 minutes
COOKING 30 minutes | **DIFFICULTY** Medium

For the coconut rice powder, dry-roast all the ingredients in a frying pan over medium heat until the rice and coconut have turned dark brown, stirring regularly so the coconut doesn't burn. Remove from the heat, allow to cool, then grind to a powder using a mortar and pestle or spice grinder. Set aside.

Place all the mustard paste ingredients in a blender. Add 125 ml (4 fl oz/½ cup) water and pulse until smooth. Set aside.

Leaving the skin on, cut the pumpkin into 2 cm (¾ inch) cubes, removing the seeds. Place in a large heavy-based saucepan, along with the onion, curry leaves and chilli. Add all the spices, the coconut milk and 2 tablespoons of the coconut rice powder and bring to the boil. (Store the remaining coconut rice powder in an airtight container in a cool dark place for next time.)

Cover and simmer over medium–low heat for about 15 minutes, until the pumpkin is just tender.

Stirring continuously, add the mustard paste and bring to just below the boil.

Remove from the heat, season to taste with salt and freshly ground black pepper and serve with coconut sambal.

500 g (1 lb 2 oz) Japanese or Kent pumpkin, washed well
1 large onion, finely chopped
1 fresh curry leaf sprig, leaves picked
2 small Indian green chillies, chopped
2 teaspoons ground cumin
2 teaspoons ground coriander
1 teaspoon ground turmeric
1 tablespoon Dark roasted curry powder (page 25)
½ cinnamon stick
1 litre (35 fl oz/4 cups) coconut milk
Coconut sambal (page 253), to serve

COCONUT RICE POWDER
100 g (3½ oz/½ cup) long-grain white rice
100 g (3½ oz) freshly grated coconut, or desiccated coconut
1 fresh curry leaf sprig, leaves picked
1 teaspoon green cardamom pods

MUSTARD PASTE
1 tablespoon brown mustard seeds
2 cm (¾ inch) knob of fresh ginger, peeled
4 garlic cloves, peeled
2½ tablespoons coconut cream

Stuffed banana chillies with plantain & mung beans

Two dishes in one! The mung bean curry is wonderful on its own, and even though it contains a lot of chilli, the plantain works as a counter to the heat.

The fire-grilled banana chillies would also go well in a salad, but as a combination it makes for a very tasty dish..

REGION Sri Lanka | **SERVES** 4 | **PREPARATION** 20 minutes + 2 hours soaking
COOKING 40 minutes + 10 minutes for grilling the banana chillies | **DIFFICULTY** Medium

150 g (5½ oz/⅔ cup) dried green mung beans (moong dhal)
8 whole banana chillies
250 g (9 oz) onions, chopped
250 g (9 oz) plantain, peeled and cut into 7.5 cm (3 inch) cubes
3 garlic cloves, chopped
3 Indian green chillies, chopped
2 cm (¾ inch) knob of fresh ginger, peeled and chopped
3 tablespoons Raw curry powder (page 25)
1 teaspoon ground turmeric
1 teaspoon chilli powder
150 g (5½ oz) ripe tomatoes, chopped
2 tablespoons chopped coriander (cilantro)
50 g (1¾ oz) Greek-style yoghurt

FOR TEMPERING
3 tablespoons virgin coconut oil
1 onion, finely chopped
1 pandan leaf, torn
3 fresh curry leaf sprigs, leaves picked
½ cinnamon stick
½ teaspoon coarsely ground black pepper

Soak the mung beans in a bowl of water for 2 hours.

Fire-roast the whole banana chillies on an open flame or hot barbecue for about 5–10 minutes, until the skins are black and starting to blister, turning regularly.

Place the grilled chillies in a heatproof bowl, cover with plastic wrap and leave to steam for 10 minutes.

Remove the plastic and split the chillies down the centre, keeping the stalks intact. Pull off and discard the skin, gently scrape out all the seeds and set the chillies aside.

Place the mung beans, onion, plantain, garlic, green chilli, ginger, curry powder, turmeric and chilli powder in a heavy-based saucepan, mixing together well. Stir in 1.5 litres (52 fl oz/6 cups) water and bring to the boil. Reduce the heat to a simmer and cook for 5 minutes.

To temper the spices, heat the coconut oil in a heavy-based saucepan until smoking. Add all the remaining tempering ingredients and cook, stirring often, over medium heat for 3 minutes, or until fragrant.

Stir the tempered spices through the mung beans, along with the chopped tomatoes. Cook at a slow simmer for about 30 minutes, until the mung beans are soft and the liquid has evaporated, stirring in a little more water if the mixture becomes dry.

To serve, spoon a generous dollop of the mung bean curry into the split chillies. Garnish with chopped coriander and a dollop of yoghurt and serve.

Ala thel dala
Fried potato curry

In Sri Lanka, this was one of my favourite dry curries. You can add it to a dosai to make masala dosai, serve it with Puri (page 38), or just roll it up in a roti and enjoy it as a snack with tamarind chutney.

REGION Sri Lanka | **SERVES** 4 | **PREPARATION** 25 minutes
COOKING 40 minutes | **DIFFICULTY** Easy

Boil the whole potatoes in their skins in a large saucepan of water over high heat for about 20 minutes. Make sure the potatoes aren't too soft — they need to have some remaining bite to them.

Drain the potatoes and leave to cool slightly, then peel them and cut into 2.5 cm (1 inch) cubes. Set aside.

Heat the coconut oil in a heavy-based, deep-sided saucepan over medium–high heat. Add the mustard seeds. As soon as the mustard seeds start to crackle, add the onion, cumin seeds and sesame seeds. Let them fry for a minute, or until they turn golden brown.

Add the diced potatoes, turmeric and salt, mixing until thoroughly combined.

Reduce the heat to medium–low and cook for 3 minutes, stirring regularly so the spices don't catch on the bottom of the pan. Continue to cook, stirring regularly, for 5 minutes, until the potatoes are cooked through and well coated in all the spices.

Stir in 250 ml (9 fl oz/1 cup) water, mixing well to give the curry a sticky feel.

Stir the chilli flakes through, then cook for a final 2 minutes.

Your potato curry is now ready to serve.

- 4 large russet or other boiling potatoes, washed well, skin on
- 4–5 tablespoons virgin coconut oil
- 2 teaspoons black mustard seeds
- 1 onion, chopped
- 2 teaspoons cumin seeds
- 2 teaspoons black sesame seeds
- 1 teaspoon ground turmeric
- 3 teaspoons salt, or to taste
- 2 teaspoons chilli flakes

Banana blossom curry

Preparing banana blossoms is a little fiddly, but well worth it, as this dish tastes fantastic. I have given two versions here, a wet curry style (kehel muwa vanjanaya) and a dry, fried style (kehel muwa malum); each is absolutely delicious. This recipe is from Vajira Sugathapala, Dilmah's general sales manager for Sri Lanka and the Maldives by day, and one hell of a cook at night.

REGION Sri Lanka | **SERVES** 6 | **PREPARATION** 20 minutes
COOKING 15 minutes | **DIFFICULTY** Medium

2 tablespoons salt
1 banana blossom

FOR BOTH CURRIES
1 large onion, sliced
2 garlic cloves, chopped
1 teaspoon finely grated fresh ginger
60 ml (2 fl oz/¼ cup) cider vinegar
1 teaspoon ground turmeric
300 ml (10½ fl oz) coconut milk
100 ml (3½ fl oz) coconut cream

EXTRAS FOR THE WET CURRY
½ teaspoon roasted chilli powder (chilli powder that has been dry-roasted in a pan; you can also purchase Sri Lankan roasted chilli powder)
2 tablespoons virgin coconut oil

EXTRAS FOR THE DRY FRIED CURRY
1 litre (35 fl oz/4 cups) vegetable oil, for deep-frying
1 teaspoon dried red chilli pieces
1 teaspoon Dark roasted curry powder (page 25)

Pour about 2 litres (70 fl oz/8 cups) cool water into a non-reactive bowl. Stir in the salt until dissolved.

Remove the outer set of leaves from the banana blossom. Chop the tip of the flower off, but keep the stalk on, as a handle. Carefully slice towards the stalk at least four times, cutting a cross-section of the flower, but don't detach it from the stalk. Now cut the blossom very finely across the cuts you have made, so you end up with very small pieces of the blossom. Add them to the bowl of salted water and wash vigorously, to remove the sticky sap and any bitterness. Drain and set aside.

FOR A WET CURRY Combine the onion, garlic, ginger, vinegar and turmeric in a large non-reactive bowl. Add the roasted chilli powder (from the extras list), mixing well. Add the banana blossom pieces, mixing well, and leave to marinate for 5 minutes.

Heat the coconut oil in a heavy-based saucepan until smoking. Add the banana blossom mixture and cook over high heat for 5 minutes, stirring all the time. Stir in the coconut milk and gently bring to the boil, then reduce the heat and simmer for 3 minutes. Add the coconut cream and stir for 1 minute. Season with salt if needed and serve with rice, or some wet and dry dishes such as the Fried potato curry (page 125), Stir-fried Bangladeshi spinach (page 113) and Pennywort salad (page 76).

FOR A DRY FRIED CURRY Pour the vegetable oil into a heavy-based saucepan and heat to 180°C (350°F), or until a cube of bread dropped into the oil turns brown in 15 seconds. Add the drained banana blossom and cook for 3–4 minutes, until golden brown. Remove and drain on paper towel. Deep-fry the onion for 3–4 minutes, until golden, then drain on paper towel.

Add the banana blossom and onion to a heavy-based saucepan. Stir in the garlic, ginger, vinegar, turmeric and coconut milk, and the dried chilli and roasted curry powder (from the extras list). Bring to the boil, stirring all the time, then reduce the heat and simmer for 5 minutes. Stir in the coconut cream and bring to the boil. Turn off the heat, season with salt if necessary and serve with rice, Coconut sambal (page 253), and a wet curry like the Ridged gourd curry (page 120).

Kaju maluwa
Cashew nut curry

Cashews are one of the only nuts that actually grow outside the fruit. They are very difficult to process because their shells contain caustic substances that can burn people's skin, hence their expensive price tag. Luckily, you don't need perfectly shaped cashews for this curry — you can use cashew pieces, which are more economical.

I love this curry: it is a solid dish, and very unusual. We always serve it with rice and two or three other curries, accompanied by poppadoms and a lime pickle.

REGION Sri Lanka | **SERVES** 4–6 | **PREPARATION** 20 minutes + 1 hour soaking
COOKING 20 minutes | **DIFFICULTY** Easy

250 g (9 oz) unsalted cashews
2 tablespoons ghee
1 large onion, finely chopped
1 fresh curry leaf sprig, leaves picked
10 cm (4 inch) piece of pandan leaf
2 Indian green chillies, chopped
½ teaspoon cumin seeds, dry-roasted
    and ground
½ teaspoon ground turmeric
1 teaspoon chilli powder
1 cinnamon stick
300 ml (10½ fl oz) coconut milk
150 ml (5 fl oz) coconut cream, plus extra
    to serve
a pinch of Dark roasted curry powder
    (page 25)

Soak the cashews in a small bowl of water for 1 hour. Once softened, strain and set aside to dry off.

Heat the ghee in a medium-sized frying pan over high heat. Once hot, add the onion, curry leaves, pandan leaf and green chilli and stir. When the onion is fragrant and starting to change colour, add the ground cumin, turmeric, chilli powder and cinnamon stick and stir for a few minutes, until the spices are lightly roasted.

Add the drained cashews and stir to combine. Stir in the coconut milk and boil for about 5 minutes, until the sauce has thickened and reduced.

Stir in the coconut cream, bring to the boil, then remove from the heat.

Season to taste with salt and freshly ground black pepper, then transfer to a serving bowl. Garnish with an extra drizzle of coconut cream and a sprinkling of roasted curry powder and serve.

Mustard greens bhutuwa

I have always loved mustard greens. They are slightly hot, and if cooked quickly have a nice crunch. They are also versatile, and bring something unique to the table. I have cooked them with roast pork, wrapped fish in them, and finely sliced them into salads.

I also love the inclusion of sichuan pepper in this dish, which shows how food and ingredients were traded across the Himalayas. You can also use this recipe for spinach instead of mustard greens.

Enjoy this flavour discovery, and I hope you make some of your own too.

REGION Nepal | **SERVES** 4 as a side dish | **PREPARATION** 10 minutes
COOKING 5 minutes | **DIFFICULTY** Easy

In a large non-stick frying pan, heat the mustard oil over high heat. Add the lovage, mustard and cumin seeds, watching and stirring until they turn dark and start to spit — be careful not to let them turn too dark, or they will become bitter.

Add the dried chillies and fry for 15 seconds, just until they darken.

Stir in the garlic, ginger, turmeric and sichuan peppercorns and stir-fry for a minute or so over low heat.

Add the mustard greens and stir-fry for about 2 minutes. Season with salt, increase the heat to high and cook until the mustard greens are wilted and the excess liquid has evaporated. Do not overcook the greens.

Add the pepper and season with salt to taste. Garnish with the dill and serve.

60 ml (2 fl oz/¼ cup) mustard oil
½ teaspoon lovage seeds; if unavailable, you can use celery seeds or dill seeds
½ teaspoon brown mustard seeds
½ teaspoon cumin seeds
3 dried red chillies, broken in half
1 tablespoon crushed garlic
1 tablespoon finely grated fresh ginger
½ teaspoon freshly grated turmeric, or ½ teaspoon ground turmeric
1 teaspoon sichuan peppercorns
450 g (1 lb) mustard greens, washed well, chopped into small pieces
½ teaspoon freshly ground black pepper
2 tablespoons finely chopped fresh dill

Mooli sabzi
Dry radish curry

In the West, white radish is underutilised as a vegetable. In India and Sri Lanka it is not just a garnish or salad item, but a highly regarded vegetable for curries such as this. The leaves of the radish are said to contain more vitamin C than the roots — so instead of throwing the leaves away (as we do with many of our root crops in the West), wash them well, chop them up and stir them through your curries right at the end and they will add a vibrant green colour and crunch.

REGION India | **SERVES** 2 | **PREPARATION** 20 minutes
COOKING 25 minutes | **DIFFICULTY** Easy

To make the ginger green chilli paste, use a spice grinder or mortar and pestle to grind the ginger and chillies into a paste. Scrape into a bowl, add the remaining ingredients and mix until well combined. You won't need all the paste for this recipe; the rest will keep in an airtight container in the fridge for 8–10 days, or indefinitely in the freezer, to use in other recipes.

Heat the coconut oil in a large frying pan over high heat. Add the ajwain seeds and cumin seeds. When they splutter, add the 2 teaspoons ginger green chilli paste and stir. Add the remaining dry spices and cook, stirring, for 2 minutes.

Stir in the tomatoes and cook for about 5 minutes, until they become mushy.

Add the chopped radish and cook, stirring, for a few minutes, then stir in 60 ml (2 fl oz/¼ cup) water. Cover and cook over low heat for about 10 minutes, until the radish becomes soft. Remove the lid.

The curry is meant to be dry, so if there is any water left in the pan, let it reduce before adding the leafy greens.

Stir in the radish leaves and spinach and let them wilt for 2–3 minutes. Do not overcook, or they will become brown and mushy.

Season to taste with salt. Serve hot, with chapatti or rice.

2 tablespoons virgin coconut oil
½ teaspoon ajwain seeds
½ teaspoon cumin seeds
2 teaspoons Ginger green chilli paste (see below)
¼ teaspoon ground turmeric
2 teaspoons ground coriander
1 teaspoon chilli powder
2 tomatoes, chopped
200 g (7 oz/1½ cups) chopped large white radish
200 g (7 oz/4 cups) chopped radish leaves, or even mustard greens
45 g (1½ oz/1 cup) roughly chopped English spinach
salt, to taste

GINGER GREEN CHILLI PASTE
100 g (3½ oz) young fresh ginger, thinly peeled, then finely grated or chopped
100 g (3½ oz) green chillies (preferably hot), stalks removed, roughly chopped
1 tablespoon mustard oil
1 tablespoon lemon juice
1 teaspoon salt

Khoresht-e-laboo
Beetroot hot pot

In Persia (Iran), a khoresht is a casserole. This dish usually contains beef, but I have found it is beautiful simply made with vegetables. Carrots are regularly used, as are plums and even quinces, so feel free to strike out with other vegetables besides beetroot.

REGION Afghanistan | **SERVES** 4 | **PREPARATION** 25 minutes
COOKING 30 minutes | **DIFFICULTY** Easy

50 ml (1¾ fl oz) rice bran oil
1 large brown onion, chopped
1 teaspoon ground turmeric
a pinch of saffron threads
½ cinnamon stick, broken
1 teaspoon ground cumin
4 green cardamom pods, crushed
1 tablespoon tomato paste
    (concentrated purée)
1 cm (½ inch) knob of fresh ginger,
    peeled and finely grated
2 hot red chillies, chopped
4 carrots, peeled and cut into 3 cm
    (1¼ inch) chunks
3 medium–large beetroot (beets), peeled
    and cut into 3 cm (1¼ inch) chunks
60 g (2¼ oz/¼ cup) dried yellow
    split peas
2 tablespoons pomegranate molasses

In a heavy-based saucepan, heat the rice bran oil over medium–high heat until nearly smoking. Add the onion and cook for 2 minutes, or until golden brown.

Add the spices and tomato paste and stir for 2–3 minutes.

Stir in the ginger, chilli, carrot and beetroot and add enough water to cover the vegetables by about 3 cm (1¼ inches). Bring to the boil, then reduce to a simmer and cook for about 10 minutes, until the beetroot is tender.

Add the split peas and give the mixture a gentle stir, then cook together at a rapid simmer for 5 minutes.

Bring to the boil, then simmer over medium–low heat for 10 minutes, or until the gravy is thick, stirring in a little more water if required.

Just before serving, stir in the pomegranate molasses and season to taste with salt.

Serve with rice.

Thakkali, wamatu, kaju vanjanaya
Green tomato, cashew & eggplant curry

Green tomatoes are tangy, and eggplant is silky, while cashews have a crunch and work as a thickening agent — a marvellous combination in this really tasty curry.

It takes a little effort to fry the eggplant, but when that yellow oil comes out of the curry you will know it was worth it.

REGION Sri Lanka | **SERVES** 4 | **PREPARATION** 25 minutes
COOKING 40 minutes | **DIFFICULTY** Medium

1 litre (35 fl oz/4 cups) vegetable oil, for deep-frying
4 eggplants (aubergines), cut into 1 cm (½ inch) cubes
1 teaspoon ground turmeric
2½ tablespoons virgin coconut oil
1 onion, thinly sliced
1 garlic clove, thinly sliced
1 fresh curry leaf sprig, leaves picked
1 teaspoon Raw curry powder (page 25)
100 g (3½ oz/⅔ cup) cashews, chopped
5 green (unripe) tomatoes, roughly chopped
1 teaspoon chilli flakes
½ teaspoon freshly ground black pepper
juice of 1 lime
¼ bunch coriander (cilantro), chopped

Pour the vegetable oil into a heavy-based saucepan and heat to 180°C (350°F), or until a cube of bread dropped into the oil turns brown in 15 seconds.

Dust the eggplant cubes in the turmeric. Working in batches, carefully add them to the hot oil and cook for about 5 minutes, or until golden. Drain on paper towel, set aside and keep warm.

Meanwhile, heat the coconut oil in a heavy-based saucepan or small wok. Add the onion, garlic and curry leaves and cook for 8–10 minutes, or until the onion is golden.

Stir in the curry powder and cashews and cook for 2 minutes. Add the chopped tomatoes and cook for a further 5 minutes, or until the tomato is pulpy.

Stir in the chilli flakes and pepper and cook for another 2 minutes, to bring the flavours together.

Remove from the heat, then stir in the eggplant, lime juice and coriander. Season to taste with salt.

Serve with rice, and our choice of another two or three curries from this book.

Gajar matar sabzi
Carrots with green peas

Colourful and flavoursome, this simple dish is said to hail from the northern regions of India. Don't add the peas until the carrot is cooked through, to keep them green and retain their 'pop'. Serve with rice, roti, paratha or Puri (page 38).

REGION India | **SERVES** 4 | **PREPARATION** 15 minutes
COOKING 25 minutes | **DIFFICULTY** Easy

Heat the coconut oil in a heavy-based saucepan over high heat. Add the cumin seeds and mustard seeds. When they start to pop, add the onion and curry leaves and cook, stirring, for 2–3 minutes, or until the onion is translucent.

Stir in the garlic and ginger green chilli paste and cook for 1–2 minutes.

Add the garam masala, chilli powder, amchur and turmeric, season with salt and fry for about 1 minute. Add the carrot and cook, stirring, for a further 3 minutes, or until all the carrot is well coated in the spices and fragrant.

Stir in 125 ml (4 fl oz/½ cup) water and bring to the boil. Reduce the heat to low, then cover and simmer for 5 minutes.

Stir in the peas, cover the pan again and cook for a further 3 minutes, or until the peas are just tender but still very green. Remove from the heat.

Transfer to a bowl and serve, garnished with dollops of yoghurt, a sprinkling of garam masala and chopped coriander.

2 tablespoons virgin coconut oil
¼ teaspoon cumin seeds
¼ teaspoon brown mustard seeds
2 brown onions, finely chopped
1 fresh curry leaf sprig, leaves picked
1 teaspoon crushed garlic
1 teaspoon Ginger green chilli paste (page 131)
1 teaspoon Garam masala (page 24)
¼ teaspoon chilli powder
½ teaspoon amchur (dried mango powder)
2 cm (¾ inch) knob of fresh turmeric, peeled and grated, or ¼ teaspoon ground turmeric
5 large carrots, cut into 3 cm (1¼ inch) chunks
150 g (5½ oz/1 cup) fresh or frozen green peas

TO GARNISH
2 tablespoons Greek-style yoghurt
a pinch of Garam masala (page 24)
1 tablespoon chopped coriander (cilantro)

Black-eyed pea & bamboo shoot tarkari

This Nepalese recipe is prepared with soaked black-eyed peas and fermented bamboo shoots curried in spices. It makes a great side dish, or just a simple meal with rice or roti.

REGION Nepal | **SERVES** 4 | **PREPARATION** 30 minutes + overnight soaking
COOKING 40 minutes | **DIFFICULTY** Easy

250 g (9 oz/1⅓ cups) black-eyed peas

150 ml (5 fl oz) vegetable oil or rice bran oil

150 g (5½ oz/1 cup) Mesu pickle (page 233) or fermented bamboo shoots, drained

3 dried red chillies, broken in half

1 brown onion, finely chopped

1 tablespoon Garam masala (page 24)

1 teaspoon chilli powder

1 teaspoon crushed garlic

1 teaspoon finely grated fresh young ginger

2 cm (¾ inch) knob of fresh turmeric, peeled and grated, or ½ teaspoon ground turmeric

1 tablespoon Mustard paste (page 123), or use a ready-made one from a jar

350 g (12 oz) sebago or other waxy potatoes, peeled and cut into 3 cm (1¼ inch) cubes

400 g (14 oz) diced tinned or fresh roma (plum) tomatoes

435 ml (15¼ fl oz/1¾ cups) coconut water

1 tablespoon chopped coriander (cilantro)

Soak the black-eyed peas in a bowl of water overnight.

In a frying pan, heat half the oil over medium heat. Fry the bamboo shoots for about 2–3 minutes, or until light brown, then set aside on a plate.

Heat the remaining oil in a heavy-based saucepan over high heat. Fry the dried chillies for 2–3 minutes, stirring often, until they turn dark.

Add the onion and cook, stirring, for about 2 minutes, until lightly browned. Turn the heat down to low, then stir in the spices and mustard paste. Season with salt and freshly ground black pepper and cook for 1 minute, stirring often.

Add the potato and cook over medium heat for 5 minutes, stirring well to coat the potato in all the spices, and sprinkle with water if the mixture starts to burn.

Drain the beans and add them to the pan with the sautéed bamboo shoots, tomatoes and coconut water. Stir well, bring to the boil, then leave to simmer over low heat for 15–20 minutes, or until the potato is fork-tender, and the gravy has reached the desired consistency.

Garnish with the coriander and serve.

Begare baingan
Spiced eggplant with tamarind

I love the creamy texture of eggplant; it is such a flavour magnet. This is a very simple dish, with a twist of sourness from the tamarind. Serve with rice or roti, or as a condiment for other dishes.

REGION Pakistan | **SERVES** 4 | **PREPARATION** 15 minutes
COOKING 15 minutes | **DIFFICULTY** Easy

Leaving the skin on, cut the eggplant into 2.5 cm (1 inch) chunks. Place in a bowl and sprinkle with the spices and salt. Toss to coat the eggplant with the spices. Mix the chopped green chilli and ginger through and set aside.

Heat the coconut oil in a heavy-based saucepan over medium heat. Add the onion, along with the ginger garlic paste and garlic paste. Cook, stirring, for 2–3 minutes, until fragrant.

Add the eggplant and mix well to combine. Stir in the tamarind paste, coriander and mint and cook for 10 minutes, stirring now and then.

Just before serving, stir the lemon juice through. Serve garnished with green chilli, coriander and lemon slices.

8 long, thin eggplants (aubergines)
2 tablespoons crushed dried red chillies
1 tablespoon cumin seeds
½ teaspoon ajwain seeds
½ teaspoon fennel seeds
1 tablespoon ground turmeric
2 tablespoons salt, or to taste
4 Indian green chillies, chopped
1 tablespoon chopped fresh ginger
2 tablespoons virgin coconut oil
2 onions, chopped
1 tablespoon Ginger garlic paste
    (page 241)
1 tablespoon fresh Garlic paste (page 241)
2 tablespoons tamarind paste,
    tamarind pureé or Tamarind chutney
    (page 220), mixed with a little water
1 bunch coriander (cilantro), chopped
½ bunch mint, leaves picked
2 tablespoons lemon juice

TO GARNISH
sliced Indian green chillies
coriander (cilantro) sprigs
lemon slices

Kewa datshi
Potatoes 'n' cheese

My first thought on encountering this truly unique dish, which is one of Bhutan's national favourites, was a crazy spicy fondue! Try it, if only once, and keep it spicy, as it should be. You can garnish it with chopped spring onion (scallion) and more fresh chilli if you want. The more chillies, the better.

REGION Bhutan | **SERVES** 4 | **PREPARATION** 20 minutes
COOKING 20 minutes | **DIFFICULTY** Easy

Pour 500 ml (17 fl oz/2 cups) water into a saucepan. Add the potato, onion, chillies, salt and rice bran oil and bring to the boil.

Leave to cook for 5–7 minutes, or until the potato is tender. Add the tomatoes and bring back to the boil.

Add the cheese and mix it through; it's fine if the potato breaks up a bit.

As soon as the cheese melts, your kewa dashi is ready to serve.

2 waxy potatoes, such as Dutch cream or pink-skinned potatoes, peeled and sliced into thin rounds
1 small red onion, chopped
4–6 fresh red chillies, halved lengthways
1 teaspoon salt
1 tablespoon rice bran oil
2 ripe tomatoes, diced
50 g (1¾ oz/⅓ cup) crumbled or grated queso fresco or feta cheese

Spicy spinach & tofu

Tofu, a curd made from soy beans, is an extremely healthy food, full of protein, low in calories and easy to digest. On its own tofu is pretty bland, but it has a remarkable ability to absorb the flavours of whatever other ingredients it is cooked with, making it very versatile.

Serve this dish with plain rice or noodles.

REGION Nepal | **SERVES** 4 | **PREPARATION** 15 minutes
COOKING 20 minutes | **DIFFICULTY** Easy

300–400 g (10½–14 oz) block of firm tofu
60 ml (2 fl oz/¼ cup) rice bran oil
1 onion, cut in half and sliced horizontally into half-moons
1 tablespoon crushed garlic
3–4 Indian green chillies, thinly sliced
250 g (9 oz/1 cup) diced tomatoes
½ teaspoon ground turmeric
1 teaspoon ground cumin
1 teaspoon chilli flakes
1 spring onion (scallion), finely chopped
1 tablespoon light soy sauce
2 tablespoons tomato sauce, such as the Velvet tomato catsup on page 248
250 g (9 oz) baby English spinach leaves
1 teaspoon sichuan peppercorns, crushed

Gently press the block of tofu to remove as much water as possible. Pat dry with paper towel, then cut the tofu into cubes or rectangular pieces.

Heat 1 tablespoon of the rice bran oil in a non-stick frying pan over medium heat. Fry the tofu pieces for 1–1½ minutes, or until lightly browned underneath, then gently turn the pieces over, taking care they don't break, and lightly brown the other side. Don't overcook the tofu, or it will become tough. Drain on paper towel and set aside.

In the same pan, heat the remaining 2 tablespoons of oil and cook the onion, garlic and green chilli for about 3 minutes, or until the onion becomes soft. Add the tomatoes, turmeric, cumin and chilli flakes. Season with a pinch of salt and cook, stirring, for 2 minutes.

Stir in 125 ml (4 fl oz/½ cup) water and cook for another few minutes, until the gravy starts to thicken. Add the spring onion, soy sauce, tomato sauce and spinach, mixing well.

Lastly, add the pan-fried tofu and the sichuan pepper and gently coat the tofu with the gravy. Adjust the seasonings and serve.

Muttaikose poriyal
Sautéed cabbage

In this very traditional southern Indian dry vegetable curry, cabbage is power cooked with a very simple seasoning of mustard seeds, curry leaves, salt and freshly grated coconut. At home we simply love the fresh flavours of cabbage when we add the least amount of spices.

Serve for lunch or dinner with your favourite sambal, and some steamed rice topped with ghee.

REGION Southern India | **SERVES** 4 | **PREPARATION** 15 minutes
COOKING 10 minutes | **DIFFICULTY** Easy

Heat the coconut oil in a large heavy-based frying pan over medium heat.

Add the mustard seeds and urad dhal and cook, stirring often, for 2–3 minutes, or until lightly browned.

Add the curry leaves, chilli and cabbage. Season with salt and give the mixture a stir. Sprinkle some water over, then cover the pan and simmer for about 5 minutes, or until the cabbage is firmly steamed and ready to eat.

Stir the grated coconut through, taste and season with more salt if required.

Serve immediately.

1 teaspoon coconut oil
1 teaspoon brown mustard seeds
1½ teaspoons white urad dhal (hulled dried black lentils)
1 fresh curry leaf sprig, leaves finely chopped
1 Indian green chilli, slit in half lengthways
500 g (1 lb 2 oz) cabbage, roughly chopped or thinly sliced
20 g (¾ oz/¼ cup) freshly grated coconut

Shamu datshi
Mushrooms & cheese

Bhutan is blessed with rich natural forests that are home to many species of mushrooms, which find their way into this typical Bhutanese dish. Serve this simple, warming meal with some bread or boiled potatoes.

REGION Bhutan | **SERVES** 2 | **PREPARATION** 15 minutes
COOKING 15 minutes | **DIFFICULTY** Easy

100 g (3½ oz) butter

1 large brown onion, sliced

250 g (9 oz) oyster mushrooms, torn, or any type of mushroom you like; a mixture would be lovely too

1 very ripe tomato, sliced into wedges

2 Indian green chillies, halved lengthways

30 g (1 oz/¼ cup) crumbled feta cheese

100 g (3½ oz/1 cup) grated cheddar cheese

2 tablespoons thin (pouring) cream

Melt the butter in a heavy-based saucepan over medium heat. Add the onion and allow to sweat for 2–3 minutes.

Add the mushrooms and season with a pinch of salt. Fry together, stirring lightly, for about 3 minutes. Add the tomato and chilli and continue cooking for 2 minutes.

Pour in 100 ml (3½ fl oz) water and bring to the boil. Sprinkle in the feta and cheddar cheese, then cover and cook for 2–3 minutes, or until the cheeses melt.

Reduce the heat to very low and stir in the cream. Let the mixture sit for a minute, then remove from the heat.

Serve immediately.

Vegetable jalfrezi

Vegetable jalfrezi is said to have originated in India during the time of the British Raj. Once a creative way to use up leftovers, it has since evolved into a flavourful and texture-rich dish — a popular Indian restaurant menu item. Try this recipe with a mixture of vegies, or highlight just one or two. Either way, vegetable jalfrezi will add a colourful splash to your plate.

REGION India | **SERVES** 4–5 | **PREPARATION** 15 minutes
COOKING 35 minutes | **DIFFICULTY** Easy

Bring a saucepan of water to the boil, and have a bowl of iced water at the ready.

Add the salt and ground turmeric to the pan of boiling water. Add the cauliflower and carrot and boil for 3 minutes. Strain the vegetables, then immediately drop them into the iced water to stop the cooking process. Drain for 1–2 minutes, then set aside.

In a non-stick frying pan, dry-roast the coriander seeds over low heat for about 5 minutes, until they start to dance in the pan, being sure to stir them often so they don't burn. Tip onto a small plate, leave to cool, then grind using a mortar and pestle. Set aside.

Heat the rice bran oil in the same pan. Add the onion and cook, stirring, for 2–3 minutes, or until lightly golden. Add the ginger and garlic and fry for 1 minute. Stir in the tomato sauce and cook for about 10 minutes, stirring occasionally to prevent sticking, until the oil separates from the sauce.

Stir in the capsicum and peas and cook for 2–3 minutes. Now add the blanched cauliflower and carrots, along with the reserved ground coriander, the garam masala and chilli powder, if using. Mix well, and season to taste with salt.

Cook for about 5 minutes, or until the vegetables are tender, but still retain their crunch, sprinkling a little water over them occasionally so that the spices don't burn.

Stir in the chopped tomato and cook for a final 1–2 minutes. Stir in a splash of lemon or lime juice, to taste.

Serve hot, with rice, roti, chapatti or naan.

1 teaspoon salt
¼ teaspoon ground turmeric
375 g (13 oz/3 cups) cauliflower florets
1 carrot, chopped
2 tablespoons coriander seeds
1 tablespoon rice bran oil
½ onion, chopped
1 teaspoon finely grated fresh ginger
2 teaspoons crushed garlic
125 ml (4 fl oz/½ cup) tomato sauce, such as the Velvet tomato catsup on page 248
½ red capsicum (pepper), chopped into bite-sized pieces
75 g (2½ oz/½ cup) frozen green peas, thawed
1 teaspoon Garam masala (page 24)
chilli powder, to taste (optional)
1 small tomato, seeded and chopped
lemon or lime juice, to taste

Chapter 6

Rice

In the West, we don't give rice enough respect.

Farmed for almost 7000 years, it is a founding grain that has long sustained some of the most populous parts of our planet. There are estimated to be some 40,000 varieties of rice, typically classified by size and texture, such as long, medium and short-grained, and by their strain, such as white, brown, red, black or purple.

In Asian countries, particularly, this tiny grain is revered as a source of sustenance and a giver of life. Friendships can be made and lost over a humble bowl of rice, a simple foodstuff consumed in nightly dinners and celebrated in holy holidays and festivals.

Across the subcontinent, people don't just eat rice because they can't get anything else; there are often other crops that would feed them more cheaply and consistently. They go to the enormous trouble of cultivating rice because in flavour, texture and satisfaction, no other basic staple comes close. The varietals and types of preparation are endless and nothing short of wondrous — and if you try hard enough to source it, you could enjoy a different type of rice each week and never hit repeat.

In the subcontinent, you cannot live without rice. Rice needs to go into the centre of your plate; rice is the anchor that brings everything together. If you are having rice just to fill your stomach, you are not giving it the reverence it deserves.

I come from a family with a deep appreciation for food and culinary culture. My diverse lineage, with my mother's Austrian roots and my dad's Sri Lankan heritage, and the many places we called home as I was growing up have meant that I have tried — and I mean really tried — pretty much every way in which this wondrous grain has been cooked. And I have never been bored. My palate has never reached fatigue. In fact, I crave rice, and not a week goes by without enjoying rice in some form.

Rice is an adventure in itself. There is samba rice in Sri Lanka which smells like a paddy when you cook it — so much so it has to be cooked with pandan leaf just to neutralise the aroma. There is also Sri Lankan red rice, which is gloriously nutty in flavour and slightly chewy in texture. In the Philippines, Tinawon rice is an heirloom grain, so deeply prized that the paddy terraces in which it is grown are World Heritage listed. Then there are the brown rices, jasmine rice, yellow rice, basmati rice, and other long and short-grain rices, each with a story to tell, and a culinary contribution to make.

My dad used to make this dish called jardi, which he nicknamed 'the rice puller'. It was a simple dish of dried fish, tomato, lime, onion and lots of chilli on rice. It was so good, you had to keep drawing the rice in and eating more. And that is my philosophy for this chapter of recipes — to entice you and pull you in, to try different rice grains and preparations, to expand your repertoire and see for yourself the inventiveness and cultural influences behind dishes made with that beautiful humble little grain called rice.

Vegetarian lovers' rice

Made to celebrate a couple's love for each other, this opulent and festive dish usually contains seafood, but the vegetarian version is just as lovely.

REGION Sri Lanka | **SERVES** 4 | **PREPARATION** 30 minutes
COOKING 40 minutes | **DIFFICULTY** Medium

200 g (7 oz) samba rice; if you can't get hold of it, use a short-grained rice
2½ tablespoons virgin coconut oil
1 fresh curry leaf sprig, leaves picked
1 carrot, finely diced
100 g (3½ oz) winter melon or pumpkin (winter squash), peeled
150 g (5½ oz/1 cup) cashews, chopped
1 tablespoon Sri Lankan vegetarian chilli paste (see below)
1 teaspoon ground turmeric
50 g (1¾ oz/⅓ cup) fresh green peas
45 g (1½ oz/¼ cup) raisins
fried shredded curry leaves, to garnish

SRI LANKAN VEGETARIAN CHILLI PASTE
100 g (3½ oz) virgin coconut oil
1 large onion, diced
½ pandan leaf, chopped
1 cinnamon stick
2 cloves
2 tablespoons chilli flakes
25 fresh curry leaves, shredded
2 teaspoons crushed garlic
2 teaspoons grated fresh ginger
2 teaspoons sugar
½ teaspoon salt

To make the chilli paste, heat the coconut oil in a heavy-based saucepan over medium heat. Fry the onion, pandan leaf, cinnamon stick, cloves and chilli flakes for about 3 minutes, or until the onion is golden. Stir in the curry leaves, garlic and ginger and cook for about 3 minutes, or until fragrant. Sprinkle with the sugar and salt and stir until dissolved, then remove from the heat and leave to cool. Blend into a paste and set aside. You will only need a small amount for this dish; the remainder will keep in an airtight container in the fridge for up to 1 month.

Wash the rice and cook according to one of the methods on page 159.

Meanwhile, in a large sturdy wok, heat the coconut oil over medium heat and add the curry leaves. When they pop, add the carrot, winter melon and cashews and cook for 5 minutes, stirring often.

Stir in the chilli paste and turmeric and cook for a few minutes, then add the peas and raisins and stir for 2 minutes.

When the rice is cooked, fluff the grains using a fork, then add the rice to the vegetable mixture, tossing in the wok until well combined.

Garnish with fried curry leaves and serve immediately, with your favourite relish or pickle.

TIP Instead of crushing the garlic and grating the ginger, you can use 1 tablespoon Ginger garlic paste from page 241, or from a jar.

Yagut palau
Pomegranate rice

The Koran mentions the pomegranate as one of the fruits found in paradise, and medical research suggests it may help those wanting to extend their stay in this world. Rich in antioxidants, the pomegranate is promoted in the West as a defence against prostate cancer, heart disease and other illnesses.

We had a few pomegranate trees in our gardens in Sri Lanka, and whenever someone had a bruise, my aunties would quickly blanch the leaves to soften them, and then apply a bandage filled with the leaves to the bruise.

Quite apart from any medicinal benefits, pomegranates are great to eat, and are a stunning addition to this lovely dish.

REGION Afghanistan | **SERVES** 4 | **PREPARATION** 20 minutes + 2 hours soaking + 5 minutes standing
COOKING 20 minutes | **DIFFICULTY** Easy

Soak the rice in a bowl of water for 2 hours.

Heat the coconut oil in a heavy-based saucepan over medium–high heat. Add the onion and garlic and cook, stirring often, for about 3 minutes, or until softened and golden brown.

Add the rice, cumin seeds, cardamom and turmeric and stir to coat all the rice.

Stir in the pomegranate juice and coconut water and bring to the boil. Reduce the heat to low and cook, partially covered, for 15–18 minutes, or until the liquid has been absorbed.

Remove from the heat, cover the pan and leave to stand for 5 minutes.

Fluff the rice grains with a fork, then fold in the spring onion and aleppo pepper. Season to taste with salt and freshly ground black pepper. Garnish with the pomegranate seeds and serve.

TIP You can make your own pomegranate juice by passing the seeds of 5–6 fresh pomegranates through a juicer.

400 g (14 oz/2 cups) white or brown basmati rice
100 ml (3½ fl oz) virgin coconut oil
1 onion, finely chopped
1 garlic clove, chopped
1 teaspoon cumin seeds
1 teaspoon ground cardamom
½ teaspoon ground turmeric
150 ml (5 fl oz) good-quality pomegranate juice (see tip)
150 ml (5 fl oz) coconut water, vegetable stock or water
2 spring onions (scallions), finely chopped
1 teaspoon aleppo pepper
1 pomegranate, seeds separated, to garnish

Bhuteko bhat
Nepalese egg fried rice

When you are in need of a quick carb boost, this is the dish! I lived on it while trekking in Nepal. It fills you up, can be made very quickly and tastes so good.

You can use any type of rice you like, although the dish will taste even better if made with cold leftover cooked rice — just make sure it isn't cold and sticky.

I have added caraway seeds to this dish, for their unique complexity of flavour.

REGION Nepal | **SERVES** 2 | **PREPARATION** 10 minutes
COOKING 10 minutes | **DIFFICULTY** Easy

3½ tablespoons virgin coconut oil
½ onion, finely diced
2 garlic cloves, chopped
1 fresh curry leaf sprig, leaves picked
    and torn
¼ teaspoon dill seeds
¼ teaspoon caraway seeds
50 g (1¾ oz/⅓ cup) fresh green peas
50 g (1¾ oz/⅓ cup) diced carrot
45 g (1½ oz/⅓ cup) diced celery
50 g (1¾ oz/¼ cup) corn kernels
45 g (1½ oz/¾ cup) broccoli florets
2 ripe tomatoes, diced
2 eggs, lightly beaten
370 g (13 oz/2 cups) leftover cooked rice,
    at room temperature
2 cm (¾ inch) knob of fresh turmeric,
    peeled and grated, or ¼ teaspoon
    ground turmeric
1 tablespoon soy sauce

Heat 2½ tablespoons of the coconut oil in a wok or heavy-based frying pan over medium heat. Cook the onion and garlic for 3 minutes, or until golden, stirring often.

Add the curry leaves, dill seeds, caraway seeds and vegetables, except the tomatoes. Toss for a few minutes, or until heated through, then stir in the tomatoes. Remove the mixture from the pan and set aside.

Wipe the pan clean with paper towel and place back over medium heat. Add the remaining coconut oil and heat until smoking. Add the beaten eggs and scramble them; while they are still moist, add the fried vegetable mixture and the rice and heat everything through, tossing regularly.

Add a splash of soy sauce, season with salt if necessary and enjoy.

Red rice kiri bath

Usually cut into diamonds and allowed to cool, these wonderful creamy rice cakes are beautiful with ripe banana and any spicy sambal. In Sri Lanka, they are served on auspicious occasions such as New Year, and every full moon, known as a poya day, when key events in Buddhism are honoured — but they are also eaten at other times because they taste so good. My dad used to love them with green mung beans in them, too.

REGION Sri Lanka | **SERVES** 6 | **PREPARATION** 25 minutes
COOKING 30 minutes | **DIFFICULTY** Easy

Wash and drain the rice, then place in a rice cooker with the cardamom pods, coconut and salt. Cook according to your rice cooker's instructions. Alternatively, cook the rice using the absorption method (see page 159).

Tip the rice into a large heavy-based saucepan. Add the coconut cream and cook over medium heat, stirring often, for about 5 minutes, until combined and sticky.

Lightly grease the banana leaf, if using.

Scoop the rice onto an oval platter, then smooth out the rice to an even 3 cm (1¼ inches) thickness, using the greased side of the banana leaf to help you.

While it is still warm, cut the kiri bath into diamonds using a wet knife and allow to cool.

The kiri bath is best enjoyed the same day. Any leftovers can be rolled into balls around some Seeni sambal (page 209), then crumbed and deep-fried, like a Sri Lankan 'arancini'.

TIP You can soften the banana leaf by running it over a gas flame, which will make it more pliable.

1.25 kg (2 lb 12 oz/6 cups) Sri Lankan red rice, or other red rice
6 green cardamom pods, bruised
75 g (2½ oz/1 cup) fresh coconut flesh
1 teaspoon salt
500 ml (17 fl oz/2 cups) coconut cream
vegetable oil, for greasing
1 banana leaf, softened (optional; see tip)

Manga sadam
Mango rice

Tangy and refreshing, this dish is similar to the lemon rice from southern India, and is a wonderful way to use leftover cooked rice. In fact, leftover rice is preferable for this dish as it is not as moist, and gives a better result.

Use a green mango for this dish, adding a little extra if you'd like a bit more sourness and tang.

REGION India | **SERVES** 2 | **PREPARATION** 15 minutes
COOKING 15 minutes | **DIFFICULTY** Easy

1 green mango, peeled and grated
370 g (13 oz/2 cups) cooked brown rice
75 g (2½ oz/½ cup) cooked peas
a pinch of salt, or to taste
1 fried curry leaf sprig, to garnish
   (optional)

FOR TEMPERING
2½ tablespoons virgin coconut oil
1 teaspoon brown mustard seeds
1 tablespoon chana dhal
1 tablespoon white urad dhal (hulled
   dried black lentils)
2 dried red chillies, broken into thirds
2 Indian green chillies, chopped
2 cm (¾ inch) knob of fresh turmeric,
   peeled and grated, or ¼ teaspoon
   ground turmeric
1 fresh curry leaf sprig, leaves picked
150 g (5½ oz/1 cup) macadamia nuts,
   chopped

If you are using cooked rice left over from another day, which is preferable, ensure it is not sticky by gently separating the grains with a fork.

To temper the spices, heat the coconut oil in a wok over medium heat. Add the mustard seeds. When they splutter, add the chana dhal, urad dhal, dried chillies and green chilli and gently cook for about 5 minutes, stirring often. When the dhal turns golden brown, stir in the turmeric, curry leaves and macadamias, and season with salt.

Add the grated mango and mix well to combine with all the spices. Cook for 3–5 minutes, until the mango turns pulpy. Add the cooked rice and peas and mix through well, so all the rice is coated with the mango mixture. Taste and season with salt, if required.

Serve hot, or at room temperature, garnished with a fried curry leaf sprig if desired.

Red rice & mung bean risotto

One of my favourite rice varieties is Bhutanese red rice. I encourage you to try it, if you can find it. It has a glorious nutty flavour, with earthy tones that pair so beautifully with other flavours. Highly valued for its antioxidant properties, it is also nutrient dense, with higher values of phosphorus, magnesium and molybdenum than other rices. Short or medium-grain brown rice works well in this dish, too.

Any leftover risotto will keep in the fridge for several days, and the flavours will only deepen. You can make a subcontinental 'arancini' by rolling the risotto into balls, filling the centres with cheese, crumbing them and deep-frying until crisp.

REGION Bhutan | **SERVES** 3–4 as a main, 6–8 as a side | **PREPARATION** 20 minutes + 20 minutes soaking
COOKING 40 minutes | **DIFFICULTY** Medium

210 g (7½ oz/1 cup) Bhutanese red rice
200 g (7 oz/1 cup) dried green
    mung beans (moong dhal)
60 ml (2 fl oz/¼ cup) virgin coconut oil
360 g (12¾ oz/4 cups) chopped fresh
    wild mushrooms, or whatever type
    you like
2 garlic cloves, crushed
2 tablespoons fresh thyme leaves,
    or a few thyme sprigs
1.25 litres (44 fl oz/5 cups) coconut water
    or vegetable stock
60 g (2¼ oz) unsalted butter
35 g (1¼ oz/⅓ cup) finely chopped
    French or red Asian shallot
60 ml (2 fl oz/¼ cup) dry rosé or
    white wine
200 g (7 oz) baby English spinach leaves
70 g (2½ oz/¾ cup) grated parmesan
    cheese, plus extra to serve

Wash the rice and mung beans twice in cold water, then drain the water off. Place the rice and mung beans in a heatproof bowl and pour 1 litre (35 fl oz/4 cups) boiling-hot water over them. Leave to soak for about 20 minutes.

Meanwhile, warm 2 tablespoons of the coconut oil in a large heavy-based frying pan over medium heat. Toss in the mushrooms, garlic, thyme, a sprinkling of salt, and a few grinds of black pepper. Cook for 10 minutes, or until the mushrooms are tender and have released their liquid. Set the mushrooms aside, pouring off any excess cooking liquid.

In a large saucepan, heat the coconut water or stock. Adjust the heat to keep it just below a simmer while cooking the risotto.

Drain the rice and mung beans, reserving the soaking liquid and adding it to the pan of warm coconut water or stock.

In a large heavy-based saucepan, heat the remaining 1 tablespoon coconut oil and 1 tablespoon of the butter over medium heat. When the butter is bubbling, add the shallot and cook for 1–2 minutes, until slightly translucent but not browned. Add the rice and stir to coat the grains with the warm fats. After 2 minutes, stir in the wine and cook for 1–2 minutes, until mostly absorbed or evaporated.

Next, add a ladleful of the warm broth to the pan, and let the rice cook and absorb most of the liquid. Add enough broth to lightly cover the rice and adjust the heat to keep a hearty simmer going. Stir regularly, adding ladlefuls of broth every few minutes to ensure the rice is always under a thin layer of broth. Continue cooking for a total of 30–40 minutes, or until the rice is plump and cooked through, but still has a toothsome quality.

Turn the heat to low and stir in the sautéed mushrooms, along with the spinach and one last ladleful of broth. Season generously with salt. Cover the pan for a few minutes, to wilt the spinach, then turn off the heat and stir in the parmesan, the remaining butter, and more salt and pepper to taste.

Cover and stand for a final 5 minutes for the flavours to come together. Serve scattered with extra parmesan.

Vegetable biriyani with paneer

When our Bangladeshi kitchen hands would make staff lunches in the restaurant, it was usually a version of this — a wholesome dish with tons of flavour. The paneer is so easy to prepare, you will wonder why you haven't made it before, once you do.

REGION Bangladesh | **SERVES** 3–4 as a main, 6–8 as a side | **PREPARATION** 20 minutes + 20 minutes soaking
COOKING 40 minutes | **DIFFICULTY** Medium

Soak the rice in plenty of cold water for 20 minutes.

Drain the rice and place in a deep non-stick saucepan, along with the bay leaf, cinnamon stick, clove and cardamom pods. Add a pinch of salt and pour in 1.125 litres (40 fl oz/ 4½ cups) water. Cover with a lid and bring to the boil, then cook over medium heat for 6 minutes, or until the rice is par-cooked. Strain the rice using a colander and set aside.

Meanwhile, for the vegetable gravy, blanch the chopped mixed vegetables in a saucepan of boiling water for a few minutes. Drain and set aside.

Heat the coconut oil in a deep non-stick frying pan over medium heat and add the cumin seeds. When the seeds crackle, add the onion and cook, stirring, over medium heat for 1–2 minutes, or until the onion is translucent.

Add the ginger, green chilli and ground spices and stir for a few seconds. Stir in the tomatoes and 2 tablespoons water, mixing well, and cook for 4–5 minutes.

Add the mixed vegetables, paneer and milk, season with salt and cook for another 2–3 minutes, stirring occasionally. Stir in the sugar and cook for a further 1 minute, then remove from the heat.

Combine the saffron yoghurt ingredients in a bowl and mix well.

Layer the rice, saffron yoghurt and vegetable gravy in a heavy-based saucepan, so you have layers of flavour and colour.

Pour the melted ghee evenly over the rice and cover with a lid. Place over low heat and allow the biriyani to steam for 10–12 minutes, and ideally form a crust on the bottom.

To serve, turn the biriyani upside down onto a serving plate. Garnish with fried onion, cashews and raisins and serve immediately.

300 g (10½ oz/1½ cups) long-grain white or brown basmati rice
1 fresh bay leaf
2.5 cm (1 inch) piece of cinnamon stick
1 clove
4 green cardamom pods
80 ml (2½ fl oz/⅓ cup) melted ghee
fried onion, to garnish
cashews, to garnish
raisins, to garnish

VEGETABLE GRAVY
300 g (10½ oz/1½ cups) chopped mixed vegetables, such as carrots, peas, cauliflower, green beans and peeled potatoes
2 tablespoons virgin coconut oil
1 teaspoon cumin seeds
1 large brown onion, finely chopped
2 cm (¾ inch) knob of fresh ginger, peeled and grated
2 small hot Indian green chillies, finely chopped
½ teaspoon ground turmeric
2 teaspoons ground coriander
1 teaspoon chilli powder
½ teaspoon Garam masala (page 24)
250 g (9 oz/1 cup) roughly chopped very ripe tomatoes
3 tablespoons crumbled Paneer cheese (page 94)
60 ml (2 fl oz/¼ cup) milk
a pinch of sugar

SAFFRON YOGHURT
70 g (2½ oz/¼ cup) Greek-style yoghurt
3 tablespoons finely chopped coriander (cilantro) leaves
a pinch of saffron threads

The delicate art of cooking rice

The cooking of rice and the 'best' method for doing so is something that divides people. I always think it depends on the rice and the dish, but I can understand this source of contention, given the variety of rices available and the many ways of cooking it.

With pasta, you know where you stand. There isn't much more to it than boiling a potato, but rice can be a temperamental little beast. It is prone to gathering in great claggy clumps, or boiling over in a torrent of unappetising foam. To be able to master rice is a feat and one worthy of your time.

PREPARATION
WASHING

Washing the rice in several changes of water is recommended in many Asian countries, but pretty useless with the highly polished rice available on our shelves, which has generally been exhaustively picked over to rid it of any remaining husks and other detritus before packaging. I certainly find very little in the stuff I buy.

Some claim it is still important to wash because it removes excess starch and will result in a fluffier grain of rice, but I think you are hard pressed to tell the difference. I also object to this, given my upbringing. My grandmother would serve me the starchy water from cooking rice whenever I was unwell — everything was looked at as a possible form of nourishment, and nothing was wasted.

You should, however, wash your rice once. Just pour cold water onto it and agitate it with your fingers; it doesn't matter if the water is still cloudy. Then simply drain the rice and cook in the required amount of fresh water.

SOAKING

The purpose of soaking rice is to help soften the grains, so the water can penetrate them more easily and stop them sticking together during cooking. Again I think this comes down to personal preference. I never do this, and think it unnecessary; most rice takes so little time to cook, except for sushi rice, and I believe this is where the idea of soaking rice came from — it is a different variety of rice, and needs to be soaked, so it is sticky, to enable you to make sushi. The rice I am talking about is always enjoyed fluffy but sticky, the perfect balance of enough starch and water to allow the grains to absorb all those beautiful subcontinental flavours.

COOKING METHODS

I often console people who get frustrated about incorrectly cooking rice by pointing out that in rice-eating cultures around the world, and in places such as Iran, a 'burnt' rice crust at the bottom of the pan is eagerly fought over as a delicacy.

The key is to try all the different methods and see what works for you. Taste is personal, but for me it's the absorption method that always delivers the most consistent results. If you follow the instructions and measurements on a rice cooker, your rice will be perfect all the time. It always astounds me when chefs in commercial kitchens deem the measuring cup unnecessary, then wonder why their rice is undercooked or gluggy.

ACCORDING TO THE PACKET INSTRUCTIONS

Unfortunately, the directions printed on a rice packet are generic and don't necessarily account for the type of grain or the end use of the rice in your dish. Proceed with caution.

THE ABSORPTION METHOD/ FINGER METHOD

This is one of the more common methods for cooking rice across the subcontinent. Rice dishes cooked in this way are meant to retain more flavour and nutrients. The basic rule of thumb for the absorption method is to put rice in a saucepan, and add water to 2.5 cm (1 inch) above the rice (this is the distance between the top of the rice and the first joint of an average adult finger). No matter how much rice you use, or how large your saucepan, the water should always come up to the first finger joint, if your fingertip is just touching the rice. Bring to the boil, cover with a tight-fitting lid, turn the heat to low and cook for 13–15 minutes. Stand covered for 5 minutes, fluff up with a fork and serve. The rice should be swollen, but still chalky to the bite.

RICE COOKER

This is another use of the absorption method, retaining similar quantities of nutrients. Follow the manufacturer's instructions. The machine switches off when the rice is cooked, but sends more heat through at intervals to keep the rice hot, dry and fluffy.

STEAMING

This approach requires steaming of parboiled rice (which has already been simmered for 8–10 minutes). The partially softened rice is transferred to a strainer and steamed over a saucepan of boiling water until cooked through. The result is good, but results in a lot of washing up compared to other methods.

THE OVEN

Once the rice has been cooked, using any of the methods outlined above, it can also be finished off in a buttered baking dish in the oven — 15 minutes at 180°C (350°F), swaddled in buttered baking paper and foil. This method gives a slightly drier result.

BOILING RICE

Boiling results in greater nutrient losses and produces a less fluffy result than the absorption method. It may be useful if cooking on an open fire where the heat cannot be turned down. For every 1 cup of raw rice, bring 4 cups water to the boil; add the rice and cook, uncovered, for 12–14 minutes, before draining the rice in a colander.

MICROWAVE

This is a variation of the absorption method. Use a microwave-safe container large enough to hold twice as much rice and water as you start with (or it will boil over). Cover with plastic wrap and use 1 cup rice with 1½ cups water and cook in the microwave for 12 minutes on HIGH; for 2 cups rice use 3 cups water and cook for 14 minutes on HIGH.

While convenient, microwaved rice is often not as fluffy as the steamed or simmered versions.

Rice & grains

Rice and grains are an absolute necessity across the subcontinent. Take these away and the very heart and soul would be ripped out of its cooking. There are some modern diets that shy away from eating rice and other grains — this would be like removing our tongues and eyes. Life would simply not be worth living. I love rice and grains!

1. SAMBA RICE Samba rice is a pungent rice native to Sri Lanka with tiny grains, about one-third the size of basmati rice, and a dense texture, making it quite filling. Adding a pandan leaf during cooking helps dissipate its powerful flavour and aroma.

2. PEARL BARLEY To make it edible for human consumption, barley must first have its tough, fibrous outer hull removed. Removing just the outer hull, but leaving the bran intact, gives a form known as hulled barley. Pearl barley, also called pearled barley, has been polished to remove the bran layer as well, so it has less fibre than hulled barley. Hulled barley has a more nutty flavour and chewy texture than pearl barley, which is paler in colour, and has a shorter cooking time.

3. DALIYA Known in Middle Eastern cuisine as burghul or bulgur, daliya is a popular breakfast cereal in northern India, where it is often made into a porridge. Daliya is made from parboiled cracked or whole wheat groats, most often durum wheat, and can be fine or coarse in texture.

4. BROWN BASMATI RICE Brown rice is a nutritional rock star in the rice family, as it retains more fibre and minerals than white rice. Basmati rice, the 'prince of rice' is a pantry staple in Afghan food. Like other rice varieties, it is available in various forms, from brown to white, depending on the degree of processing it has been subjected to. Aged (or 'classic') basmati rice has been matured for 1–2 years, intensifying the flavour and resulting in a lighter and fluffier steamed rice.

5. RED RICE Red rice is a medium-grain rice with a soft, nutty texture and a distinctive earthy flavour. It has been grown in Bhutan for thousands of years, without the use of chemicals and pesticides, and irrigated with mineral-rich glacial waters. It has a shorter cooking time than brown rice, of only about 20 minutes. You'll find red rice in health food stores.

6. PUFFED RICE Commonly used in breakfast cereals and snack foods, puffed rice has been heated until it 'puffs' out of its hull, like popcorn. It is a popular street food in India and other parts of the subcontinent.

7. BOONDI This popular Indian snack is made from a chickpea flour batter, which has been deep-fried in hot oil until crispy. You'll find a recipe for it on page 49.

Keerai sadam
Spinach rice

Filling and healthy, this simple one-pot recipe is great for the times you are feeling hungry but time poor. Use any variety of cooked rice you like — leftovers are perfect!

REGION India | **SERVES** 2 as a main, 6 as a side | **PREPARATION** 25 minutes
COOKING 15 minutes | **DIFFICULTY** Easy

550 g (1 lb 4 oz/3 cups) cooked rice
    of your choice
2½ tablespoons virgin coconut oil
1 teaspoon brown mustard seeds
1 large onion, finely chopped
5 garlic cloves, chopped
500 g (1 lb 2 oz) English spinach
    or Ceylon spinach, cleaned
    and chopped
3 Indian green chillies, chopped
½ teaspoon chilli powder
½ teaspoon ground turmeric
100 g (3½ oz/⅔ cup) roasted
    macadamia nuts, chopped

FOR TEMPERING
1½ tablespoons virgin coconut oil
1 tablespoon chana dhal
1 tablespoon white urad dhal (hulled
    dried black lentils)
2 tablespoons coriander seeds
1 tablespoon cumin seeds
½ teaspoon fenugreek seeds
½ teaspoon dill seeds, or ½ teaspoon
    chopped fresh dill
½ teaspoon fennel seeds

To temper the spices, heat the coconut oil in a small saucepan over medium heat and fry the chana dhal and urad dhal for 2–3 minutes, until lightly browned. Add the spices and cook for a minute or two until fragrant, taking care that the fenugreek seeds don't burn, or the spices will taste bitter. Remove from the heat, then grind to a paste and set aside.

If your rice is still hot, spread it out on a plate to cool, fluffing the grains with a fork to separate them. If using leftover rice, ensure the grains are well separated.

Heat the coconut oil in a large wok or heavy-based frying pan over medium heat. Add the mustard seeds and wait for them to pop, then roast, stirring often, for 1–2 minutes, or until golden.

Add the onion and garlic and cook, stirring, for a few minutes over medium heat. Stir in the spinach, green chilli, chilli powder, turmeric, along with the freshly ground tempered spice paste. Season with salt to taste.

Cover and cook for about 3 minutes, or until the spinach has wilted. If the pan gets too dry, stir in 60–125 ml (2–4 fl oz/¼–½ cup) water.

Remove the lid and gently mix the rice through, taking care not to break up the grains. If there is any excess moisture, cook for a few more minutes without the lid, until the water has evaporated.

Check the seasoning, top with the macadamias and serve.

Chapter 7
Breads

Bread, in all its glorious forms, is deeply ingrained in my upbringing.

It would be fascinating to have a collage of all the breads in the world, in all their varieties, shapes, colours, flavours and textures. I love the interplay of science, flour, our hands and our eyes in creating a fundamental staple for food cultures the world over. The sheer simplicity of ingredients draws me in.

My mum would tell me about the boys along the roadside in Afghanistan and Iran, with long breads slung over their arms, and I have such vivid memories of making coconut rotis in Sri Lanka. I also loved visiting the bakery next door, watching the bakers mix a giant master dough for the kade paan, or shop bread. There were about six men, mixing the bread on one long bench. They'd place the flour around the whole table and make a giant well, then fill about 12 buckets of water with yeast and sugar, and have a quick nap or chat while the yeast activated. One man poured the frothy, yeasty water into the well, and the others would gently mix the flour in. Sometimes, they let me join in: my job was to run around the table and block off any leaks in the flour wall. I'd be covered in flour and dog tired, but so, so happy.

Once they'd mixed it into a massive dough, weighing as much as two men, they'd knead it, working every muscle in their wiry bodies to bring it all together. Such hard work! The dough was rested and then knocked back, before being split into three parts: the largest for the loaves of bread; another for savoury breads, stuffed with delicious spicy meat, fish or vegetables; and the third for the sweet buns. (My favourite was and still is the kimbula, or 'crocodile' — a long bun rolled in coarse white sugar.)

The bread tins were painted with coconut oil, and the giant century-old oven, still hot from the last baking, was lit. All the wood had to burn down before the bread went in. When the baking was finished the next morning, the village ladies would give the baker a few rupees to bake their cakes for them; this was a time when not everyone had an oven, so the bakery was central to the community.

When the hot bread arrived at our house, I'd sandwich it with fresh coconut sambal. The heat would release the oil from the coconut and the taste was divine.

The bakery was a place of fun and awe. During daylight hours it just looked like a big room full of beaten-up bread tins with a five-metre wooden table in the middle; no one could tell what fun and excitement happened there after midnight. When we moved to Australia, making bread with my dad would instantly revive these treasured memories of our time together, taking me straight back inside that bread shop.

The concept of breaking bread is so simple and so fundamental to the stuff of life, and yet the process is underpinned by technique, knowledge and skill. At its simplest, bread making is a process of trust — and bread, like life, doesn't always go to plan. Often you have to follow the dough, instead of leading it. You have to know it. Know it to touch, to rise, to punch back and rise again. Bread making is not the scary part; it is trusting yourself that is a challenge.

Practice is the only thing that will help you to make great bread. The secret is to not overthink it. The art of bread making is centuries old, and there are only a few simple ingredients to contend with. Just imagine being in a village with no electricity or fancy equipment; better toys don't make a better baker!

Roll up your sleeves, get into it and, most importantly, have some fun.

Gwaramari
Breakfast dumplings

'Gwaramari' literally means 'a round bread' in Newari, a local language spoken by a community in the Kathmandu Valley. This famous breakfast dish is typically served with chutney or milk tea, and is best served warm. Try it with the Chutney for momos on page 221.

REGION Nepal | **SERVES** 4 | **PREPARATION** 10 minutes + overnight resting
COOKING 20 minutes | **DIFFICULTY** Easy

250 g (9 oz/1⅔ cups) plain (all-purpose) flour
1 teaspoon baking powder
¼ teaspoon ground cumin
¼ teaspoon ground coriander
½ teaspoon salt, or to taste
½ teaspoon freshly cracked black pepper, or to taste
250 ml (9 fl oz/1 cup) lukewarm water
1 litre (35 fl oz/4 cups) vegetable oil, for deep-frying

Combine the flour, baking powder, cumin, coriander, salt and pepper in a large bowl. Carefully add the water, stirring continuously, until the mixture becomes a thick paste.

Cover the bowl with plastic wrap and refrigerate overnight.

The next morning, heat the oil in a deep heavy-based saucepan over medium–high heat to 190°C (375°F), or until a cube of bread dropped into the oil turns brown in 10 seconds.

When the oil is ready, stir the dough with a large metal spoon to deflate it. Take about 1½ tablespoons of the dough (about 30 g/1 oz), shape it into a small ball and gently place it in the hot oil, being careful as the oil will spit. Cook a maximum of six dumplings at a time (so the oil doesn't cool down) for 4–5 minutes, or until golden brown and crisp on the outside.

Remove using a slotted spoon and drain on paper towel while cooking the remaining dumplings.

Serve warm.

Coconut roti

A breakfast staple in Sri Lanka, this textural and tasty roti is great with a spicy sambal, or even a ripe banana. Make sure you don't remove the seeds from the chillies — you want them to add the zing.

This roti is quite dry. If you like it a bit softer, add more water, but be careful because if the dough is too wet, the ingredients will become loose, and you'll have difficulty flipping the roti.

REGION Sri Lanka | **MAKES** 8 | **PREPARATION** 20 minutes
COOKING 2–4 minutes per batch | **DIFFICULTY** Easy

500 g (1 lb 2 oz) atta flour (high-protein durum wheat flour)
50 g (1¾ oz) ghee
3 Indian green chillies, finely chopped
1 small onion, finely chopped
1 fresh curry leaf sprig, leaves picked and finely chopped
80 g (2¾ oz/1 cup) freshly grated coconut, or 200 g (7 oz) frozen grated coconut
1 teaspoon salt
500 ml (17 fl oz/2 cups) warm water
100 ml (3½ fl oz) rice bran oil or ghee

Place the flour, ghee, chilli, onion, curry leaves, coconut and salt in a large bowl.

Gradually add the water, a little at a time, using your hands to mix it in and bring everything together into a smooth dough.

Divide the dough into eight balls, place in an oiled bowl and lightly oil the dough to stop it drying out. Set aside until ready to cook; the dough can sit for an hour or two.

Take a ball of dough and, using your fingers, spread it out to form a thin disc, about 5 mm (¼ inch) thick and 10 cm (4 inches) in diameter.

Heat a small amount of the rice bran oil or ghee on a flat round grill (such as a tawa) or in a heavy-based frying pan over high heat. Add a few roti and cook until they are loose enough to come off the pan, then flip them over and cook the other side until lightly crisped. Remove from the pan and set aside.

Repeat with the remaining dough.

Serve hot, or at room temperature. The roti are best eaten as soon as possible.

TIP You could also cook the roti on the flat plate of a hot barbecue, which would be large enough to cook them all at the same time.

Cheka paratha
Bangladeshi flat bread

Delicious with butter, and often enjoyed with tea, this is a dried, crispy bread that folds into itself so it has multiple layers, much like a croissant, or a very basic puff pastry. But don't panic, it's not as complex as the turning process required for croissants — the layers are achieved by a few simple folds.

The key is not to overthink it. You are basically making a roti with the dough recipe, and then layering the roti by rolling the roti, and then pressing it down and rolling again.

There is a special way to get the roti to be soft and crumbly; this is by putting your hands on either side and 'clapping' the roti. If this is a bit hard or the roti is too hot, try placing it in a plastic takeaway container and shaking it. The dough should be nice and flaky.

REGION Bangladesh | **SERVES** 2 | **PREPARATION** 25 minutes + 4 hours resting
COOKING 4–8 minutes per paratha | **DIFFICULTY** Medium

For the dough, add the flour, rice bran oil, salt and water (you will need enough water to make a soft but non-sticky dough) to the bowl of an electric stand mixer fitted with a dough hook. Mix the dough for 5 minutes. If making by hand, knead the mixture on a lightly floured bench really well for about 10 minutes, or until the dough is smooth and elastic, and not sticky to the touch.

Cover with a tea towel and leave to rest for 1–3 hours, then divide the dough into six portions. Roll out each portion very thinly, into rounds about 10 cm (4 inches) in diameter, and about 5 mm (¼ inch) thick.

Lay the first paratha on a floured work surface and generously spread with melted ghee. Cut the paratha from the centre to the edge, just once, so you can then roll it into a cone. Stand the cone on its end and roll it into a roti shape again. It will look like a snail pastry; this will give you the layers.

Repeat with the remaining parathas, until you have finished all six. Cover with a tea towel and set aside to rest for a further 1 hour.

Cook the parathas on the oiled flat plate of a hot barbecue, a flat round grill (such as a tawa) or in a heavy-based frying pan for 2–4 minutes on each side, until crisp and golden brown. As soon as you remove them from the grill or pan, put each one on a flat surface and clap it together two or three times to make it flaky.

The parathas are best served warm, straight away.

TIP You can freeze the uncooked parathas, after their second resting, between sheets of baking paper or plastic wrap, to cook later on. There is no need to thaw them, simply cook them from frozen.

- 300 g (10½ oz/2 cups) plain (all-purpose) flour
- 2 teaspoons rice bran oil
- 2 teaspoons baking powder
- 1 teaspoon sugar
- 1 teaspoon salt
- 125 ml (4 fl oz/½ cup) water, approximately
- 200 ml (7 fl oz) melted ghee, plus extra for greasing

Obi non
Thick naan

Also known as lepyoshka, obi non is an Afghan flat bread that is shaped like a disc and thicker than naan, and baked in a clay oven called a tandyr. A tandoor or tandyr will obviously impart a better flavour; the next best thing would be to use a coal barbecue and a pizza stone, or even a pizza oven — but a regular oven will also do.

These flat breads are traditionally stamped with patterns such as flowers using special bread stamps, but the important thing is to make an indent in the centre, so they will rise on the outside.

REGION Afghanistan | **MAKES** 6 | **PREPARATION** 20 minutes + 3–4 hours proving
COOKING 5 minutes | **DIFFICULTY** Medium

Place the water, sugar and yeast in a large bowl and set aside for 5–10 minutes, or until frothy. Add the melted ghee and stir through to combine.

Sift the flour into a large bowl and mix the salt through. Make a well in the flour mixture and pour the yeasty water into it. Bring the ingredients together and knead into a dough, adding more water or flour if needed, and turning the dough into itself, until the mixture leaves the side of the bowl and you have a soft, elastic dough. This will take at least 6–10 minutes of firm kneading.

Place in a greased bowl and cover with a damp tea towel. Leave the mixture to prove in a warm place for 3–4 hours, or until doubled in size.

Preheat the oven to 220°C (425°F). Place a large baking tray in the oven to heat up with the oven.

Remove the tea towel, punch the dough down and knead it in the bowl for 2–3 minutes. Divide the dough into six evenly sized portions and roll them into balls.

Flatten each into a round bread about 10 cm (4 inches) wide, 2–3 cm (¾–1¼ inches) thick at the edges, and 5 mm (¼ inch) thick in the centre.

Traditionally, the cook will usually then make a pattern in the centre with a chekish (bread stamp), but I have found that if you just push five fingertips of one hand into the middle, you will imprint each naan with your own unique stamp!

Transfer to the baking tray and bake for 3–5 minutes, or until golden brown.

The naan are nice straight away, but can also be gently reheated for serving. They are quite rustic and chewy.

500 ml (17 fl oz/2 cups) lukewarm water
1 tablespoon sugar
20 g (¾ oz/6 teaspoons) active dried yeast
2 tablespoons melted ghee, plus extra for greasing
1 kg (2 lb 4 oz) plain (all-purpose) flour
2 teaspoons salt

Phitti
Hunza bread

Studded with raw nuts, raisins, goji berries and dried apricot, this energy-building bread is rich in proteins and antioxidants, and has sustained the local inhabitants of the remote and spectacularly mountainous Hunza Valley region in northern Pakistan for nearly 2000 years.

I remember eating this wholesome bread while trekking through the Himalayas, after trudging into another hill town, feeling the lack of oxygen, and watching school kids running up the stairs past us as if they were on flat ground.

The Hunza people live highly secluded lives, barely mingling with neighbouring communities. Perhaps this bread is one of the keys to their famed longevity!

REGION Pakistan | **SERVES** 8 | **PREPARATION** 5 minutes + 2 hours proving
COOKING 1 hour | **DIFFICULTY** Medium

---

2 teaspoons (7 g) active dried yeast
375 ml (13 fl oz/1½ cups) lukewarm water
150 g (5½ oz/1 cup) strong ('bread-making') flour
125 g (4½ oz/1 cup) millet flour, or 150 g (5½ oz/1 cup) wholemeal (whole-wheat) flour
1 teaspoon salt
1 carrot, grated
8 dried apricots, roughly chopped
1 teaspoon goji berries
1 teaspoon raisins
1 teaspoon chopped hazelnuts
2 tablespoons melted butter, or rice bran oil
1 tablespoon honey
¼ teaspoon ground cinnamon
¼ teaspoon ground allspice

Add the yeast to the lukewarm water and whisk briefly, then set aside for 5–10 minutes, or until bubbles appear on the surface.

Combine the remaining ingredients in the bowl of an electric stand mixer fitted with a dough hook, or mix by hand with a wooden spoon until thoroughly combined.

Stir 185 ml (6 fl oz/¾ cup) of the yeasty water mixture into the flour mixture until combined. Now work in enough of the remaining yeasty water to give you a dough that isn't too wet or too dry — it should come together and not be sticky.

Set aside in a warm place to allow the yeast to work, for about 1 hour, or until doubled in size.

Grease a baking tin measuring 30 x 15 cm (12 x 6 inches), with 3 cm (1¼ inch) deep sides, and line with baking paper. Add the dough to the baking tin and leave to rise for a further 1 hour.

Preheat the oven to 150°C (300°F). When the oven has reached the right temperature, turn the setting down to 50°C (120°F) and bake the loaf for 1 hour, or until a skewer inserted into the centre comes out clean.

Traditionally this bread is enjoyed fresh, torn up and either eaten with tea, or actually put into the tea, to make a kind of porridge.

Khuli
Buckwheat pancakes

Mix up your Sunday morning pancake ritual with these deliciously healthy pancakes. Top them with fresh fruits, chia seeds, honey, maple syrup, yoghurt, ricotta or mascarpone cheese, fresh cream, chocolate chips or your favourite chocolate spread, depending on what you fancy! They make a pretty stack, too.

REGION Bhutan | **SERVES** 4 | **PREPARATION** 20 minutes
COOKING 2–4 minutes per batch | **DIFFICULTY** Easy

Combine the buckwheat flour, sugar and salt in a large bowl.

Add the egg, banana, orange zest, orange juice, butter, buttermilk, milk and lemon juice and whisk until well combined and lump-free. (You can also whiz the batter in a blender for a smooth result, but leaving it slightly chunky will give a more rustic effect.)

For fluffier pancakes, let the batter rest for 10 minutes.

Heat a large non-stick frying pan over medium heat. Once the pan is heated, turn the heat down to low and grease it using paper towel that has soaked up a bit of vegetable oil.

For each pancake, spoon 1–2 tablespoons of batter into the pan, without overcrowding it. I can usually cook about four pancakes at a time, as these are just small ones — but you can add a little more batter if you prefer bigger pancakes.

Cook for a minute or two, until bubbles appear on the surface and the underside is turning brown. Loosen the edges of the pancakes using a spatula, then carefully flip the pancakes over and cook the other side.

Serve warm, with your choice of topping.

125 g (4½ oz/1 cup) buckwheat flour
1 tablespoon sugar
1 teaspoon salt
1 large egg, lightly beaten
1 banana, mashed
zest of 1 orange
3 teaspoons orange juice
30 g (1 oz) unsalted butter
200 ml (7 fl oz) buttermilk
180 ml (6 fl oz) milk
3 teaspoons lemon juice
vegetable oil, for greasing

Flours & baking items

Without flour we would not have bread, chapatti, roti, naan and so many other delicious foods. On the subcontinent, flour is not just flour, and comes from a multitude of plants: rice, millet, lentils, chickpeas, maize and potato, to name a few, and even within the category of wheat flour there are several different types. Flours are often marketed according to their purpose, such as chapatti flour and idli flour. Read the label if confused.

---

1. ATTA FLOUR This high-protein durum wheat flour lends an earthy chewiness to chapatti and other Indian flat breads.

2. BUCKWHEAT FLOUR Despite its name, buckwheat is not a variety of wheat at all, but the grain-like seed of a plant related to rhubarb and sorrel. It is completely gluten free, so ideal for people who are sensitive to gluten. It has a slightly nutty flavour and is rich in nutrients, fibre and protein.

3. SEMOLINA Ground from the endosperm of high-protein durum wheat, semolina can be coarse or fine in texture, and gives great colour and texture to baked goods. On the subcontinent it is used in making batters for dosa, idli, uttapam and upma, and across northern Africa it is made into couscous. It is also perfect for making pasta and Italian-style breads.

4. RICE FLOUR Known as chawal ka atta, rice flour is made from ground rice grains and is gluten free. In the south of India it is used in various pancakes and breads, such as idli and dosa, which are made from a mixture of rice and lentil flours. It is also used in sweets such as sandesh and malpua.

5. EVAPORATED CANE JUICE This form of sugar is made by evaporating the juice of the sugar cane plant. It has not undergone the same degree of processing as refined white sugar, thereby retaining slightly more nutrients, and a more caramel-like flavour. It is used like palm sugar (jaggery) in sweets, and of course to sweeten tea.

6. FLOUR The only difference between plain (all-purpose) flour and self-raising flour is that the latter has had baking powder added, which reacts with heat and liquid in the oven, creating carbon dioxide bubbles that cause cake batters to rise, giving a lighter and more airy texture. You can make your own self-raising flour by mixing baking powder into plain flour; check the ratio recommended by the baking powder manufacturer.

7. FINE SEMOLINA The very finely ground endosperm of hard durum wheat. It is paler and creamier in colour than semolina with a coarser grind, and is often used in desserts and cooked into a 'porridge'.

8. GROUND ALMONDS A great gluten-free alternative to regular flour, this pantry staple is made by grinding raw almonds. Various grades are available. Almond flour, as shown here, is made by finely grinding almonds that have first been blanched to remove their brown outer skin; almond meal is coarser in texture and darker in colour, as the skin has not been removed prior to grinding.

Kulcha
Leavened wheat breads

The pitta bread of Pakistan! This beautiful flat bread can be served with dips, or enjoyed with a curry instead of rice. The key to this recipe is rolling the flat breads as thinly as possible, otherwise they will end up looking like naan. Adding oil while rolling ensures easy rolling, without the dough shrinking.

Once you've cooked them, keep your flat breads in a bamboo basket or on a clean tea towel or wire rack, to avoid soggy bases.

REGION Pakistan | **MAKES** 4 | **PREPARATION** 20 minutes + 1 hour resting
COOKING 5–7 minutes per flat bread | **DIFFICULTY** Medium

150 g (5½ oz/1 cup) plain (all-purpose) flour, plus an extra 35 g (1¼ oz/¼ cup) for dusting
½ teaspoon baking powder
¼ teaspoon bicarbonate of soda (baking soda)
1 teaspoon raw sugar
½ teaspoon salt, or to taste
60 ml (2 fl oz/¼ cup) milk
1 tablespoon buffalo curd or Greek-style yoghurt
vegetable oil, for greasing
chopped coriander (cilantro) leaves, for sprinkling
black or white sesame seeds, for sprinkling
melted butter, for brushing

Sift the flour, baking powder and bicarbonate of soda into a mixing bowl. Make a dent in the middle. Add the sugar, salt, milk and the curd or yoghurt. Gather the ingredients together into a dough and knead on a lightly floured bench for 1 minute, or until it comes together into a ball and pulls away from your fingers.

Cover with a tea towel and rest for 1 hour.

Knead again on a lightly floured work surface for about 10 minutes, or using an electric stand mixer fitted with a dough hook for 5 minutes on low, until the dough is smooth.

Divide the dough into four evenly sized balls. Oil your bench and rolling pin, then roll each portion of dough into a thin round roti, about 15 cm (6 inches) in diameter; the oil will make it easy to spread the dough out without shrinking.

Sprinkle some coriander over each flat bread. Roll the rolling pin gently over the top, so the coriander adheres to the dough.

Heat a flat round grill (such as a tawa), a barbecue hot plate or heavy-based frying pan over high heat.

Brush the flat breads with a little water, then sprinkle with sesame seeds, pressing them on. Turn each one over and brush some water over the plain side, then place on the hot grill or in the hot pan, sesame seeds facing up.

Turn the heat down to medium and cover the grill or pan for a minute or two. Once you see bubbles on the top, flip the bread over. After 3–5 minutes, when brown spots appear, brush the bread with melted butter and serve.

Serve straight away, or gently reheat for serving.

TIP If making ahead, you can freeze the uncooked flat breads between sheets of baking paper or plastic wrap. You can also cook them in a preheated 180°C (350°F) oven for 10 minutes.

Lavash

*This lavash bread is crispy and simple to make, although you'll need to plan ahead,
as the dough needs to sit for 24 hours. It isn't the easiest dough to make by hand,
so definitely use an electric mixer if you have one. If you have a pasta machine,
rolling out the dough to the paper-thin stage will be a lot easier. Otherwise, you'll just
have to use a lot of muscle and a rolling pin!*

REGION Afghanistan | **SERVES** 6 | **PREPARATION** 30 minutes + 24 hours resting
COOKING 10 minutes | **DIFFICULTY** Easy

Add the flour, salt, sugar, butter, eggs and milk to the bowl
of an electric stand mixer fitted with a dough hook and mix
for 20 minutes. (If making the dough by hand, bring the
ingredients together in a bowl, turn out onto a lightly floured
work surface, then knead into a dough that is smooth to touch,
but firm, and resembles a pasta dough.)

Remove the dough from the bowl, wrap in plastic wrap
and refrigerate for 24 hours.

When you're ready to start baking, preheat the oven to
150°C (300°F).

Roll the dough out very thinly, using a lightly floured pasta
machine or rolling pin.

Brush the surface with milk, then sprinkle the poppy seeds
and sesame seeds on top.

Place on a large baking tray and bake for 10 minutes, or
until the bread is pale golden and crisp.

Allow to cool, then break into smaller bits for serving.
The lavash will keep in an airtight container in the pantry for
3–5 days.

350 g (12 oz/2⅓ cups) plain
    (all-purpose) flour
2 teaspoons salt
1 tablespoon sugar
45 g (2½ oz) butter
2 eggs
150 ml (5 fl oz) milk, plus extra
    for brushing
poppy seeds, for sprinkling
sesame seeds, for sprinkling

Roast paan

Very crispy and fairly thin, with a lovely soft centre, this bread is still a favourite of mine. The flavour comes from its double baking and the lashings of coconut oil used. You will need a small bread tin, measuring about 20 x 10 cm (8 x 4 inches) and at least 10 cm (4 inches) deep; metal is best, as you need to control the rising of the dough so it goes upwards, not sideways, and a silicone one will stretch as the dough expands.

REGION Sri Lanka | **MAKES** 6 | **PREPARATION** 20 minutes + 1¼–1½ hours proving
COOKING 35 minutes | **DIFFICULTY** Medium

2 teaspoons (7 g) active dried yeast
(see tip)
350 ml (12 fl oz) lukewarm water,
approximately
1 large egg, beaten
675 g (1 lb 8 oz/4½ cups) unbleached,
high-gluten white wheat flour
(see tip)
45 g (1½ oz/¼ cup) rapadura sugar
2 teaspoons salt
150 ml (5 fl oz) melted virgin coconut oil

Dissolve the yeast in 60 ml (2 fl oz/¼ cup) of the lukewarm water. After about 10 minutes, when the mixture turns frothy, add the beaten egg and the remaining water and mix well.

In a large bowl, mix together the flour, sugar and salt. Add the yeast mixture and knead on a lightly floured bench for about 10 minutes, or until smooth and elastic; you may need to add a little more water or flour to achieve the right consistency. (Over-kneading can result in a heavy, non-elastic, brick-like bread — so it is good to mix the ingredients by hand, rather than using an electric mixer, so you can really feel the consistency of the dough.)

Leave the dough to prove in a warm place for about 1 hour, or until doubled in size.

Knock back the dough by punching it down to release the air bubbles. Divide into six equal portions, then flatten them out into squares the same width and depth as the bread tin.

Brush both sides of each paan with melted coconut oil, then stand them upright in the bread tin side by side, with a sheet of greased baking paper in between each one; they should fit into the tin snugly.

Leave to rise for another 20 minutes, while you preheat the oven to 160°C (315°F).

Brush the top of each paan with a bit more coconut oil and bake for 25 minutes, or until the tops are golden brown.

Turn the paan out of the tin; you will end up with individual slices or loaves. Remove the baking paper and brush them with more coconut oil. Lay them flat on a wire cake rack, turn the oven temperature up to 200°C (400°F), then bake for a final 3–5 minutes on each side, or until they are golden and crisp, but still soft and fluffy inside.

Enjoy warm, if you can, although the paan are delicious cold as well.

TIP For this recipe use a high-gluten flour, available from whole-food stores. Alternatively, use 'strong' or 'bread' flour, as it has more gluten than regular flour. Otherwise, mix regular flour with wheat gluten, as directed on the gluten packet. Also be sure to use the right amount of yeast. A little excess is okay, but you won't get a good result if you don't use quite enough.

Uttapam

Traditionally, this popular dish from southern India is made with a rice and lentil batter that can be time consuming to prepare. This bread uttapam, on the other hand, is easy to make and quick to cook, not to mention it tastes delicious.

Uttapam is a thick dosa, or pancake, topped with vegetables. Essentially it is an Indian pizza, so get creative with your ingredients and place whatever you like on top. It is divine served hot, with a side of chutney.

Make sure you use a non-stick frying pan or a well-cured pan (see page 19), as this uttapam is notoriously sticky.

REGION India | **MAKES** 9–10; serves 3 | **PREPARATION** 15 minutes + 1 hour resting
COOKING 4–5 minutes per uttapam | **DIFFICULTY** Easy

Cut the bread into small pieces, then soak in 250 ml (9 fl oz/ 1 cup) water for about 5 minutes. Drain the bread and place in a blender. Add the semolina, yoghurt and salt and blitz to a thick, smooth paste.

Pour the batter into a bowl, cover with a tea towel and set aside to rest at warm room temperature for 1 hour. The warmer and more humid, the better.

The batter should be a relatively thick consistency; stir in a little more water if needed.

Lightly grease a non-stick frying pan and place over medium heat. Be careful not to cook the uttapam on high heat, as the batter will not cook through.

For each uttapam, pour about 2 tablespoons of batter into the pan; it should spread into a thick pancake, about the size of a pikelet, and you should be able to cook several at a time, depending on the size of your pan. Pour a little rice bran oil around the pancakes. Leave to cook for about 2 minutes, then sprinkle some of the cumin seeds, chaat masala, tomatoes, chilli, coriander and ginger on top. Press the topping ingredients down lightly, turn the pancake over, and cook for another 2 minutes, until golden brown on both sides.

Serve hot, with chutney or yoghurt.

3 slices white bread, crusts removed
180 g (6 oz/1 cup) coarse semolina
70 g (2½ oz/¼ cup) Greek-style yoghurt
1 teaspoon finely ground black salt
rice bran oil, for greasing
¼ teaspoon cumin seeds
1 teaspoon Chaat masala (page 24)
60 g (2¼ oz/¼ cup) finely chopped tomatoes, seeds removed
1 Indian green chilli, or to taste, finely chopped
2 tablespoons finely chopped coriander (cilantro)
2 teaspoons finely shredded fresh ginger
Green coconut chutney (page 208), Coriander chutney (page 215) or Greek-style yoghurt, to serve

Roghni roti
Griddle-grilled wheat flour roti

Cooked on a flat or slightly concave iron griddle called a tawa, this deliciously soft roti is served hot, brushed with ghee or butter. It can be used to scoop other foods, or stuffed with a savoury filling such as the potato in the Vada pav (Mumbai burgers) on page 46, or the cabbage filling from the Buckwheat & cabbage momos on page 31.

REGION Bangladesh | **MAKES** 6 | **PREPARATION** 20 minutes + 1 hour proving
COOKING 3–5 minutes per roti | **DIFFICULTY** Easy

375 g (13 oz/1½ cups) plain (all-purpose) flour, plus extra for dusting
375 g (13 oz/1½ cups) wholemeal (whole-wheat) flour
1 tablespoon raw sugar
1 teaspoon salt
1 teaspoon active dried yeast
3 heaped tablespoons ghee
125 ml (4 fl oz/½ cup) milk
60 ml (2 fl oz/¼ cup) thin (pouring) cream
melted butter or extra ghee, for brushing

In a large bowl, mix together the flours, sugar, salt, yeast and ghee using your hands, until the mixture resembles breadcrumbs.

Add the milk and cream and knead to form a soft dough. Cover and set aside to rise for 1 hour, or until doubled in size.

Divide the dough into six evenly sized portions, then roll each one out on a lightly floured work surface into a circle about 12 cm (4½ inches) wide, and 1 cm (½ inch) thick.

Heat a flat round grill (such as a tawa), a solid heavy-based frying pan or barbecue hot plate over high heat. Turn the heat down to medium.

Cook each roti for 1½–2½ minutes, or until it starts puffing up, then turn and cook the other side for another 1½–2½ minutes. You will need to cook them one at a time if using a tawa or pan; on a barbecue you can cook them all at once.

Serve hot, brushed with melted butter or extra ghee.

Chapatti

Chapatti is another name for roti, a favourite staple across the whole subcontinent Different people call it by different names, but the method for preparing it is the same.

REGION India | **MAKES** 10 | **PREPARATION** 15 minutes + 10 minutes resting
COOKING 2–4 minutes per chapatti | **DIFFICULTY** Easy

Add the flour, rice bran oil, salt and hot water to a large bowl and mix with a spoon until combined.

Turn out onto a floured work surface. When cool enough to handle, knead the mixture for about 5 minutes, until you have a soft dough, dusting with the extra flour to prevent sticking. The dough should be smooth and soft, and not sticky to touch.

Cover the dough with a tea towel and leave to rest for 10 minutes.

Break the dough into 10 evenly sized portions. Roll them out on a lightly floured work surface, into circles about 18 cm (7 inches) wide and 5 mm (¼ inch) thick.

Heat a flat round grill (such as a tawa), a solid heavy-based frying pan or barbecue hot plate over medium heat. Brush with a little ghee and add a chapatti (or several, if using a barbecue). Brush the top of the chapatti with more ghee and cook for 1–2 minutes on each side, or until golden brown and puffed.

Keep warm inside a clean tea towel while cooking the remaining chapatti, and until ready to serve.

250 g (9 oz/1⅔ cups) durum wheat flour, atta flour or unbleached white flour, plus 75 g (2½ oz/½ cup) for dusting
30 ml (1 fl oz) rice bran oil
1 teaspoon salt
125 ml (4 fl oz/½ cup) hot water, approximately
2 tablespoons ghee, melted

Makki ki roti
Corn bread

Literally, 'makki ki roti' means 'bread of corn' in the Punjabi language. It is a bit trickier than the usual roti made from wheat flour, as the dough is crumblier and more difficult to handle. This is why I have suggested that you leave each roti on a sheet of plastic wrap, very similar to making a Mexican tortilla, then simply place the roti straight onto the hot grill or pan. Don't forget to remove the plastic!

REGION India | **MAKES** 8–10 | **PREPARATION** 25 minutes
COOKING 5–6 minutes per roti | **DIFFICULTY** Medium

270 g (9½ oz/1½ cups) cornmeal
    or polenta
35 g (1¼ oz/¼ cup) wholemeal
    (whole-wheat) flour
1 teaspoon salt
125–185 ml (4–6 fl oz/½–¾ cup)
    lukewarm water
4 tablespoons rice bran oil or ghee,
    for cooking
melted butter, for brushing

Mix the cornmeal, flour and salt together in a bowl. Work in the lukewarm water, a little at a time, to make a medium-soft dough that is just tacky and sticky to the touch.

Divide the dough into 8–10 evenly sized portions.

Wet your hand with a little water and flatten each portion on a wet sheet of plastic wrap, into a disc about 10 cm (4 inches) in diameter. Leave them on the sheets so it is easy to transfer them to your grill.

Heat a flat round grill (such as a tawa), a heavy-based frying pan or barbecue hot plate over high heat. Turn the heat down to medium and grease the grill with a little rice bran oil or ghee.

Carefully transfer the corn breads to the grill or pan, being sure to remove the plastic sheet; you will probably need to cook them one at a time if using a tawa or pan, or in two batches on a barbecue.

Spoon a little more oil or ghee on the sides of the bread and fry over low heat for up to 3 minutes on each side, until crunchy and light golden brown.

Generously brush the hot corn breads with melted butter and serve.

Gothamba roti with brinjal pickle

*This is a variation on a street food called elawalu roti, or vegetable roti.
The gothamba roti takes a bit of practice, as it has to be paper thin; you can go
online and learn how to toss it, or just roll it out paper thin on your kitchen bench.
I like to serve it with my pumpkin curry on page 123.*

REGION Sri Lanka | **SERVES** 4; makes 8 | **PREPARATION** 30 minutes + at least 2 hours resting
COOKING 4–5 minutes per roti | **DIFFICULTY** Medium

For the roti dough, combine the flour and salt in a large bowl. Add the rice bran oil and knead in enough lukewarm water to form a smooth dough. Cover with a damp tea towel and rest in a warm place for 1 hour, or even overnight.

Divide the dough into eight small balls, about 6 cm (2½ inches) in diameter. Rub some vegetable oil over them, cover with a damp tea towel and rest for another 1 hour, so the dough becomes soft and stretchy.

When you're ready to serve, heat a griddle, barbecue flat plate or large frying pan over medium heat.

Liberally oil a substantial area of a clean work surface. Place one dough ball in the middle and press down with the palm of your hand, while moving it in a circular motion, to flatten and smooth out the dough as much as possible before you start to stretch it. It takes a bit of practice to throw a roti the professional way, so an equally effective way is to work around the edges of the dough, gently stretching them outwards as far and as thinly as you can, before holes start to appear. The end result should be as thin as tracing paper, and about 60–70 cm (24–27½ inches) in diameter.

Pull opposite edges of the roti towards one another, to overlap in three layers, drizzling a little oil between each. Fold this elongated shape into thirds again, drizzling more oil between each layer, and spreading the roti with about 2 tablespoons of the brinjal pickle; you should end up with a triangular roti.

Lightly oil your cooking surface and fry the roti for 1–2 minutes on each side, until golden blisters appear on each side. As the roti will be thick with the filling, also cook all the edges, so you have a brown and well-formed triangle, measuring about 5 cm (2 inches) along each edge.

Keep warm while shaping and cooking the remaining roti. Serve immediately.

Brinjal pickle (page 232); you'll need about 2 tablespoons per roti

ROTI DOUGH
450 g (1 lb/3 cups) plain (all-purpose) flour
1 teaspoon salt
2½ tablespoons rice bran oil
200 ml (7 fl oz) vegetable oil, for brushing and greasing

Chapter 8

Soups

Given the harshness and diversity of the subcontinent's climates, its widespread poverty and the remoteness of many of its communities, soup is truly life sustaining.

U nless you have travelled to some of the harsh mountainous regions, it is hard to fully comprehend the bone-chilling cold and sometimes the scarcity of ingredients, as well as the soul-restoring powers of a truly humble bowl of soup.

Most cookbooks that delve into the cuisine of the subcontinent rarely have a full chapter dedicated to soups, so it was important to me to try to capture the diversity of soups from this region, as well as their life-giving nature. The recipes in this chapter are very considered. There is a full balanced diet right here. This chapter could sustain you, even if you didn't have any teeth!

The cooking of the subcontinent is genuinely regional — more so even than in France or Italy. Recipes vary from town to town and state to state. Many of the differences are determined by the ingredients available in each area, and so the soups in this chapter are closely linked to their local environment, reflecting their role in the local diet, and the comfort and vigour they provide.

I will never forget spending my 21st birthday on the banks of the Ganges. India's prime minister, Indira Gandhi, had been assassinated 11 days earlier, so it was a time of great uncertainty, and many places we travelled to were deserted. We were living on a houseboat, on the Dal Lake in the Kashmir Valley, and had gone into the local village to find food. We were hungry but the market was empty, like a ghost town. There were no tourists; there was nothing to eat in this beautiful, magnificent and yet desolate environment. When you are truly cold and hungry, you will eat anything you can find. We sourced scraps from the marketplace floor. I literally collected cabbage leaves and foraged what I could (being a cook helps sometimes!) before making my way back to the boat. We used a military pack to spark fire for our little pot of water and boiled up these vegetable scraps. To this day the warmth and heartiness of that meagre meal locks soup in my memory as survival food, with ferocious intensity.

Soup is important. Soup is hearty. Soup is good. You will need a fork to get through many of the soups in this chapter; they are healthy and robust, full of good slow-release carbs and proteins, the kind of food that fuels and energises the body and helps protect against the cold. With our increasingly busy lifestyles, soup makes sense. From a convenience perspective, you can put a soup on in the slow cooker before you go to work and have a delicious, nutritious meal waiting for you when you get home. Soup is also easy to share among lots of people, and very cost effective.

When making soups, try using your vegetable offcuts to make a vegetable stock. Pop them in a saucepan with a bay leaf and peppercorns. Use the stock in these soup recipes in place of water, or even try an unsweetened coconut water to add a different dimension to your soups.

Badam ka shorba
Almond soup

The Indian almond is a different nut to the almond we're familiar with in the West. Also known as the Bengal almond, tropical almond, Malabar almond and country almond, Terminalia catappa is a large tropical tree from the leadwood family, native to South-East Asia. It thrives in coastal, tropical areas, and is now also grown in Australia, Polynesia, Madagascar, West Africa, India, Pakistan, South and Central America, and parts of the Caribbean.

If you can't find Indian almonds, just use regular almonds in this lovely rich soup, as the flavours are similar.

REGION India | **SERVES** 4 | **PREPARATION** 15 minutes
COOKING 30 minutes | **DIFFICULTY** Easy

160 g (5½ oz/1 cup) raw almonds
1 tablespoon butter
2½ teaspoons plain (all-purpose) flour
500 ml (17 fl oz/2 cups) milk
1 teaspoon sugar
½ teaspoon ground white pepper,
   or to taste
1 litre (35 fl oz/4 cups) boiling water
60 ml (2 fl oz/¼ cup) thin (pouring) cream

Soak the almonds in hot water for a few minutes. Drain them, then peel off the skins. Slice 10–12 almonds and reserve as a garnish. Grind the remaining almonds to a smooth paste, using a blender.

Melt the butter in a heavy-based saucepan over medium heat. Add the flour and stir for 1 minute, then gradually add the milk, stirring continuously to avoid lumps.

Add the sugar, white pepper and salt to taste. Cook, stirring continuously, until the mixture comes to the boil.

Reduce the heat and simmer for 5 minutes, stirring occasionally.

Stir in the almond paste and boiling water and simmer for 10–15 minutes, stirring occasionally, until the soup has thickened.

Meanwhile, lightly toast the reserved sliced almonds in a frying pan over low heat, taking care they don't burn.

Just before serving, sprinkle the toasted almonds over the soup and drizzle with the cream. Serve piping hot.

Mosh awa
Afghani vegetable soup

There are soups like this in traditional Persian and Turkish cuisine. Usually this one is made with a chicken or lamb stock, but this vegetarian version is just as delicious. It's so much fun to discover and experiment with such dishes; I have found adding sautéed oyster mushrooms makes it the perfect meal. The yoghurt makes this dish unique, but if you are a vegan, omit the yoghurt and butter, and fry the mushrooms in olive oil.

REGION Afghanistan | **SERVES** 3–4 as a main, 6–8 as a side | **PREPARATION** 20 minutes + 2–12 hours soaking
COOKING 1¼ hours | **DIFFICULTY** Medium

95 g (3¼ oz/½ cup) dried chickpeas,
　　or 400 g (14 oz) tinned chickpeas
200 g (7 oz/1 cup) dried green mung
　　beans (moong dhal)
150 ml (5 fl oz) olive oil
2 onions, finely chopped
4 garlic cloves, crushed
1 teaspoon dried red chilli pieces
6 ripe tomatoes, roughly chopped
1 tablespoon tomato paste
　　(concentrated purée)
250 g (9 oz) Greek-style yoghurt
1 teaspoon chickpea flour (besan)
2 teaspoons crushed black peppercorns
50 g (1¾ oz) butter
150 g (5½ oz) oyster mushrooms,
　　torn in half
1 Indian green chilli, chopped
3 tablespoons torn mint
¼ bunch of dill, leaves picked

If using dried chickpeas, soak them overnight in plenty of cold water.

Next day, soak the mung beans in cold water for 2 hours.

Drain the mung beans, and the dried chickpeas, if using. Place them in a saucepan with at least 2 litres (70 fl oz/8 cups) water and bring to the boil. Cook for about 30 minutes, or until they are tender. Remove from the heat and allow to cool in the liquid.

Heat the olive oil in a large heavy-based saucepan over medium heat. Add the onion and garlic and cook for a few minutes, stirring occasionally, until they start to brown. Add the chilli pieces and cook for a further 3 minutes.

Reduce the heat to low and stir in the tomatoes and tomato paste. Continue to cook, stirring occasionally, for about 10 minutes, or until the mixture becomes pulpy.

Add 500 ml (17 fl oz/2 cups) of the cooking liquid from the mung beans and 500 ml (17 fl oz/2 cups) fresh water, along with the mung beans and chickpeas (if using tinned chickpeas, drain and rinse them first). Bring to the boil, then reduce the heat and leave to simmer for 20 minutes.

Mix the yoghurt with a little bit of water to thin it, then stir in the chickpea flour; this will help stop the soup 'splitting'.

Stirring continuously, slowly add the yoghurt to the soup. Turn off the heat, stir in the crushed peppercorns and season to taste with salt.

In a frying pan, melt the butter over medium heat. When it starts to froth, add the mushrooms and cook for a few minutes, until tender and soft. Stir in the green chilli, mint and dill, then season to taste.

Serve the soup immediately, with a spoonful of the mushrooms on top.

TIP If using a pressure cooker, follow the manufacturer's instructions for cooking the soup ingredients, then thicken with the yoghurt and chickpea flour once the pressure has abated.

Sambar

Sambar, a popular soupy lentil curry served with rice, idli or vadai, has become a symbol of Tamil food, but came about by accident, back in the 1600s. The story goes that Sambhaji, the eldest son of the first Maratha ruler Shivaji, one day returned home very hungry, only to find his wife and daughter away. He tried to make himself some rice and dhal, but added some tamarind to his dhal by mistake, giving it an entirely different complexion. There are so many variations to this simple yet very tasty soup, but this is a lovely version to start with.

REGION India | **SERVES** 4 | **PREPARATION** 15 minutes + 30 minutes soaking
COOKING 30 minutes | **DIFFICULTY** Medium

Soak the tamarind in 750 ml (26 fl oz/3 cups) warm water for 30 minutes.

Meanwhile, heat 2 tablespoons of the coconut oil in a heavy-based saucepan and cook the onion, garlic and vegetables over medium heat for 5–6 minutes, stirring occasionally to prevent too much colouring. Stir in the red lentils and set aside.

In a separate saucepan, heat the remaining coconut oil and add the coconut, cumin seeds, chillies and chana dhal. Fry for a few minutes, or until the coconut starts to brown, then remove from the heat. Using a spice grinder or bullet blender, grind the mixture to a slightly coarse paste with a little water. Set the coconut paste aside.

Squeeze the juice of the soaked tamarind out, into the soaking water. You should now have at least 750 ml (26 fl oz/ 3 cups) of tamarind water; if not, top up with a little more water.

Add the tamarind water to the sautéed vegetables and place over high heat. When the mixture starts boiling, stir in the coconut paste, palm sugar and salt. Allow to boil for 10–15 minutes, or until the soup thickens slightly, stirring now and then. Cook together for a few more minutes, or until the lentils are well combined into the soup. Remove from the heat.

In a small frying pan, heat another 1 teaspoon coconut oil over medium heat. Add the mustard seeds. When they splutter, add the curry leaves and turmeric.

Pour the spices over the soup and serve immediately.

TIP Different implements will give quite different results when grinding spices and other ingredients. Using a mortar and pestle is traditional, and with patient and persistent grinding will give you a fine paste, but the process can be slow and tiring. A bar blender will result in a coarse mixture, unless the recipe uses liquid, whereas a modern bullet blender is excellent, and can handle volume. A spice grinder or coffee blender generally works well, for small volumes of ingredients.

150 g (5½ oz) tamarind pulp
  (a lemon-sized ball)
2 tablespoons virgin coconut oil
1 onion, finely diced
2 garlic cloves, sliced
100 g (3½ oz) diced potato
100 g (3½ oz) diced carrot
100 g (3½ oz) diced radish
100 g (3½ oz) diced eggplant (aubergine)
200 g (7 oz/1 cup) dried split red lentils
40 g (1½ oz/½ cup) freshly grated
  coconut
2 tablespoons cumin seeds
6–7 dried red chillies, broken in half
2 tablespoons chana dhal
1 tablespoon palm sugar (jaggery)
3–4 teaspoons salt, or to taste
1 teaspoon brown mustard seeds
1 fresh curry leaf sprig, leaves picked
¼ teaspoon ground turmeric

Daal aur chawal
Pakistani-style dhal

We ate a lot of dhal during our journey through the subcontinent in 1969. Dhal is comfort food, and variations of it abound. When I first encountered this dish, the first thing that struck me was the use of dried split mung beans, instead of orange or yellow lentils. Every household in this region has a slightly different version, so feel free to tailor the taste to suit your own family.

REGION Pakistan | **SERVES** 6 | **PREPARATION** 20 minutes
COOKING 1 hour | **DIFFICULTY** Easy

150 g (5½ oz/⅔ cup) dried split yellow
    mung beans (moong dhal)
1 teaspoon ground cumin
1½ teaspoons ground coriander
½ teaspoon ground turmeric
¼ cinnamon stick

FOR TEMPERING
1 tablespoon virgin coconut oil
1 teaspoon cumin seeds
1 teaspoon brown mustard seeds
3 dried red Kashmiri chillies, broken
    in half
6 cherry tomatoes, halved
a pinch of asafoetida
2 garlic cloves, crushed
1 fresh curry leaf sprig, leaves picked

TO GARNISH
chopped coriander (cilantro)
1 tablespoon fried onion
a pinch of Chaat masala (page 24)

Wash the dried mung beans in cool water and drain. Place in a large heavy-based saucepan with the ground spices and cinnamon stick. Pour in 750 ml (26 fl oz/3 cups) water.

Bring to the boil and boil rapidly for about 45–50 minutes, until the mung beans are soft and pulpy, and the water has reduced considerably. Remove the cinnamon stick, transfer the dhal to a bowl and set aside.

In the same saucepan you cooked the dhal, heat the coconut oil for tempering over high heat. When it starts to smoke, add the cumin seeds, mustard seeds and dried chillies. When the mustard seeds start to pop, stir in the tomatoes, asafoetida and garlic and cook, stirring, until the garlic is golden.

Stir in the curry leaves, followed by the dhal. Bring to a simmer and cook for a final 10 minutes, stirring regularly.

Just before serving, season to taste with salt. Garnish with chopped coriander, fried onion and a sprinkling of chaat masala for colour.

Serve as an accompaniment, or with steamed rice or bread.

Tamatar shorba
Spiced tomato soup

*Everyone loves tomato soup. To me it is full of memories — of my mum attending to me when I was sick, or camping and cooking a one-pot warmer, or coming home from school and settling down to watch **The Saint** or **The Man From U.N.C.L.E.** with my brothers.*

This is a simple recipe packed with flavour. Kashmiri chilli powder isn't hot, but adds a vibrant colour to this soup; omit the milk and it can also be vegan. I would serve it with chapatti.

REGION India | **SERVES** 6 | **PREPARATION** 10 minutes
COOKING 30 minutes | **DIFFICULTY** Easy

In a heavy-based saucepan, heat the coconut oil over high heat until it starts to smoke. Add the onion, garlic and curry leaves and reduce the heat to medium–low. Cook, stirring often, for about 5 minutes, or until the onion is translucent; do not allow to brown. Stir in the garam masala, tomatoes and chilli powder.

Increase the heat to high and bring to the boil. Add the coriander, peppercorns, cinnamon stick and cloves. Pour in the milk and 1 litre (35 fl oz/4 cups) water and bring back to the boil.

Reduce the heat and leave to simmer for 10 minutes. Remove from the heat, then season to taste with salt.

Purée the soup using a hand-held stick blender, or allow to cool slightly and whiz in a blender. (You can pass the soup through a coarse strainer if you'd like it smooth; otherwise just enjoy it as is.)

Garnish with fried curry leaves and serve with sliced mozzarella, if desired.

TIP To fry curry leaves, heat a little bit of vegetable oil in a pan. When hot, add the curry leaves. Let them pop and splutter for a few seconds, then remove with a slotted spoon and drain on paper towel.

2 tablespoons virgin coconut oil
1 onion, diced
4 garlic cloves, crushed
1 fresh curry leaf sprig, leaves chopped
1 teaspoon Garam masala (page 24)
500 g (1 lb 2 oz) ripe tomatoes, roughly chopped
¼ teaspoon Kashmiri chilli powder
¼ bunch coriander (cilantro), washed and chopped, including the roots
1 teaspoon black peppercorns
¼ cinnamon stick
2 cloves
435 ml (15¼ fl oz/1¾ cups) full-cream milk
fried curry leaves (see tip), to garnish
sliced buffalo mozzarella (optional), to serve

Peter's green lentil & spiced tempeh soup

Writing recipes is a journey of discovery. It is like meeting people through food: their tastes and culture come to life firstly on the page, and then on your tongue. I got very hungry writing this book, inspired to experience and create new dishes. This is one of those dishes.

A special tip for all those tempeh fanatics, courtesy of Michael Joyce from Mighty Bean on Australia's Sunshine Coast. You already know the amazing health properties of this fermented soy bean cake, but I bet you've struggled to marinate it, because it is too dense to absorb your marinade. Well here is how to make the mighty tempeh thirsty for your marinade: just freeze it, then thaw it slowly in your fridge. So simple! Freezing makes the water in the cell walls of the soy expand, and when the tempeh thaws, the cell walls break down, allowing your marinade to soak in.

REGION Sri Lanka | **SERVES** 4 | **PREPARATION** 20 minutes + 6 hours soaking
COOKING 1 hour | **DIFFICULTY** Easy

50 g (1¾ oz/¼ cup) dried white beans
200 g (7 oz) tempeh or spiced tofu, sliced 2 cm (¾ inch) thick
110 g (3¾ oz/½ cup) split yellow lentils (toor dhal)
110 g (3¾ oz/½ cup) dried green lentils
½ teaspoon ground turmeric
100 ml (3½ fl oz) virgin coconut oil
1 onion, finely chopped
4 garlic cloves, crushed
½ teaspoon cumin seeds
¼ teaspoon fennel seeds
¼ teaspoon black sesame seeds
¼ teaspoon dill seeds
5 whole dried red chillies
½ teaspoon Garam masala (page 24)

TO SERVE
3 tablespoons chopped spring onion (scallion)
3 tablespoons chopped coriander (cilantro)
2 Indian green chillies, sliced (optional)
100 g (3½ oz) Greek-style yoghurt (optional)

Soak the dried white beans in plenty of cold water for 6 hours. Meanwhile, if using tempeh, freeze the tempeh slices for a few hours, then leave them in the fridge to thaw.

Drain the white beans, then cook them in a saucepan of boiling water for about 10–15 minutes, or until partly cooked. Drain and set aside.

Wash the yellow and green lentils, then place in a saucepan with the drained white beans. Add the turmeric and 1 litre (35 fl oz/4 cups) water and bring to the boil.

Meanwhile, in a small heavy-based frying pan or wok, heat the coconut oil over medium heat. When smoking, add the onion and garlic and cook, stirring often, for about 2 minutes, until the onion starts to brown. Add all the spice seeds, and the whole dried chillies, stirring well for about 2 minutes, until the spices become fragrant. Stir in the garam masala and cook for a further minute, then add the tempeh or tofu, stirring to coat with the spices.

Pour the spiced oil mixture into the boiling pulses. Reduce the heat to low and cook for 30–40 minutes, or until all the pulses are soft, adding more water if needed.

Season to taste with salt. Serve garnished with spring onion and coriander, and chilli and yoghurt if desired.

Bagthuk
Bhutanese potato & noodle soup

*This rich potato soup with wholemeal hand-cut noodles will warm you up,
give you energy and fill you up too. I love the garlic chives and sichuan peppercorns:
they are both very strongly flavoured, but make this soup unique.*

*I have not been to Bhutan, but I have visited Sikkim and the Hindu Kush
mountains, as well as Darjeeling and Srinagar, all hill stations. In such places the
locals are hardy, and things take on their own life: the climate is cooler, the air is
fresh, the terrain is mountainous — and all these elements conspire to make your
body crave carbohydrates. It just seems right to eat lots of potatoes while trekking!
You are burning so much energy that soups like this are not only tasty,
but give you the boost you need to keep climbing higher.*

REGION Bhutan | **SERVES** 6 | **PREPARATION** 45 minutes
COOKING 45 minutes | **DIFFICULTY** Medium

---

4 potatoes, peeled and cut into 5 mm
   (¼ inch) thick rounds
65 g (2¼ oz/½ cup) thinly sliced daikon
   (white radish)
2 ripe tomatoes, chopped
1 litre (35 fl oz/4 cups) vegetable stock
2 tablespoons virgin coconut oil
1 teaspoon chilli flakes, or to taste
1 large garlic clove, crushed
½ bunch garlic chives, cut into 3 cm
   (1¼ inch) lengths
1 teaspoon sichuan peppercorns,
   crushed using a mortar and pestle

NOODLES
500 g (1 lb 2 oz/3⅓ cups) wholemeal
   (whole-wheat) flour, plus extra
   for dusting
½ teaspoon salt
200 ml (7 fl oz) water

Start by making the dough for the noodles. Place the flour and salt in a large mixing bowl and mix in enough of the water to make a soft pliable dough. Knead the dough by hand for 4 minutes, or until elastic. Cover and set aside while starting the soup, to allow the gluten in the dough to relax.

Place the potato slices in a large saucepan, along with the radish and tomatoes. Pour in the stock, cover and bring to the boil.

Take a small handful of the dough and roll it out on a floured surface into a fairly thin, large circle, using a rolling pin. Use a sharp knife to cut the dough into two semicircles.

Lay one half on a chopping board, with the straight edge facing you. Cut strips about 1 cm (½ inch) wide from the curved edge to the straight edge, creating noodles.

Gently place the noodles in a bowl that has been generously dusted with an extra 1 tablespoon flour, then continue with the remaining dough.

Once all the noodles have been cut, add them to the soup. Continue boiling for another 10 minutes, or until the noodles are glossy and have no flour residue, stirring occasionally so they don't clump together.

Meanwhile, just before serving, heat the coconut oil in a small frying pan until very hot. Add the chilli flakes, garlic and garlic chives, stirring to coat in the oil. Cook over medium heat for 2 minutes, or until the mixture is fragrant and the garlic is slightly browned.

Remove the soup from the heat and add the fried garlic mixture, including the oil. Stir in the crushed sichuan peppercorns and season with salt to taste. Your bagthuk is ready to serve.

Ema datshi
Chilli 'n' cheese

Translating as 'chilli' and 'cheese', this intensely hot and spicy soup hails from Bhutan, where it is considered the national dish. It is also adored by Tibetans, who call it churu, or 'rotten cheese' soup.

The cheese that is actually used in this soup cannot be found outside Bhutan. It is a strongly flavoured local farmer's cheese, with a unique texture that doesn't dissolve in boiling water. Using feta as a substitute calms the flavours down a little — but remember, this dish is very fiery, so it's best served with a generous portion of red rice or polished white rice.

REGION Bhutan | **SERVES** 4 | **PREPARATION** 15 minutes
COOKING 20 minutes | **DIFFICULTY** Easy

Cut each chilli lengthways, into quarters. Place in a saucepan with the onion and about 400 ml (14 fl oz) water. Stir in the rice bran oil and bring to the boil, then boil over medium heat for about 10 minutes.

Stir in the tomatoes and garlic and allow to boil for another 2 minutes.

Add the cheese and cook for a further 2–3 minutes.

Finally, stir in the coriander and turn off the heat.

Cover and stand for 2 minutes, then serve.

250 g (9 oz) green chillies, of medium hotness
1 onion, cut into long strips
2 teaspoons rice bran oil
2 tomatoes, sliced
5 garlic cloves, finely crushed
250 g (9 oz) Danish feta, crumbled
a handful of coriander (cilantro) leaves

Kola kenda
Pennywort rice soup

In every hotel in Sri Lanka you will see this soup at the breakfast buffet, rich green in colour, quite thin, with pieces of red rice in the bottom. Beside it you will also see a bowl of palm sugar, to nibble on as you drink the soup.

Traditionally enjoyed before breakfast, this soup is deeply adored by the locals, including truck drivers on their way to the fish markets at 4 am, and actually in the markets, where stallholders will have a jar or thermos of this healthy, warming soup. At home, it is served like a rice gruel to people who are sick, and can be made with any green leaves, although the gotu kola, or pennywort, is the most prized.

REGION Sri Lanka | **SERVES** 6 | **PREPARATION** 15 minutes
COOKING 30 minutes | **DIFFICULTY** Easy

250 g (9 oz/11/4 cups) raw red rice
½ teaspoon salt
1 cup tightly packed pennywort, or any
    green leaves of your choice
1 small garlic clove, peeled
750 ml (26 fl oz/3 cups) coconut milk
a squeeze of lemon juice
½ teaspoon freshly ground black pepper
100 g (3½ oz) dark palm sugar (jaggery),
    cut into chunks for serving

Wash the rice and place in a heavy-based saucepan with the salt and 500 ml (17 fl oz/2 cups) water. Bring to the boil, reduce the heat and leave to simmer.

Meanwhile, place the pennywort, garlic and 250 ml (9 fl oz/1 cup) of the coconut milk into a blender and whiz until totally emulsified. Strain through a coarse sieve.

After about 15 minutes, when the rice starts to soften, stir in the blended pennywort and remaining coconut milk. Bring to the boil.

Turn off the heat and stir in the lemon juice and black pepper. Check the seasoning, adding more salt if necessary.

Serve hot, with the palm sugar to nibble on as you drink the soup.

Thukpa
Tibetan vegetable noodle soup

Possibly introduced in the distant past via China, this Tibetan soup is now a staple in Bhutan and Nepal, and very popular in the north-eastern states of India as well, with subtle variations depending on what is locally available.

Easy to make, this no-frills soup will help you stay a little warmer on those cold days.

REGION Nepal | **SERVES** 2 | **PREPARATION** 15 minutes
COOKING 30–35 minutes | **DIFFICULTY** Medium

In a pressure cooker or heavy-based saucepan, heat the grapeseed oil over medium heat. Add the garlic and green chilli and cook for 30 seconds. Add the onion and cook for about 3 minutes, or until translucent, stirring frequently.

Stir in the tomato and cabbage and cook for about 5 minutes, until the vegetables are soft. Add the chilli powder, garam masala, and salt to taste, mixing well, and cook for about 30 seconds. Stir in the stock, soy sauce and 750 ml (26 fl oz/3 cups) water.

Seal the pressure cooker, if using, and cook on low pressure for 10–12 minutes, or according to the manufacturer's instructions for making soup. Remove from the heat and allow the pressure to release. Once safe, remove the lid. Just before serving, stir in the chopped coriander, then adjust the spices to suit your taste.

If making the soup in a saucepan, cook the mixture for 20–25 minutes, stirring now and then.

Meanwhile, for the noodles, bring a large saucepan of water to the boil. Add the salt, then add the noodles and cook for the length of time recommended on the packet instructions. Drain, return to the saucepan and mix the rice bran oil through. Set aside and keep warm.

Just before serving, make the omelette. Crack the eggs into a bowl and beat well. Add the salt. Heat the rice bran oil in a small frying pan over medium heat. Pour in the egg mixture, swirl it around the pan and allow it to set underneath. Flip it over and cook on the other side, taking care not to overcook it so it doesn't become rubbery. Quickly turn out onto a chopping board, then cut the omelette into strips.

To serve, divide the noodles between two deep bowls and ladle the hot soup over them. Top with the omelette strips, garnish with coriander and serve straight away.

1 tablespoon grapeseed oil
1 tablespoon crushed garlic
1–2 Indian green chillies, chopped
    (vary the quantity according to taste)
1 small onion, chopped
1 tomato, chopped
75 g (2½ oz/1 cup) chopped cabbage
½ teaspoon chilli powder, or to taste
1½ teaspoons Garam masala (page 24)
300 ml (10½ fl oz) vegetable stock
a splash of mushroom soy sauce
5 coriander (cilantro) sprigs, chopped,
    plus extra to garnish

NOODLES
½ teaspoon salt
150 g (5½ oz) Tibetan noodles, or any
    noodles of your choice
1 teaspoon rice bran oil

OMELETTE
2 eggs
a pinch of salt
1 teaspoon rice bran oil

Quantee
Curried soup with mixed sprouted beans

Anything sprouted is better for you, right? Well, whatever the health claims, this soup is delicious, thanks to the sprouted pulses, which really do have their own unique flavour, with all the spices adding another dimension. Once you realise how easy it is to sprout your own dried pulses, you might begin to toss them through fresh salads, too.

Serve this wonderfully tasty soup with rice.

REGION Nepal | **SERVES** 4 | **PREPARATION** 15 minutes + 2–3 days sprouting
COOKING 20 minutes | **DIFFICULTY** Medium

Fill a large bowl with water, add the beans and leave to soak overnight.

Next day, drain off the water and rinse the beans well. Cover the bowl with a damp tea towel and set it in a warm place to allow sprouting. It will take about 2–3 days, depending on what length you'd like your sprouts; remember to gently rinse them every 12 hours or so (see page 64).

When your sprouts are ready, heat the rice bran oil in a large heavy-based saucepan. Fry the lovage, fennel and mustard seeds over low heat for about 2 minutes, until lightly browned, stirring often. Add the sprouted beans and stir for about 2 minutes over medium heat.

Stir in the onion, chilli, garlic, ginger, turmeric and curry powder. Season with salt and freshly ground black pepper to taste. Mix for about 2 minutes, to thoroughly coat the sprouted beans in all the spices.

Now stir in the tomatoes, capsicum and stock, then season again, to taste.

Bring to the boil, reduce the heat to low and simmer for about 10 minutes, until the sprouts are tender, and the soup is the desired consistency.

Garnish with herbs or sprouts and serve immediately, with rice.

400 g (14 oz/2 cups) mixed dried beans, such as kidney beans, black-eyed peas, chickpeas, soy beans, mung beans, black beans, white beans
60 ml (2 fl oz/¼ cup) rice bran oil
½ teaspoon lovage seeds
1 teaspoon fennel seeds
1 teaspoon brown mustard seeds
2 small onions, chopped
3 fresh red chillies, finely chopped
1 tablespoon crushed garlic
1 tablespoon finely grated fresh ginger
½ teaspoon ground turmeric
1 tablespoon curry powder
500 g (1 lb 2 oz) fresh tomatoes, chopped
2 small red capsicums (peppers), chopped
1 litre (35 fl oz/4 cups) vegetable stock or water
coriander (cilantro), dill sprigs or sprouts, to garnish

Chapter 9
Chutneys

In the cuisine of the subcontinent, the 'extras' provide a beating heart to many dishes, and at the centre of this food narrative lies the condiment.

Often, it is the chutney on the side that elevates a meal, playing a key role in the depth of a dish. It would be unthinkable to have a meal in Sri Lanka, or indeed across most of the subcontinent, without any accompaniments. Chutneys awaken the tastebuds and enhance the flavours of curries and other dishes. For me, the word 'chutney' is an essential part of any sentence that involves rice and curry. Chutneys are used to great effect all across the subcontinent, and can turn the humble or simple into an otherworldly taste sensation with serious kick and intent. They can cool, add sweetness, add fat or sourness, as well as contributing spice and aromatic herbs. Spicy, tangy, sweet, sour, salty — all of these flavours can be in a chutney, ranging from savoury eggplant (aubergine) and tomato pickles, tangy lime and date chutneys, to fiery sambals based on salt, lime, Maldive fish, chilli and onion. Added to a scalding hot curry, a dollop of chutney with some curd will give a spectacular cooling effect, as will a sweet chutney. A coconut chutney is great with root vegetables, stirred into rice or slathered on a piece of Roast paan from page 178.

Growing up, we made all our own chutneys; whenever we had fresh fruits and vegetables in excess, we'd extend their shelf life by making a chutney with them.

Making chutney is very simple: take the main ingredient, add sugar, vinegar and spices, and then cook and cook and cook. But there are also chutneys that don't get cooked for long, or aren't even cooked at all.

For a superb depth of flavour, always use the freshest ingredients possible, and use non-reactive pans, as some metals can react with the acid in the chutney; stainless steel and glass pans work well.

If a recipe looks heavy on the sugar, do not be tempted to reduce the amount, or to substitute the sugar with alternatives. High sugar levels preserve food, protecting against microbial invasions by drawing water out of the microbes, causing them to shrivel up and die. Without adequate sugar, your chutney may spoil.

Have all your ingredients and implements ready before you begin, especially with chutneys that require cooking. With cooked chutneys, you really do need to vigorously boil the chutney and ensure it gets piping hot. This will ensure the chutney is the right texture and not too runny. And remember to watch, watch, watch! Cooked chutneys can easily burn, and there is no saving a chutney once that burnt flavour has taken hold.

Hot chutneys, jams and preserves should be ladled into hot sterilised jars. Never put hot mixtures into cold jars, as the glass may crack. This also assists with preservation: the air at the top of the jar will expand with the heat, so when you seal the jar — which you should do immediately once you've poured in the mixture — the cooling air will contract and tighten the seal, ensuring your chutney lasts and lasts.

Vegetable chutneys containing lots of vinegar can be left to cool before being added to sterilised jars, as the vinegar will self-preserve them.

Sterilising jars and bottles

Every jar or bottle you are storing food in needs to be sterilised first, even if it is brand new. Any receptacle that has a tight lid will preserve the food inside it, protecting it from bacteria outside the jar — but if it has not been properly sterilised, you could be trapping harmful bacteria within. Bacteria will rapidly reduce the shelf life of your food, and can also cause serious illness, so it's very important to sterilise your jars.

Thankfully, sterilising jars and bottles is not that hard at all! One of the most important things to remember is to make sure the jar or bottle, and the food you are putting in it, are the same temperature, to avoid any glassware breakages. Hot food into hot jars, and cold food into cold jars.

Sterilising basically just means giving your jars and bottles a really good clean. So you need to wash the inside of the jars, then steam or heat them to ensure they remain clean while drying. There are two ways to do this.

IN THE DISHWASHER

This is the easiest of the two methods, so if you have a dishwasher, it's the best option to go for.

Fill your dishwasher with your clean jars or bottles. Set your dishwasher to the highest setting, or a steam setting if it has one, and put them through a cycle.

Leave to cool slightly in the dishwasher, removing each jar as you need it.

IN THE OVEN

Wash your jars or bottles thoroughly using warm water and detergent, then rinse them clean.

Place a sheet of baking paper on one of the racks of your oven (not at the bottom of the oven) and place the jars on the rack, making sure they're not touching each other.

Heat your oven to 140°C (285°F) and dry the jars out for 15–20 minutes.

WHAT ABOUT THE LIDS?

Lids can be left in boiling hot water to sterilise them. If you are using preserving jars, you may want to remove the rubber seals and soak them in boiling water, too.

Surkh-e-murch
Capsicum chutney

Simple and tasty, this is a really fresh chutney to be eaten on the day of making, with anything from barbecued vegetable kebabs to a really good cheddar cheese. It's also great on a sandwich.

REGION Afghanistan, Pakistan | **MAKES** 1 x 250 ml (9 fl oz/1 cup) jar
PREPARATION 15 minutes | **DIFFICULTY** Easy

Place all the ingredients in a blender and pulse into a chunky chutney.

Cover and refrigerate until required; bring to room temperature for serving. This chutney is best enjoyed the same day it is prepared.

3 large red capsicums (peppers), cut into small cubes
3 garlic cloves, or 2 large garlic cloves, chopped
½ teaspoon finely chopped fresh ginger
60 ml (2 fl oz/¼ cup) malt vinegar
40 g (1½ oz/¼ cup) sugar
2 red bird's eye chillies
¼ teaspoon freshly cracked black pepper
a pinch of salt, or to taste

Sandwich chutney

Use this vibrant green chutney to accompany tiffin or snack items, or for a true subcontinental sandwich, add it to a sandwich with slices of steamed or boiled plantain, and some refreshing Pakistani Cabbage salad from page 82.

REGION Bangladesh | **MAKES** 1 x 250 ml (9 fl oz/1 cup) jar
PREPARATION 15 minutes | **DIFFICULTY** Easy

1 bunch coriander (cilantro), leaves picked
1 bunch mint, leaves picked
1 Lebanese (short) cucumber, peeled, seeded and chopped
3–4 Indian green chillies, roughly chopped
1 tablespoon Tamarind chutney (page 220)
a pinch of salt, or to taste

Bring a saucepan of water to the boil, and have a bowl of iced water on standby.

Shock the mint and coriander leaves in the boiling water for 3–5 seconds, then remove with tongs and plunge straight into the iced water. When cooled, dry the leaves on paper towel. (Blanching the leaves helps keep the chutney green and makes it easier to blend.)

Put the coriander and mint leaves in a blender. Add the remaining ingredients and about 1 tablespoon water. Blend until smooth and well combined.

Use straight away, or spoon into a sterilised jar, seal and refrigerate. Being a fresh chutney, it will discolour quickly, and should be used within 2–3 days.

Rhubarb chutney

*This sweet and sour spiced chutney is an excellent accompaniment to just about
any meal. Remove the seeds from the chillies if you'd like a milder chutney.*

REGION India | **MAKES** 1 x 300 ml (10½ fl oz) jar | **PREPARATION** 15 minutes
COOKING 45 minutes | **DIFFICULTY** Easy

¼ teaspoon dill seeds
1½ tablespoons coriander seeds
1 tablespoon fennel seeds
1 teaspoon cumin seeds
2 tablespoons virgin coconut oil
500 g (1 lb 2 oz) rhubarb, cut into 2 cm
    (¾ inch) lengths
4 Indian green chillies, cut into 2 cm
    (¾ inch) pieces
2 tablespoons thinly sliced fresh ginger
¼ teaspoon ground turmeric
1½ teaspoons salt, or to taste
¼ teaspoon Kashmiri chilli powder
75 g (2½ oz/⅓ cup) sugar, or to taste

Using a mortar and pestle, coarsely grind the dill, coriander, fennel and cumin seeds.

Heat the coconut oil in a heavy-based saucepan, then add all the ingredients except the sugar, stirring until thoroughly combined. Cook over medium heat for 10–15 minutes, or until the rhubarb is tender, stirring occasionally to ensure the mixture doesn't stick to the pan or burn.

Stir in the sugar and cook over low heat for about 30 minutes, or until the chutney has thickened.

Spoon into a hot sterilised jar, seal and leave to cool.

Store in the fridge, and allow to settle for a day or two before using. The chutney will keep in the fridge for 2–3 weeks.

Green coconut chutney

This is the go-to chutney in India, served with virtually everything. It is particularly popular at breakfast, but you'll also find it on thali plates, served with idli, dosa or vada (savoury fried snacks), and offered as a condiment with dinner.

REGION India | **MAKES** 1 x 250 ml (9 fl oz/1 cup) jar | **PREPARATION** 15 minutes
COOKING 5 minutes | **DIFFICULTY** Easy

25 g (1 oz/¾ cup) coriander (cilantro) leaves
60 g (2¼ oz/¾ cup) freshly grated coconut, or frozen coconut
1 Indian green chilli, chopped
1 cm (½ inch) knob of fresh ginger, peeled and chopped
1½–2 tablespoons roasted chana dhal
a pinch of salt, or to taste
1 teaspoon sugar, or to taste
½ teaspoon lemon juice, or to taste

FOR TEMPERING
1 tablespoon virgin coconut oil
½ teaspoon brown mustard seeds
¾ teaspoon dried black lentils (urad dhal)
8–10 fresh curry leaves

Place the coriander, coconut, chilli, ginger and chana dhal in a blender. Add 100 ml (3½ fl oz) water and blend until smooth. Season to taste with salt, sugar and lemon juice, mixing well.

For tempering, heat the coconut oil in a small heavy-based frying pan over medium–high heat. Add the mustard seeds and lentils. Cook for a minute or two, until the mustard seeds splutter and the lentils brown. Add the curry leaves and fry for a few seconds, until fragrant.

Stir the tempering mixture through the chutney.

Serve straight away, or spoon into a sterilised jar, seal and refrigerate. The chutney will keep in the fridge for 2–3 days.

Seeni sambal
Sugar sambal

Although its Sinhalese name translates as 'sugar sambal', this condiment contains very little sugar. Such an aromatic sambal, it goes with just about everything, not just vegetarian meals, but also meat, chicken and egg curries.

REGION Sri Lanka | **MAKES** 1 x 250 ml (9 fl oz/1 cup) jar | **PREPARATION** 15 minutes + 15 minutes soaking
COOKING 20 minutes | **DIFFICULTY** Easy

Soak the tamarind pulp in the hot water for 15 minutes. Push the mixture through a fine sieve, into a bowl, and discard any fibres.

Heat the coconut oil in a heavy-based saucepan. Add the onion, chilli powder, curry leaves, garlic, cloves, cinnamon stick, cardamom pods and pandan leaf and cook over medium heat, stirring regularly, for 5 minutes, or until the onion is caramelised, but not too dark.

Stir in the sugar, salt, lime juice and tamarind water and cook, stirring regularly, for another 15 minutes, or until the onion is glossy and the mixture is piping hot.

Spoon into a hot sterilised jar, seal and leave to cool.

The sambal will keep in the fridge for 2–3 weeks, but should be left at least overnight to let the flavours combine and settle. The sambal will harden upon refrigeration, so will need to be warmed gently before serving.

80 g (2¾ oz) seedless tamarind pulp (about 4 tablespoons)
150 ml (5 fl oz) hot water
2 tablespoons virgin coconut oil
2 red onions, halved and thinly sliced
1 teaspoon chilli powder
1 fresh curry leaf sprig, leaves shredded
4 garlic cloves, crushed
3 cloves
1 cinnamon stick
2 green cardamom pods, bruised
5 cm (2 inch) piece of pandan leaf, shredded
1 tablespoon caster (superfine) sugar
2 teaspoons salt
juice of 1 lime

Nuts & dried fruits

Nuts and dried fruits feature extensively in subcontinental cooking. Drying fruit greatly extends its shelf life, and because most of the water has been extracted, their nutrients are more concentrated; however they are also high in sugar, so should not be eaten in large amounts. Nuts are also highly nutritious, and rich in healthy fats. Try to buy organic dried fruits and nuts, to minimise exposure to preservatives and chemical residues.

1. BLANCHED SLIVERED ALMONDS Blanched almonds have been heated to remove their brown outer skin. You can buy them whole, or cut into long thin slivers, or as flaked almonds, which have been thinly sliced into oval-shaped flakes.

2. TAMARIND The brown pulp of ripe tamarind fruit has a sweet and sour flavour. The dried pulp is ground into a paste with water, to be used in curries and chutneys, and to tenderise meat. Preferable to the sometimes bitter concentrate, tamarind pulp adds a sour tang to desserts and savoury dishes. You can make tamarind water by soaking 250 g (9 oz) tamarind pulp in 1 litre (35 fl oz/4 cups) hot water and pushing it through a sieve. You can also buy tamarind pulp without the seeds, but it's not as tangy.

3. WALNUTS Known to the ancient Romans as 'Jupiter's royal acorn', walnuts have been harvested since at least 7000 BCE, and were traded along the Silk Road. They are high in protein, manganese, healthy fatty acids, and several vitamins and minerals.

4. SULTANAS (GOLDEN RAISINS) Often featuring in rice dishes and sweets, and rich in antioxidants, sultanas and raisins are simply dried white grapes. Raisins are often slightly larger and darker than sultanas, but they are essentially interchangeable.

5. CASHEWS These wonderful nuts are rich in minerals, protein, fibre and healthy fat. Delicious to eat, they are notoriously difficult to harvest, as the shells contain caustic substances that can cause terrible burns for the workers who process them.

6. DRIED GOJI BERRIES Also known as wolf berries, these brightly coloured berries are native to Asia and are packed with antioxidants.

7. PEPITAS These are simply the seeds of certain varieties of pumpkin and squash. They are incredibly nutritious and make an excellent snack.

8. RAW ALMONDS These are unblanched almonds, perfect for eating out of hand.

9. PISTACHIOS Native to the Middle East and Central Asia, these health-giving nuts are synonymous with Persian cuisine, and have been enjoyed since ancient times.

10. SHREDDED/DESICCATED COCONUT This is coconut meat that has been shredded, then dried. They are essentially the same, except shredded coconut has a coarser texture than desiccated coconut.

11. DRIED APRICOTS Organic ones are dark in colour, as they have been dried without the use of sulfur dioxide, which preserves the fruit's bright orange colour.

Peanut chutney

Keep this beautiful, unique chutney in your fridge and I am sure you will find many uses for it. It is great as a condiment for any curries, as well as dosa (an Indian pancake) and idli (steamed rice-lentil cake).

REGION India | **MAKES** 1 x 250 ml (9 fl oz/1 cup) jar | **PREPARATION** 20 minutes
COOKING 15 minutes | **DIFFICULTY** Easy

250 g (9 oz/1¾ cups) raw peanuts
2½ tablespoons virgin coconut oil
3 teaspoons white urad dhal
   (hulled dried black lentils)
2 Indian green chillies, roughly chopped
2 garlic cloves, peeled
2 fresh curry leaf sprigs, leaves picked
a pinch of salt, or to taste
1 tablespoon tamarind purée

FOR TEMPERING
1 teaspoon cumin seeds
2½ tablespoons virgin coconut oil
¼ teaspoon brown mustard seeds
1 dried red chilli, broken
1 teaspoon dried black lentils (urad dhal)

In a heavy-based frying pan, dry-roast the peanuts over low heat for about 5 minutes, or until golden, stirring frequently. Remove from the pan and set aside to cool.

Place the frying pan back over medium–high heat and add the coconut oil. Fry the white lentils for 3 minutes, or until golden, then add the chilli, garlic and curry leaves. After a minute or two, when the curry leaves turn crisp, remove the mixture from the heat.

Once cooled, add the mixture to a blender, along with the salt and tamarind purée, and blend until smooth.

For tempering, toast the cumin seeds in a small dry frying pan over low heat for 5 minutes, or until fragrant. Remove from the pan. Heat the coconut oil in the pan, then fry the remaining tempering ingredients over medium–high heat for 3 minutes, or until the seeds turn golden.

Add the mixture to the peanut mixture in the blender and whiz until smooth.

Use straight away, or spoon into a sterilised jar, seal and refrigerate. This chutney will keep in the fridge for up to 2 weeks.

Nepalese tomato achar

A favourite among Nepal's many ethnic communities, achar increases the appetite and is generally eaten as a side dish with roti, or dhal bhat tarkari (lentils with rice and vegetable curry), enhancing the flavour of the whole meal. Try dolloping it on your curries; it's also great spread on burgers and wraps. Add a splash of lemon juice if you'd like it tangy.

REGION Nepal | **MAKES** 1 x 250 ml (9 fl oz/1 cup) jar | **PREPARATION** 15 minutes
COOKING 30 minutes | **DIFFICULTY** Easy

Heat a non-stick frying pan or wok over medium–low heat. Once the pan is hot, add the whole tomatoes to the dry pan. Cook for about 10 minutes, turning as necessary, until the skins are slightly wrinkled and split.

Add the chillies to the pan and dry roast them for a further few minutes.

Remove the tomatoes and chillies from the pan. Roughly chop the tomatoes, and chop the chillies a bit more finely.

Heat the rice bran oil in the pan and add the fenugreek seeds, mustard seeds, ginger and garlic. Fry for about 2 minutes, or until the fenugreek seeds are just browning. Add the cumin, ground coriander, tomatoes and chillies, stirring well. Cook over medium–low heat for about 10 minutes, until there is no liquid left, and the mixture is like a thick paste.

Stir the chopped coriander through just before serving.

This chutney is best served straight away, but will keep for a day or two in the fridge.

2 large tomatoes
3 red chillies
2 tablespoons rice bran oil
½ teaspoon fenugreek seeds
½ teaspoon mustard seeds
1 tablespoon grated fresh ginger
6 garlic cloves, thinly sliced
1 teaspoon ground cumin
1 teaspoon ground coriander
1–2 tablespoons chopped fresh coriander (cilantro)

Chatni gashneez
Coriander chutney

Quickly plunging the coriander in boiling water, then straight into iced water, helps keep this chutney vividly green. Serve it with kebabs.

REGION Afghanistan | **MAKES** 1 x 250 ml (9 fl oz/1 cup) jar | **PREPARATION** 15 minutes
COOKING 5 minutes | **DIFFICULTY** Easy

Bring a small saucepan of water to the boil, and have a bowl of iced water on standby.

Plunge the coriander leaves into the boiling water for 3–5 seconds, then remove with a slotted spoon and immediately refresh in the iced water. When cooled, dry on paper towel and roughly chop.

Place the coriander, garlic, chilli and walnuts in a blender or food processor and whiz until a textured paste is achieved, gradually adding the lemon juice or vinegar while processing. Add salt to taste. (Or you could pass the ingredients through a food grinder with a fine screen, or chop them finely, then pound together using a mortar and pestle, gradually stirring in the lemon juice and salt to taste.)

Place in a small bowl, cover and chill until required.

The chutney will keep in the fridge for a day or two, but is so tasty it will quickly be used up, so only make whatever quantity you need for each meal.

30 g (1 oz/1 cup) coriander (cilantro) stems and leaves
2 garlic cloves, roughly chopped
1 Indian green chilli, seeded and roughly chopped
60 g (2¼ oz/½ cup) roughly chopped walnuts
60 ml (2 fl oz/¼ cup) lemon juice or vinegar
a pinch of salt, or to taste

Aaloo bukhara
Plum & almond chutney

A festive Pakistani chutney, designed to complement some of their amazing rice dishes, such as pilaf and biriyani. It can also be used as a dip for savoury snacks, or as a side dish with chapatti. If you want real heat in your chutney, break up the dried red chillies before frying them, otherwise leave them whole.

REGION Pakistan | **MAKES** 1 x 300 ml (10½ fl oz) jar | **PREPARATION** 15 minutes
COOKING 20 minutes | **DIFFICULTY** Easy

1 teaspoon virgin coconut oil
½ teaspoon brown mustard seeds
½ brown onion, chopped
2 dried red chillies
3 ripe plums, seeded and chopped
1 cinnamon stick
1 tablespoon balsamic vinegar
60 ml (2 fl oz/¼ cup) lime juice
a pinch of salt, or to taste
2 tablespoons sugar
50 g (1¾ oz/⅓ cup) slivered almonds,
    lightly toasted, then chopped
2 tablespoons raisins

In a heavy-based saucepan, heat the coconut oil over medium heat. Add the mustard seeds and cook for a minute or two, until they start to pop.

Add the onion and dried chillies and cook for a further 3 minutes, or until the onion is fragrant and translucent

Stir in the chopped plums, then add the cinnamon stick, vinegar, lime juice and salt, stirring well. Let the plums soften for a minute or two, then add 250 ml (9 fl oz/1 cup) water and cook over medium–high heat for about 5 minutes, or until the plums disintegrate.

When the plums have cooked down to a fairly thick sauce, stir in the sugar and let the mixture simmer for another 3–4 minutes.

Remove from the heat and stir in the toasted almonds and raisins.

Spoon into a hot sterilised jar, seal and leave to cool.

Store in the fridge, and allow to settle for a day or two before using. The chutney will keep in the fridge for up to 2 weeks.

Babari ko achar
Mint chutney

*Mint really is quite a universal herb, used in many cuisines across the globe.
I love it for its versatility, and its hardy tenacity in the garden.*

*Serve this smooth, bright green and ever-popular chutney with any
tandoori snack or starter.*

REGION Nepal | **MAKES** 1 x 250 ml (9 fl oz/1 cup) jar | **PREPARATION** 15 minutes
COOKING 5 minutes | **DIFFICULTY** Easy

Bring a small saucepan of water to the boil, and have a bowl of iced water on standby.

Add the mint and coriander to the boiling water for a few seconds, then immediately refresh them in the iced water, to help lock in the chlorophyll so your chutney will stay bright green. Pat dry with paper towel and set aside.

In a bowl, beat the curd or yoghurt with a whisk until smooth. Add the cumin, chaat masala, amchur and salt and mix until combined.

Add the mint and coriander leaves to a blender, along with the onion, ginger and chilli, and the garlic if using. Add 1–2 tablespoons water and blend to a very smooth paste.

Stir the herb paste through the curd mixture until the chutney becomes uniform in colour.

Cover and refrigerate until required. This chutney is best enjoyed the same day it is prepared.

30 g (1 oz/1½ cups) mint leaves
30 g (1 oz/1 cup) coriander (cilantro) leaves
3–4 tablespoons fresh curd, Greek-style yoghurt or cashew yoghurt
1 teaspoon ground cumin
1 teaspoon Chaat masala (page 24)
1 teaspoon amchur (dried mango powder)
a pinch of black salt or rock salt, or to taste
1 small onion, chopped
1 cm (½ inch) knob of fresh ginger, peeled and chopped
1 Indian green chilli, chopped
2–3 chopped garlic cloves (optional)

Tamarind chutney

Tamarind chutney is like the subcontinent's Vegemite – delicious as a condiment and great when added to a curry to thicken and enhance the flavours.

Sweet but tart, and sometimes very sour, the flavour of tamarind is potent, so a little goes a long way, which is why it is often mixed with sugar, and/or diulted, to mellow its strong taste. Tamarind makes a great base for sauces, marinades and stews.

REGION Sri Lanka | **MAKES** 2 x 500 ml (17 fl oz/2 cup) jars | **PREPARATION** 30 minutes
COOKING 1¼ hours | **DIFFICULTY** Easy

---

450 g (1 lb) tamarind pulp
150 g (5½ oz) ghee
1 onion, finely chopped
5 garlic cloves, crushed
10 cm (4 inch) knob of fresh young
    ginger, peeled and thinly sliced
650 g (1 lb 7 oz) raw sugar
1 teaspoon chilli flakes
350 ml (12 fl oz) white vinegar
2 fresh curry leaf sprigs, leaves picked
2 tablespoons black mustard seeds
1 teaspoon salt

Soak the tamarind pulp in 350 ml (12 fl oz) warm water for 5 minutes, then push through a fine sieve, into a bowl. Reserve the liquid and discard any fibres.

Heat half the ghee in a heavy-based saucepan over medium–low heat and cook the onion, garlic and ginger for 3–5 minutes, or until the onion is translucent, stirring regularly.

Add the reserved tamarind water, the sugar, chilli flakes and vinegar and bring to the boil. Reduce the heat to low and cook, stirring continuously, for 1 hour, or until the mixture has reduced by about three-quarters and is thick and pulpy.

Heat the remaining ghee in a small heavy-based frying pan over medium heat. Add the curry leaves and mustard seeds and shake the pan until the mustard seeds begin to pop, then immediately add to the tamarind mixture with the salt, stirring well. Cover and cook for a further 10 minutes.

Spoon into two hot sterilised jars, seal and leave to cool.

Store in the fridge, and allow to settle for a week or two before using. This chutney will keep in the fridge for up to 1 year.

Date & tamarind chutney

Thick, spicy and rich, this is the most amazing chutney. It goes with any kind of curry, and you can even use it as a rub on your favourite vegetable before putting it on the barbecue — or spread it on a roti and make a curried potato wrap.

REGION Sri Lanka | **MAKES** 1 x 500 ml (17 fl oz/2 cup) jar | **PREPARATION** 15 minutes
COOKING 50 minutes | **DIFFICULTY** Easy

Pour the vinegar into a heavy-based frying pan and place over medium heat. Stir in the sugar, ginger garlic paste and all the spices. Cover and cook for 2 minutes.

Stir in the dates and tamarind pulp and cook over low heat for about 40 minutes, until the liquid has thickened, but the dates are not pulpy.

Gently mash the mixture with a big spoon, then add the raisins and cook for a further 2 minutes. Discard the cinnamon stick and stir in the salt.

Spoon into a hot sterilised jar, seal and leave to cool.

Store in the fridge, and allow to settle for a day or two before using. This chutney will keep in the fridge for up to 3 months.

185 ml (6 fl oz/¾ cup) malt vinegar
150 g (5½ oz/¾ cup, lightly packed) brown sugar
1 tablespoon Ginger garlic paste (page 241)
1 teaspoon brown mustard seeds, crushed
1 tablespoon chilli flakes
4 whole cardamom pods, crushed
2 cloves, crushed
3 cm (1¼ inch) piece of cinnamon stick
160 g (5½ oz/1 cup) pitted dates, chopped
200 g (7 oz) tamarind pulp
1 tablespoon raisins
¾ teaspoon sea salt

Chutney for momos

Plenty of countries claim the momo, but it seems these delicious little dumplings originated in Tibet, and everyone has a special chutney for them. I really like the tomato base in this version, which is similar to the one I enjoyed while trekking in Nepal.

REGION Nepal, Bhutan, India | **MAKES** 1 x 250 ml (9 fl oz/1 cup) jar | **PREPARATION** 10 minutes
COOKING 10–15 minutes | **DIFFICULTY** Easy

Heat a small heavy-based saucepan over medium heat. Add the rice bran oil and once hot, add the tomato and lightly cook for 5–7 minutes, until it starts to soften.

Stir in the remaining ingredients and gently cook for 3–5 minutes, or until fragrant.

Allow to cool slightly, then transfer to a food processor and blend until smooth, adding a little water if the chutney is too thick.

Check the seasoning and serve hot, or spoon into a sterilised jar, seal and refrigerate. This chutney will keep in the fridge for up to 1 week.

2 tablespoons rice bran oil
2 tomatoes, finely chopped
2 red bird's eye chillies, chopped
1 onion, finely chopped
4 garlic cloves, chopped
½ teaspoon grated fresh ginger
1 teaspoon curry powder
1 teaspoon salt

Akhrot chutney
Walnut chutney

The walnut tree is revered by the Kalash people in Pakistan, who traditionally believe it protects them from harm and evil. In their spring festival they offer fennel and ground walnuts to the earth spirits to appease them.

Cool and refreshing, nutritious and yummy, this absolutely awesome chutney is unlike any you have tried before. This versatile side dish can be enjoyed as an accompaniment with almost anything. For me it also brings back great memories of life on the houseboats in Kashmir, where this chutney is also served.

REGION Pakistan | **MAKES** about 2 cups
PREPARATION 20 minutes + 1–2 hours chilling | **DIFFICULTY** Easy

4–5 dried red Kashmiri chillies
115 g (4 oz/1 cup) walnut halves
130 g (4½ oz/½ cup) fresh buffalo curd
　　or thick Greek-style yoghurt
a pinch of salt, to taste
½ teaspoon sugar
1 teaspoon lime juice
1 tablespoon olive oil
flat-leaf (Italian) parsley, to garnish

Soak the dried chillies in a bowl of warm water for 10 minutes.

Drain the chillies and pound together with the walnuts using a mortar and pestle, or blitz together in a blender. I like it smooth, but you can also leave it a bit chunky if you prefer.

In a small bowl, thoroughly mix together the curd or yoghurt, salt and sugar.

Add the pounded walnut mixture to the curd mixture, mixing well. Stir the lime juice through.

Cover and chill for an hour or two before serving. This chutney will keep for a day or two in the fridge, but is best enjoyed freshly made.

Just before serving, drizzle with the olive oil and garnish with parsley.

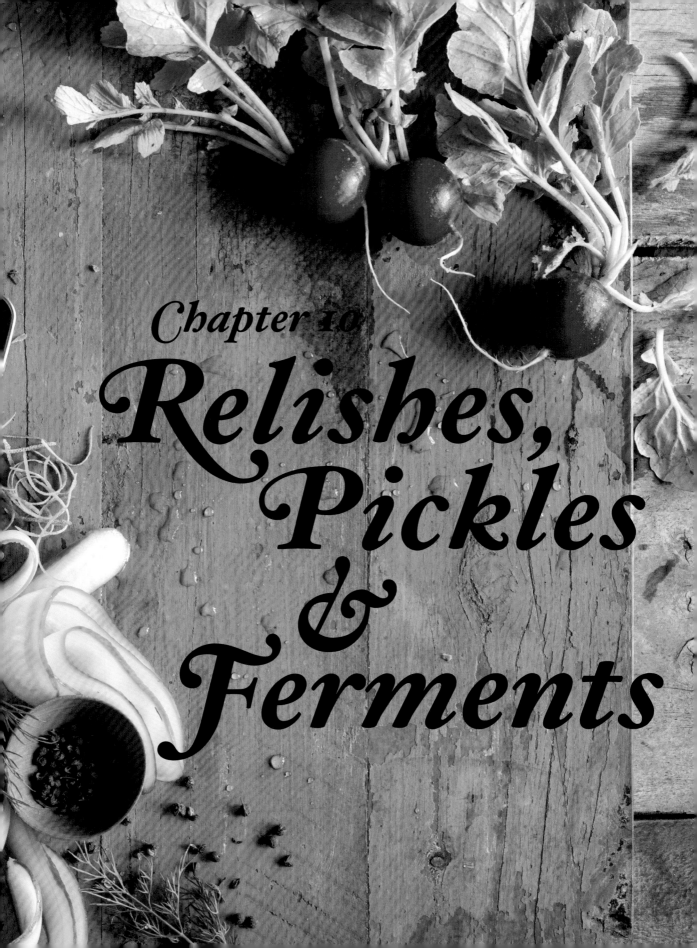

Chapter 10
Relishes, Pickles & Ferments

When I go home to Sri Lanka or travel the subcontinent for work, or just for pure enjoyment, there is one thing I really look forward to: the pickles.

Pickles and relishes are fantastic, served on top of dhal, slathered on flaky flat breads, or with curries. There is nothing like their immediacy to liven the senses.

I remember my first taste of the Sinhalese pickle known as achcharu (page 228), a mix of all the vegetables and chillies found in the markets: upcountry carrots, green papaya, very small Bombay onions and super-hot green chillies, all pickled in a mixture of ground brown mustard seeds and coconut vinegar. It made my mouth come alive.

At home I'd make lime pickle, one of Sri Lanka's signature pickles, with my aunties and grandmother. We'd buy limes in season and then cut them in quarters nearly all the way through, keeping the ends at the bottom joined. My job was to stuff coarse rock salt and black pepper into them. I loved it, getting into the kitchen with my aunties and grandmother, but I remember even more distinctly the excruciating pain — I would constantly have nicks on my hands and feet from running around wearing no shoes and minimal clothing; my mum used to call me Mowgli! The lime and salt would get into these tiny cuts, and it was enough to make my eyes water. The lime pickles were then boiled in an earthenware crockpot, then left in the liquid in a dark place for a few months.

Lime pickle and Sinhalese pickle were always on our table at every meal. Now these pickles make an appearance on my restaurant dinner tables, still as they were made all those years ago.

The repertoire of recipes and uses for fruit-based relishes and pickles across the subcontinent are endless. The preservation of foods when they are abundant and in season was born out of necessity, but has over the centuries become an art form across the subcontinent. Prior to refrigeration, preserving was the way to keep produce well beyond its natural use-by date, but people came to realise that pickled and fermented foods were also good for you.

It may have come on trend recently, but pickling is one of the most ancient and universal methods of food preservation. Everywhere, fruits and vegetables are salted or sun-cured, then bottled in spice-infused oil, where their flavour intensifies, transforming into condiments that perk up meals. They take on a very fundamental role — often multiple roles — across a single dish. They cool, they sweeten, they add sourness or lively spice, even heat.

More than simply safeguarding seasonal produce, the art of relishes and pickles preserves the culinary heritage of the entire subcontinent.

Mixed fruit relish

The whole subcontinent loves fruit relish — perhaps because we are always trying to find the balance between spicy and sweet. This relish could be from anywhere on the subcontinent. Don't be too limited in what you put into your relish — just experiment a little with whatever is fresh and seasonal. Always add your choice of dried fruits, to keep the relish pulpy and rich.

REGION Bangladesh | **MAKES** 2 x 500 ml (17 fl oz/2 cup) jars | **PREPARATION** 30 minutes
COOKING 40 minutes | **DIFFICULTY** Medium

100 ml (3½ fl oz) virgin coconut oil
1 fresh bay leaf
1 teaspoon yellow mustard seeds
½ pineapple, cored and diced
2 teaspoons salt
2 granny smith apples, cored and diced
90 g (3¼ oz/½ cup) seedless grapes, halved
80 g (2¾ oz/½ cup) dried mango, diced
110 g (3¾ oz/½ cup) sugar
2 tablespoons raw cashews
100 g (3½ oz/½ cup) dried apricots, diced
95 g (3¼ oz/½ cup) dried figs, diced
320 g (11¼ oz/2 cups) pitted dates, diced
1 tablespoon raisins
½ cup fresh pomegranate seeds
½ orange, peeled and diced

ROASTED SPICE MIX
½ teaspoon cumin seeds
½ teaspoon fennel seeds
½ teaspoon fenugreek seeds
3 dried red chillies
3 cinnamon sticks
6 cardamom pods

Put all the ingredients for the roasted spice mix in a dry frying pan and toast for a few minutes over medium–high heat until fragrant, stirring often and making sure the fenugreek seeds don't burn, or the whole mixture will taste bitter. Tip onto a plate and leave to cool, then grind to a powder using a mortar and pestle or spice grinder. Set aside.

Heat the coconut oil in a heavy-based saucepan over medium–high heat for 30 seconds. Add the bay leaf and mustard seeds. After a minute or two, when the mustard seeds begin to pop, add the pineapple and salt and mix well.

Cover with a lid and cook over low heat for 5 minutes, or until the pineapple is soft.

Stir in the apple, grapes and mango and cook for a further 10 minutes. Add the sugar, stirring it in well.

Add a little water, just enough to stop it all sticking, then cover the pan again and cook for a further 6–7 minutes.

Now stir in the cashews, dried fruits, pomegranate seeds and orange and cook for 3–4 minutes.

Stir in the roasted spice powder, again mixing well. Turn the heat down to low and let the mixture cool down for 10 minutes at a low simmer, stirring constantly.

Once cooled, the relish is ready to eat straight away. It is best eaten on the day of making, as the fruit will break down. However, the flavours will develop if left to sit for a while, so if you don't mind soggy fruit, reheat the remaining relish, spoon into hot sterilised jars and seal. Store in the fridge and use within 1–2 days.

Apple relish

Apples used to be hard to obtain in Sri Lanka. I clearly remember biting into my first one. My mum helped an East German sailor, named Christian, defect from his ship while he was in Sri Lanka; the operation had been planned for years, and was finally executed with Jason Bourne–like precision. During the planning we would visit Christian's ship in Colombo harbour and he'd invite us into his cabin, where he'd lavish us with German sausage, sweets, apples and oranges —flavours that would burst in our unsuspecting mouths.

Apples are now grown in the hill country, and here's a lovely way to enjoy them.

REGION Sri Lanka | **MAKES** 2 x 500 ml (17 fl oz/2 cup) jars | **PREPARATION** 15 minutes
COOKING 25 minutes | **DIFFICULTY** Easy

Toast the cumin and coriander seeds in a dry frying pan over low heat for 3–5 minutes, or until lightly browned and aromatic. Coarsely pound using a mortar and pestle and set aside.

Sweat the onion, garlic and ginger in a frying pan over medium heat with the salt for about 5 minutes, or until the onion is translucent and the mixture is fragrant.

Stir in the pounded spice mix and the cinnamon sticks and cook for another minute or two, or until fragrant.

Add the remaining ingredients, stirring well, and cook over low heat for 5–10 minutes, or until the apple is tender. Season generously with salt and freshly ground black pepper, take off the heat and cool quickly.

Once cooled, the relish is ready to eat straight away.

However, you could also spoon the hot relish into hot sterilised jars, seal, refrigerate and use within 2–3 days.

2 teaspoons cumin seeds
2 teaspoons coriander seeds
2 red onions, finely diced
4 garlic cloves, finely diced
1 small knob of fresh ginger, peeled and finely diced
a generous pinch of salt
2 cinnamon sticks
6 granny smith apples, peeled, cored and diced
250 ml (9 fl oz/1 cup) white wine vinegar
110 g (3¾ oz/½ cup) sugar

Achcharu
Sinhalese mixed pickle

Achcharu is a spicy Sri Lankan pickle or salad. Variations of this simple condiment abound, but here is the Kuruvita version. You will have to track down the right green chillies for this one, but it will be well worth the effort.

REGION Sri Lanka | **MAKES** 2 x 500 ml (17 fl oz/2 cup) jars | **PREPARATION** 15 minutes + 2 weeks pickling | **COOKING** 10 minutes | **DIFFICULTY** Easy

1 small carrot
50 g (1¾ oz) green papaya
50 g (1¾ oz) Indian green chillies,
    with stalks
100 g (3½ oz) Bombay onions, or
    1 red onion, roughly chopped
50 g (1¾ oz) baby green beans
3 garlic cloves, sliced
2 tablespoons brown mustard seeds
1 teaspoon salt
350 ml (12 fl oz) malt vinegar

Peel the carrot and papaya, then cut them into thin batons, 3 cm (1¼ inches) long and about 5 mm (¼ inch) thick. Place in a bowl.

Using a sharp knife, cut the chillies in half lengthways, keeping them connected by the stalk. Add to the carrot mixture with the onion, beans and garlic and mix to combine. Divide the mixture evenly between two sterilised jars.

Place the mustard seeds, salt and vinegar in a small saucepan, bring to the boil, then pour over the vegetable mixture, ensuring there is just enough liquid to cover them.

Seal and leave to cool, then store in the fridge for 2 weeks before using. The pickles will keep getting tastier and hotter, and will keep in the fridge for up to 2 months.

Green chilli paste

Keep this condiment handy, as it pops up in so many recipes. It will keep in an airtight container in the fridge for 8–10 days, or indefinitely in the freezer.

REGION India | **MAKES** 100 g (3½ oz) | **PREPARATION** 15 minutes | **DIFFICULTY** Easy

100 g (3½ oz) Indian green chillies
½ teaspoon salt
2 teaspoons mustard oil
2 teaspoons lemon juice

Wash the chillies well and remove the stalks. Grind the chillies to a paste, using a mortar and pestle, then mix in the salt, mustard oil and lemon juice.

VARIATION
Mustard green chilli paste: Grind together 1 tablespoon black mustard seeds, 1 tablespoon yellow mustard seeds, 2 chopped green chillies, 1 teaspoon sugar and 375 ml (13 fl oz/1½ cups) water. Season to taste with salt. The temperature of the water determines the spiciness of the paste; cold water produces a hotter flavour.

Weralu achcharu
Olive pickles

Sold as a snack by the roadside and by beach vendors all over Sri Lanka, these olives have a great flavour and texture — and once you've eaten one, you keep going back for more. They also make a great chaser for a beer or a glass of coconut arrack.

REGION Sri Lanka | **MAKES** 1 x 1 litre (35 fl oz/4 cup) jar | **PREPARATION** 15 minutes + 2 weeks pickling
COOKING 20 minutes | **DIFFICULTY** Easy

Boil the olives in a saucepan of salted water for 10 minutes, then drain and set aside.

Heat the rice bran oil in a large heavy-based saucepan. Add the garlic and fry over medium heat for about 3 minutes, or until golden brown.

Add the other ingredients, except the olives, and mix well. Now add the boiled olives and mix until all the ingredients are well distributed.

Transfer to a large sterilised glass jar, seal and store in a cool dark place for 2 weeks before eating.

Once opened, the olives will keep in the fridge for up to 3 weeks.

50 ripe green olives
2 tablespoons rice bran oil
1 teaspoon chopped garlic
1 tablespoon chilli flakes
5 fresh curry leaves
1 tablespoon malt vinegar
2 tablespoons tomato sauce, such as the Velvet tomato catsup on page 248
1 tablespoon sugar
¼ teaspoon coarsely ground black pepper
1 teaspoon salt

Tomato chilli jam

I have used this simple jam for over 30 years. In the 1980s and 1990s it was served with just about everything, but it still tastes lovely. Try it on a vegie burger, or with one of the snacks from the street food chapter.

REGION Afghanistan | **MAKES** 1 x 500 ml (17 fl oz/2 cup) jar | **PREPARATION** 20 minutes
COOKING 40 minutes | **DIFFICULTY** Easy

Blitz the tomato, chilli and garlic in a blender until smooth.

Scrape the mixture into a saucepan and stir in the remaining ingredients. Bring to the boil over high heat, then reduce the heat and simmer for 30–35 minutes, or until the mixture thickens, stirring regularly.

Leave to cool slightly, then spoon into a sterilised jar, seal and refrigerate. The relish can be used straight away, but the flavours will intensify on sitting. It will keep in the fridge for 1–2 weeks.

5 large ripe tomatoes, roughly chopped
3 long red chillies, roughly chopped
2 garlic cloves, finely chopped
240 g (8½ oz/1¼ cups, lightly packed) brown sugar
125 ml (4 fl oz/½ cup) white wine vinegar
1 teaspoon finely grated fresh ginger
2 tablespoons soy sauce
½ teaspoon sea salt

Fruit chaat

*Traditionally, in India and Pakistan, fruit chaat, a type of spiced fruit salad,
is made with apples, oranges, bananas and guava, if they are in season. Any fruit
of your choice can be used, but the vital element that makes a fruit mixture a fruit
chaat is the chaat masala. We used to have this wrapped in a banana leaf and eat it
like a snack.*

*Tangy, sweet, savoury and sour, it is great for refreshing the palate. You can also
add a tablespoon of sugar, honey, date syrup or palm sugar (jaggery) syrup for extra
sweetness, and a few fresh mint leaves.*

REGION India | **SERVES** 6 | **PREPARATION** 15 minutes + 2–3 hours chilling | **DIFFICULTY** Easy

---

1 large apple, diced

1 banana, sliced

45 g (1½ oz/¼ cup) seedless grapes, halved lengthways

225 g (8 oz/1½ cups) diced watermelon, or 280 g (10 oz/1½ cups) diced papaya

1 orange, peeled and cut into thin segments

160 g (5½ oz/1 cup) diced pineapple

¼ cup fresh pomegranate seeds (optional)

½ teaspoon cumin seeds, dry-roasted and ground

½ teaspoon Chaat masala (page 24)

½ teaspoon black salt

¼ teaspoon freshly ground black pepper

Place all the cut fruit in a bowl, with the pomegranate seeds, if using. Sprinkle with the spices, salt and pepper and gently toss together well.

Cover the bowl with plastic wrap and chill in the refrigerator for 2–3 hours.

Serve the fresh chilled relish in small individual bowls, on the day of making.

Brinjal pickle

The brinjal pickle is a beautiful condiment, even on a piece of toasted sourdough.
It is used all across the subcontinent, and is loved for its flavour, texture and colour.

REGION Sri Lanka | **MAKES** 1 x 500 ml (17 fl oz/2 cup) jar | **PREPARATION** 15 minutes + overnight pickling
COOKING 30 minutes | **DIFFICULTY** Medium

6 eggplants (aubergines)
12 long red chillies
10 French or red Asian shallots, peeled
2 tablespoons ground turmeric
vegetable oil, for deep-frying
1 tablespoon ghee
15 fresh curry leaves
1 tablespoon brown mustard seeds
4 cm (1½ inch) knob of fresh ginger,
    peeled and finely grated
5 garlic cloves, crushed
3 tablespoons ground cumin
100 g (3½ oz) sugar
150 ml (5 fl oz) white vinegar
½ teaspoon salt

Cut the eggplants, chillies and shallots into 3 cm (1¼ inch) chunks or pieces. Place in a large bowl and sprinkle with the turmeric, stirring well to thoroughly coat.

Pour about 5 cm (2 inches) of vegetable oil into a heavy-based saucepan and heat to 180°C (350°F), or until a cube of bread dropped into the oil turns brown in 15 seconds.

Working in batches, add the turmeric-coated vegetables to the hot oil and cook for about 5 minutes, or until deep golden brown. Remove each batch with a slotted spoon and set aside.

Strain the excess oil into a heatproof container, leave to cool, then chill in the fridge to use in other recipes, as a flavoured oil.

Heat the ghee in a clean heavy-based saucepan and fry off the curry leaves and mustard seeds until the mustard seeds pop, being careful not to burn the mustard seeds.

Add the ginger and garlic and cook for another minute or two, until fragrant. Stir in the cumin and fry briefly, then add the sugar, vinegar and salt, cooking for about 3 minutes, until the sugar breaks down.

Stir the mixture through the vegetables until well combined. Leave to cool, then spoon into a sterilised jar.

The pickle is best left to steep overnight before using, and will keep in the fridge for about 1 week.

Chilli lime pickle

One of my go-to condiments, this pickle is sour, tangy and really tasty, and enjoyed across the entire subcontinent, in many similar versions. A tiny dollop in a mouthful of curry just brightens your day. Try mixing it with some yoghurt and fresh chilli.

REGION Pakistan | **MAKES** 1 x 1 litre (35 fl oz/4 cup) jar
PREPARATION 25 minutes + 5–6 days pickling | **DIFFICULTY** Easy

Grind the mustard seeds to a coarse powder, using a mortar and pestle. Cut each of the limes into eight pieces. Slit the chillies and cut them into 2 cm (¾ inch) pieces.

Toss the ground mustard seeds in a bowl with the turmeric, salt and chilli and lime pieces, mixing until well combined.

Transfer the mixture to a sterilised glass bottle or earthenware jar. Pour the vegetable oil on top and shake the bottle or jar well. Cover with muslin (cheesecloth) and secure with kitchen string.

Keep in a cool dark place with good air flow, stirring the contents of the jar at least once a day for the first few days.

Leave to pickle for 5–6 days before using. Once opened, the pickle will keep in the fridge indefinitely — although it's so tasty it probably won't last very long at all!

3 tablespoons brown mustard seeds
10 large limes
200 g (7 oz) Indian green chillies
1½ teaspoons ground turmeric
25 g (1 oz) coarse sea salt
200 ml (7 fl oz) vegetable oil

Mesu
Fermented bamboo shoots

The use of mesu as a pickle and as the base of curries is a long tradition in the hills of Darjeeling and the state of Sikkim in north-east India. Made with fermented bamboo shoots, this very popular pickle has a tangy and sour taste that is hard to forget.

REGION India | **MAKES** 1 x 1 litre (35 fl oz/4 cup) jar
PREPARATION 20 minutes + 6 hours fermenting | **DIFFICULTY** Easy

Place all the ingredients in a bowl and mix until well combined.

Spoon into a sterilised jar. Cover the opening with a piece of muslin (cheesecloth), then secure the lid.

Store in a cool dark place for at least 6 hours, until pickled to your liking; the fermented bamboo shoots will keep for up to 4 weeks. During this time, the flavour will keep getting stronger, and the shoots more tender.

250 g (9 oz) blanched or tinned
    bamboo shoots
4 garlic cloves, crushed
3 teaspoons chilli powder
1 teaspoon brown mustard seeds,
    dry-roasted
1 teaspoon mustard oil
1 teaspoon salt

Turshi
Radish pickle

Radishes originated in China, but the ancient Egyptians and Romans also loved them. This is a pickle that I use as a condiment. Everything stays crisp, and the flavours marry beautifully.

REGION Afghanistan | **MAKES** 1 x 500 ml (17 fl oz/2 cup) jar
PREPARATION 20 minutes + 30 minutes pickling | **COOKING** 10 minutes | **DIFFICULTY** Easy

Place all the pickling brine ingredients in a small non-metallic saucepan. Add 100 ml (3½ fl oz) water and bring to the boil. Remove from the heat and set aside to cool.

Put the remaining ingredients in a bowl, pour the cooled pickling brine over and gently toss to coat well.

Cover with plastic wrap and stand in the fridge for 30 minutes, or until lightly pickled.

Enjoy straight away, or pour into a sterilised jar, seal and refrigerate. This pickle will keep in the fridge for up to 2 weeks.

1 Lebanese (short) cucumber, thinly shaved lengthways
6 baby radishes, thinly sliced
10 coriander (cilantro) sprigs, leaves picked
10 dill sprigs, leaves picked
zest of 1 lime

PICKLING BRINE
100 ml (3½ fl oz) Chinese black vinegar
100 g (3½ oz/¾ cup) finely grated palm sugar (jaggery)
4 dill sprigs
1 tablespoon freshly cracked black pepper
1 garlic clove, crushed
juice of 1 lemon

Simple fermented bok choy

This method of fermentation has been used for centuries. You can use it with any vegetable and it will keep for months — but I prefer the pickle fairly fresh, at about 4–6 days old. I have loosely based this recipe on the Nepalese version; try it in a vegie burger with some grilled eggplant (aubergine) and haloumi cheese.

REGION Nepal | **MAKES** 2 x 500 ml (17 fl oz/2 cup) jars
PREPARATION 15 minutes + 1 hour salting + 4–6 days fermenting | **DIFFICULTY** Easy

---

450 g (1 lb) bok choy (pak choy),
    washed thoroughly and chopped
1 onion, chopped
2 celery stalks, chopped
3 garlic cloves, crushed
1 tablespoon prepared horseradish
1 tablespoon fresh thyme leaves
1 tablespoon coarse sea salt
fresh or dried hot chillies, to taste

Combine all the ingredients in a crockpot or food-grade bucket, making sure the salt is distributed evenly.

Press the mixture down with your fist, then set aside for 1 hour, or until the salt has drawn out enough moisture to submerge the vegies in the brine.

If not enough moisture is drawn out, add enough water to almost cover the vegies.

Cover the mixture with a non-metallic plate. Place some tins of food on top of the plate, to press the mixture down, ensuring no metal comes in contact with it.

Cover the crock or bucket with a clean T-shirt or cloth, then tie some kitchen string around the fabric to secure it in place.

Press the mixture down once a day, and check the flavour every day until it tastes sour enough to you; for me this is usually 4–6 days.

At this point, transfer the mixture to sterilised glass jars, seal and refrigerate. The vegies will keep in the fridge for up to 2 months.

TIP Instead of bok choy, you can also try fermenting vegetables such as cabbage, radish, daikon, kohl rabi and leafy Asian greens.

Kamrakh lonji
Star fruit relish

We still don't use it much in the West, but star fruit or carambola — just like most ingredients in the cuisines of the subcontinent — has an impressive list of health benefits. It is sweet and sour and looks beautiful. Try this relish with hot chapattis, parathas or rice, and perhaps you'll start using star fruit a little bit more in salads and even as a garnish.

REGION Bangladesh, India | **MAKES** about 1 cup | **PREPARATION** 15 minutes
COOKING 20 minutes | **DIFFICULTY** Easy

4 star fruit (carambola), about 200 g (7 oz) in total; make sure they are not too ripe
1 tablespoon virgin coconut oil
½ teaspoon brown mustard seeds
½ teaspoon cumin seeds
½ teaspoon fenugreek seeds
¼ teaspoon ground turmeric
1 teaspoon ground coriander
½ teaspoon ground fennel
2 teaspoons salt
¼ teaspoon chilli powder
2 tablespoons sugar
½ teaspoon Garam masala (page 24)

Wash the star fruit, cut into small pieces and set aside.

Heat the coconut oil in a heavy-based saucepan over medium–high heat and add the mustard seeds, cumin seeds and fenugreek seeds. Toast, stirring frequently, for 3–5 minutes, or until fragrant, ensuring they don't burn.

Stir in the turmeric, coriander and fennel and cook for a further 2 minutes, or until fragrant.

Now stir in the star fruit, salt and chilli powder, cover the pan and leave to cook for 3–4 minutes over medium heat. Once the star fruit softens, stir in the sugar, garam masala and 250 ml (9 fl oz/1 cup) water. Let the mixture boil, uncovered, for 7–8 minutes over medium heat.

Once cooled, the relish is ready to eat straight away. It is best eaten on the day, as the star fruit will start to wilt.

However, you could also spoon the hot relish into a hot sterilised jar, seal, refrigerate and use within 10 days.

Green tea & jasmine pickled cucumbers

Several experiences have culminated in this pickle, which I originally created to accompany some torched kingfish. As a vegetarian condiment, try using it to top one of the pulse recipes in chapter 2 — or a salad made of Paneer (page 94) and chickpeas, tossed with the dressing from the Bhutanese red rice salad on page 90. It's very important to use a pure, unadulterated green tea here, one that is infused with pure jasmine flowers, with no chemical or pesticide residues.

REGION Sri Lanka | **SERVES** 4–5 | **PREPARATION** 15 minutes
COOKING 10 minutes | **DIFFICULTY** Easy

Peel the cucumbers, leaving alternating green stripes. Slice the cucumbers in half lengthways and scrape the seeds out with a spoon, discarding the seeds.

Using a food processor or sharp knife, very thinly slice the cucumbers, then place in a double layer of paper towel and squeeze gently to remove the excess moisture. Set aside.

In a saucepan, combine the vinegar, tea leaves, sugar and salt and heat gently, stirring to dissolve the sugar and salt. Cover and leave to steep for 5 minutes, then strain the tea leaves out.

Add the cucumber and sesame seeds, tossing well to combine. Serve immediately.

TIP To toast sesame seeds, spread them out on a baking tray and bake in a preheated 180°C (350°F) oven for 5–7 minutes, or until golden brown.

2 medium-sized telegraph (long) cucumbers, or 1 large English (green) cucumber
125 ml (4 fl oz/½ cup) rice vinegar
2 teaspoons purest-quality jasmine green tea leaves, such as Dilmah Green Tea With Jasmine
1 teaspoon sugar
¼ teaspoon salt
2 tablespoons sesame seeds, toasted (see tip)

Himalayan relish

Something quite unusual here, but very tasty! Try it alongside the momos on pages 31 and 99, and as another condiment for Puri chana chaat masala (page 45) — or simply scoop it up with one of the breads in this book.

REGION Nepal, Bhutan, Pakistan | **MAKES** 1 x 500 ml (17 fl oz/2 cup) jar
PREPARATION 10 minutes | **DIFFICULTY** Easy

Place the coriander and lemon juice in a high-speed blender. Add 125 ml (4 fl oz/½ cup) water and pulse until well combined.

Add the remaining ingredients and blend into a paste.

Spoon into a sterilised jar, seal and refrigerate. The relish will keep in the fridge for up to 1 week.

- 2 bunches coriander (cilantro), including the roots, roughly chopped
- 125 ml (4 fl oz/½ cup) lemon juice
- 55 g (2 oz/1 cup) dried coconut flakes
- 7.5 cm (3 inch) knob of fresh ginger, peeled and chopped
- 1 tablespoon raw honey
- 1 teaspoon Himalayan pink salt

Ginger garlic paste

Fresh ginger and garlic are indispensable to many dishes across the subcontinent; keep a jar of this paste in the fridge, as you'll find so many brilliant uses for it. The key is to use equal amounts of ginger and garlic. You can also add green chillies, or use vinegar or lime juice instead of lemon juice, to help preserve the paste.

REGION India | **MAKES** 1 x 250 ml (9 fl oz/1 cup) jar | **PREPARATION** 20 minutes | **DIFFICULTY** Easy

Thinly peel the ginger, and peel all the garlic cloves.

Finely grate or chop the ginger, then grind to a paste with the garlic cloves, using a spice grinder or mortar and pestle. Mix in the salt, mustard oil and lemon juice until well combined.

The paste will keep in a sterilised container in the fridge for 8–10 days, or indefinitely in the freezer.

- 100 g (3½ oz) young fresh ginger
- 100 g (3½ oz) garlic cloves
- 1 teaspoon salt
- 1 tablespoon mustard oil
- 1 tablespoon lemon juice

VARIATIONS

Ginger paste: Thinly peel 100 g (3½ oz) young fresh ginger, then finely grate or chop it. Grind to a paste using a spice grinder or mortar and pestle, then mix in ½ teaspoon salt, 2 teaspoons mustard oil and 2 teaspoons lemon juice.

Garlic paste: Peel 100 g (3½ oz) garlic cloves and grind to a paste, then mix in ½ teaspoon salt, 2 teaspoons mustard oil and 2 teaspoons lemon juice.

Gundruk
Spicy fermented vegetables

This is Nepal's kimchi, made with the vegetables from the summer harvest and kept as a staple through the colder months. It is also sometimes made into a curry, but this pickle makes a great accompaniment to dhal and rice and adds a tang to your meals. You can also serve it alongside some steamed rice or pilaf, and the Masala dahi (spiced curd) from page 109.

This is also an excellent pickle to put on a burger. Try Paneer (page 94), grilled eggplant (aubergine) and Gundruk on your next vegie burger.

REGION Nepal | **MAKES** 1 x 1 litre (35 fl oz/4 cup) jar
PREPARATION 20 minutes + 6 days fermenting | **DIFFICULTY** Easy

500 g (1 lb 2 oz) Chinese cabbage
  (wong bok)
500 g (1 lb 2 oz) daikon (white radish)
200 g (7 oz) carrot
4 tablespoons coarse salt
4 spring onions (scallions), cut into 5 cm
  (2 inch) lengths
1 tablespoon roughly chopped garlic
1 tablespoon thinly sliced fresh ginger
1 tablespoon chilli flakes
1 tablespoon mild Kashmiri chilli powder
1 teaspoon black peppercorns
1 teaspoon sichuan peppercorns
¼ teaspoon asafoetida
2 tablespoons sugar

Cut the cabbage into 5 cm (2 inch) squares, and the daikon and carrot into thin slices about 5 cm (2 inches) long. Place them in a large mixing bowl, add 3 tablespoons of the salt and mix thoroughly. Cover and leave to sit in a warm place for at least 6 hours.

Drain the vegetables into a colander and rinse well, then return them to the mixing bowl. Add the remaining ingredients, including the remaining 1 tablespoon of salt, along with 250 ml (9 fl oz/1 cup) water. Toss well to combine the vegetables with all the spices.

Transfer the mixture to a large sterilised jar, gradually pressing down on each layer as it is spooned in, to make it all fit; the mixture will break down with time.

Place a piece of muslin (cheesecloth) on top of the jar and secure it in place with a rubber band. In the first few days, keep the jar in a bowl, as some of the liquid from the vegetables will overflow.

After 3 days, seal the jar tightly and leave to ferment in a warm place for at least 3 days.

Once the vegetables are fermented enough for your taste, store the jar in the fridge. This pickle will keep for up to 4 weeks.

Chapter 11
Sauces

So often it is the sauces spiced with the flavours from my life and travels that spark feelings of family and home.

All of us are brought up on certain foods — ones our mothers and fathers, and their mothers and fathers, were fond of, were able to cook, and most of all could afford. We really do tend to continue to eat the foods and dishes we have known all of our lives, and one of these for me is kiri hodi, a wonderful mild coconut milk gravy.

When we first arrived in Sri Lanka, my beautiful grandmother kept me very close to her, and made the first kiri hodi I ever tried. It really was an amazing experience for my little English tastebuds, an explosion of flavour and intensity that was unfamiliar to me but completely exciting.

I love the power of a sauce to shock the tastebuds. Across the subcontinent, where religion and geographical climate ensure vegetarianism is a common way of life, elements such as sauces are given great consideration and care. Their impact on the look and taste of a final dish can be huge.

Sauces easily levitate the simplest and the humblest of foods into something legendary. Like chutneys and pickles, sauces play a vital role in adding colour, sweetness, saltiness, sourness or a hit of chilli to a dish. They can be tangy, smooth, soft, pungent, zesty, salty and sweet, all the while providing balance to the overall flavour and texture of a dish.

Sauces should evoke memories and be the 'glue' in a dish, but never ever take over the flavour of the main ingredient.

Here are some of my favourites, gathered from my travels across the subcontinent.

Kukhra alainchi sanga
Gurkha cardamom sauce

This is a sauce from the Gurkha people in Nepal, who are famed for their courage and tenacity. Trekking through the Himalayas, trudging up to 4800 metres (16,000 feet), also made me realise how resilient they are, as we were passed in both directions by the same Ghurka speeding up and down the mountain, delivering everything from beer to beds up to base camp, so we could enjoy pizza and beer among the highest peaks in the world.

Try this aromatic sauce with anything from grilled eggplant (aubergine) to Paneer cheese (page 94).

REGION Nepal | **MAKES** 2 x 500 ml (17 fl oz/2 cup) jars | **PREPARATION** 30 minutes
COOKING 25 minutes | **DIFFICULTY** Medium

1 tablespoon rice bran oil
2 white onions, finely chopped
2 cinnamon sticks
4 cloves, crushed
1 teaspoon cumin seeds
1 teaspoon cardamom pods, crushed
1 fresh bay leaf
4 vine-ripened tomatoes, chopped
250 g (9 oz) Greek-style yoghurt

NEPALESE MASALA PASTE
1 brown onion, sliced
2 teaspoons grated fresh ginger
5 green cardamom pods, crushed
5 garlic cloves, crushed
2 teaspoons fennel seeds
1 teaspoon hot chilli powder
2 teaspoons ground cumin
2 teaspoons ground coriander
1 teaspoon ground turmeric

Place all the masala paste ingredients in a food processor and blend until a smooth paste forms. Set aside.

Heat the rice bran oil in a large saucepan over medium heat. Add the onion, cinnamon sticks, cloves, cumin seeds, cardamom pods and bay leaf. Cook, stirring occasionally, for about 5 minutes, or until the onion is golden brown.

Add the masala paste and tomatoes and continue to cook for about 10 minutes, stirring lightly to stop the sauce sticking to the bottom; you will see the oil slowly rising to the surface.

At this stage, carefully stir in 350 ml (12 fl oz) cold water and bring the sauce to the boil. Reduce the heat and leave to simmer for 5–10 minutes, or until the sauce is thick and there is a nice layer of masala-infused oil on top.

Remove the bay leaf and cinnamon sticks, then blend the sauce using a hand-held stick blender. Stir in the yoghurt until well combined.

Spoon into hot sterilised jars, seal and refrigerate. The sauce will keep in the fridge for 1–2 weeks.

Toum
Cold garlic cream sauce

Serve this deliciously simple white sauce with grilled vegetable kebabs, or as a finisher for a salad or rice. It also makes a great dip for naan or any other flat breads.

REGION Afghanistan | **MAKES** 1 x 250 ml (9 fl oz/1 cup) jar
PREPARATION 10 minutes | **DIFFICULTY** Easy

Crush the garlic cloves using a garlic crusher, or chop them as finely as you can. Transfer to a bowl.

Add the salt, then gradually add the rice bran oil, stirring continuously.

Stir in the sour cream, yoghurt and coriander.

Spoon into a sterilised jar, seal and refrigerate.

This sauce will keep in the fridge for 2–3 days; just stir it together really well before using.

10 garlic cloves, peeled
1 teaspoon salt
2½ tablespoons rice bran oil
100 g (3½ oz) sour cream
50 g (1¾ oz) curd or Greek-style yoghurt
1 teaspoon chopped coriander (cilantro)

Kiri hodi

I think of this coconut milk gravy as 'L plates for curry eaters' — a wonderful mild sauce mostly served with steamed breads and the bowl-shaped pancakes known as hoppers, pairing beautifully with them. Several variations exist across the subcontinent.

REGION Sri Lanka | **MAKES** about 750 ml (26 fl oz/3 cups) | **PREPARATION** 10 minutes
COOKING 10 minutes | **DIFFICULTY** Easy

Place the onion, garlic, chilli, curry leaves and pandan leaf in a heavy-based saucepan. Add the goraka, spices and the fish flakes, if using. Stir in 250 ml (9 fl oz/1 cup) water and simmer over low heat for 5 minutes, or until the onion is soft.

Stirring continuously, add the coconut milk, and keep stirring for 1–2 minutes, without letting the mixture boil. It is important to keep stirring the mixture after adding the coconut milk, to stop the milk coagulating.

Remove from the heat, stir in the lime juice and season to taste with the salt. Serve hot.

Any leftovers will keep in the fridge in an airtight container for several days; gently reheat for serving.

1 onion, thinly sliced
2 garlic cloves, thinly sliced
1 small green chilli, halved lengthways
4–6 fresh curry leaves
2 cm (¾ inch) piece of pandan leaf
½ piece of dried goraka
½ teaspoon ground turmeric
½ teaspoon fenugreek seeds
1 teaspoon Maldive fish flakes (optional)
500 ml (17 fl oz/2 cups) thick coconut milk
1 tablespoon lime juice
1 teaspoon salt, or to taste

Pakora dipping sauce with tamarind

More like a tamarind water, this is a very simple version of a tamarind chutney, and is easy to make. Serve as an accompaniment to hot pakoras, such as the Vegetable and chickpea flour fritters on page 40.

REGION Pakistan | **MAKES** 1 x 250 ml (9 fl oz/1 cup) jar
PREPARATION 10 minutes + 1 hour soaking (optional) | **DIFFICULTY** Easy

115 g (4 oz) tamarind pulp
1 teaspoon salt
½ teaspoon chilli powder
2 teaspoons sugar

If your tamarind pulp is very firm, soak it in a bowl of hot water for about 1 hour. Drain the tamarind and push it through a sieve, into a small bowl, discarding the fibres and seeds. Add the remaining ingredients, stir in 125 ml (4 fl oz/½ cup) water and mix until well combined.

If your tamarind pulp is already ground into a paste, then just mash it and mix it with the other ingredients.

Spoon into a sterilised jar, seal and refrigerate. The sauce will keep in the fridge for 1–2 weeks.

Meetha tamatar
Velvet tomato catsup

This fabulously spiced tomato sauce is proudly served across the subcontinent as a sauce with everything from samosas to kebabs, and in my house is eaten on everything. Make it in bulk, adjust the seasonings to suit your family's tastebuds, and you'll never want to buy bottled tomato sauce again.

REGION India | **MAKES** 1 x 250 ml (9 fl oz/1 cup) jar | **PREPARATION** 15 minutes
COOKING 30 minutes | **DIFFICULTY** Easy

2 tablespoons sugar
1½ tablespoons virgin coconut oil
1 fresh bay leaf
1 teaspoon ground cumin
2 teaspoons ground coriander
1 teaspoon Garam masala (page 24)
a pinch of freshly grated nutmeg
a pinch of ground cloves
a pinch of ground ginger
6 very ripe tomatoes, chopped
salt, to taste

In a bowl, combine the sugar and 60 ml (2 fl oz/¼ cup) water, stirring to dissolve the sugar. Set aside.

Heat the coconut oil in a heavy-based saucepan over medium heat. Add the bay leaf and the spices and fry for a few minutes, or until aromatic.

Stir in the tomatoes and the sugar water. Season to taste with salt, then leave to simmer for 20 minutes, or until thick.

Blend using a hand-held stick blender, then pass the mixture through a fine sieve. Spoon into a hot sterilised jar, then seal and leave to cool.

Store in the fridge, and use within 5–7 days.

Kebab sauce

Originating in Iran, the humble kebab found its way throughout the Middle East, and is now popular the world over. This sauce is actually the marinade used to tenderise and flavour beef and chicken kebabs, but will work just as well with vegetable kebabs and cheese. It is also very good with rice.

REGION Afghanistan | **MAKES** 1 x 500 ml (17 fl oz/2 cup) jar | **PREPARATION** 20 minutes
COOKING 10 minutes | **DIFFICULTY** Easy

Liquefy all the ingredients together in a food processor or blender.

Transfer to a saucepan and simmer for about 10 minutes, or until the sauce has thickened slightly and the flavours have set.

Allow to cool slightly, then spoon into a sterilised jar, seal and refrigerate; the sauce will keep in the fridge for up to 1 week.

Use the sauce as a marinade for meat, vegetables or cheese. Allow meat to marinate in it overnight; vegetables and cheese such as Paneer (page 94) will only need about 1 hour.

- 2 onions, peeled
- 250 g (9 oz) plain yoghurt
- juice of 1 lemon
- 1 teaspoon sugar
- ½ teaspoon freshly ground black pepper
- 2 tablespoons ground cumin seeds
- 2 tablespoons ground coriander seeds
- 1 tablespoon Garam masala (page 24)
- ½ teaspoon ground turmeric
- ½ teaspoon ground aleppo pepper, or smoked paprika
- 1 teaspoon fresh Ginger paste (page 241)
- 1 teaspoon fresh Garlic paste (page 241)
- 1 teaspoon chopped fresh coriander (cilantro), or to taste

Afghan white sauce for kebabs
Tzatziki

We know this sauce so well, thanks to all our Middle Eastern brothers and sisters; it is also very Greek and Mediterranean. Light and tangy, it goes with just about anything. Try it with vegetable kebabs and Vegetable jalfrezi (page 145).

REGION Afghanistan | **MAKES** 1 x 500 ml (17 fl oz/2 cup) jar
PREPARATION 15 minutes | **DIFFICULTY** Easy

Peel and grate the cucumber, then place in a blender. Add the salt and blend for about 20 seconds.

Pour the blended cucumber through a strainer to separate the liquid from the pulp. Discard the liquid and place the pulp in a mixing bowl. Add the remaining ingredients and mix well with a wooden spoon.

Cover and refrigerate until ready to serve; it is best made on the day it will be consumed.

- 1 telegraph (long) cucumber
- 1 teaspoon salt
- 250 g (9 oz) Greek-style yoghurt
- 1 teaspoon lemon juice
- 1 teaspoon crushed garlic
- 1 teaspoon olive oil
- 1 teaspoon white vinegar
- ½ teaspoon ground white pepper

Chatni sauce
Hot green sauce

Very similar to the Argentinian chimichurri, this deliciously hot sauce, made with green chillies and fresh herbs, is served in Afghanistan with just about every meal, four seasons of the year. If there is no chatni or 'chatney' in the house, people will use fresh or dry pepper with their meal, to fire their tastebuds.

You'll also find a very similar version of this hot green sauce enjoyed in India, Pakistan and some other countries — so do as all the locals do, and serve it with everything!

REGION Afghanistan | **MAKES** 1 x 250 ml (9 fl oz/1 cup) jar
PREPARATION 20 minutes | **DIFFICULTY** Easy

½ bunch flat-leaf (Italian) parsley
¼ bunch coriander (cilantro)
¼ bunch mint
4 garlic cloves, crushed
2 Indian green chillies, chopped finely
   with the seeds
3 teaspoons lemon or lime juice
30 ml (1 fl oz) white vinegar
½ teaspoon ground cumin
1 teaspoon salt
1 teaspoon freshly cracked black pepper
2 tablespoons olive oil

Very finely chop the parsley, coriander and mint, then place in a bowl.

Add the garlic, chilli, lemon or lime juice, vinegar, cumin, salt and pepper and mix together using a whisk.

Add the oil and continue to whisk until the mixture has emulsified.

Spoon into a sterilised jar, seal and refrigerate. The sauce will keep in the fridge for several days — but you'll be lucky if there is any left by then!

Bring to room temperature for serving.

Yoghurt pakora dipping sauce

Used in cooling drinks and refreshing dipping sauces such as this, as well as for marinating meats for the tandoor, yoghurt has long been an important part of Pakistan's cuisine, thanks to its centuries-old Mughlai influences. The tandoor oven was in fact invented in Pakistan, so feel free to also serve this refreshing sauce with anything pulled out of the tandoor's fiery depths.

REGION Pakistan | **MAKES** 1 x 250 ml (9 fl oz/1 cup) jar
PREPARATION 15 minutes | **DIFFICULTY** Easy

1 tablespoon crushed garlic
1 tablespoon grated fresh ginger
250 g (9 oz) plain yoghurt

Using a mortar and pestle, mix the garlic and ginger together. Transfer to a bowl, add the yoghurt and mix well.

Use straight away, or spoon into a sterilised jar, seal and refrigerate. This sauce will keep in the fridge for 2 days.

Chilli sesame momo dipping sauce

This again is a very familiar sauce, very much like a Mexican salsa roja. If you can cook the tomatoes over coals, you will get that authentic village taste in your sauce. For added smokiness, instead of the three dried long red chillies, you could use three Mexican chipotles, which are dried and smoked jalapeño chillies.

This sauce is great of course with momos (pages 31 and 99), but it could also become your go-to sauce for anything from burgers to grilled paneer cheese.

REGION Nepal | **MAKES** 1 x 375 ml (13 fl oz/1½ cup) jar | **PREPARATION** 15 minutes
COOKING 15 minutes | **DIFFICULTY** Easy

3 tablespoons sesame seeds
5 dried long red chillies
3 tomatoes
3 garlic cloves, unpeeled
1 tablespoon chopped coriander
   (cilantro)
juice of ½ lime

Heat a heavy-based frying pan over medium heat. Add the sesame seeds and toast for about 1 minute, stirring often, until lightly browned. Remove from the pan and set aside.

In the same dry pan, heat the dried chillies for 2–3 minutes, turning every so often to ensure even roasting. Remove from the pan and set aside with the sesame seeds.

Place the tomatoes in the pan with the garlic cloves and cook for 5–7 minutes, or until the tomato skins start to blister.

Transfer the tomatoes to a food processor. Squeeze the garlic cloves, so the beautiful cooked garlic oozes out of the skins, and add them to the tomatoes with the sesame seeds, chillies, coriander and 60 ml (2 fl oz/¼ cup) water. Blend for a minute or two, into a sauce.

Spoon into a sterilised jar, seal and refrigerate. This sauce will keep in the fridge for up to 1 week.

Aam kasundi
Bengali mustard sauce

Enjoy this tangy sauce with tandoori dishes, kebabs, and even on sandwiches.

REGION Bangladesh | **MAKES** 1 x 500 ml (17 fl oz/2 cup) jar
PREPARATION 10 minutes | **DIFFICULTY** Easy

If you have a blender like the ones popular for juicing, use it for this recipe, as it is compact and chops very well. Otherwise a normal blender will do, but it might not crush the mustard seeds — so it may be good to grind them a bit first, using a mortar and pestle.

Add all the ingredients to the blender and blend to a smooth paste.

Spoon into a sterilised jar, seal and refrigerate. This sauce will keep in the fridge for 2 days.

- 3 tablespoons yellow mustard seeds
- 2 teaspoons black mustard seeds
- 300 g (10½ oz) green mango, peeled and grated
- 3 tablespoons chopped green chillies
- ½ teaspoon freshly grated turmeric
- 1½ tablespoons salt
- 1 tablespoon sugar
- 2½ tablespoons malt vinegar
- 60 ml (2 fl oz/¼ cup) mustard oil

Coconut sambal

In Sri Lanka, this fresh sambal is served with nearly every meal. We loved putting a big spoonful of it on our bread, still hot from the bakery next door. You really need fresh coconut for this sambal. When we first arrived in Australia in 1979 it was very hard to get a fresh coconut, so we'd reconstitute the desiccated version with warm water. Not as good as fresh, but acceptable.

I have used paprika here solely to give the sambal its distinctive rich red colour; you can use extra chilli powder if you'd like it very hot.

REGION Sri Lanka | **SERVES** 6 | **PREPARATION** 15 minutes | **DIFFICULTY** Easy

Using a large mortar and pestle, grind the peppercorns. Add the onion, crushing it well. Stir in the chilli powder and paprika and work the mixture into a coarse paste.

Add the coconut and pound together, so the coconut and paste are thoroughly combined.

Add the lime juice a little at a time, making sure the sambal doesn't taste sour, and season to taste with salt.

This sambal will keep in a clean airtight container in the fridge for 2–3 days, or in the freezer for up to 1 month.

- 1 teaspoon black peppercorns
- 60 g (2¼ oz/⅓ cup) chopped red onion
- 2 teaspoons chilli powder
- 1 teaspoon paprika
- 1 large fresh coconut, flesh scraped, or 100 g (3½ oz/1 cup) desiccated coconut soaked in 100 ml (3½ fl oz) water
- juice of 1 lime

Chapter 12

Sweets & Desserts

There is no denying the subcontinent's love for sweets. Far beyond the realm of staple fare, every happy moment is celebrated by sharing sweets.

They are often presented in places of worship as sacred offerings, and play a huge part in socialising, community and hospitality. At festive occasions, weddings and religious ceremonies, sweets are often served before any other foods. When you go and visit people you take sweets; when you arrive you are offered sweets. Sweets are the crux of so many social exchanges across the subcontinent, it would be impossible to imagine life without them.

Most of us have a memory from our childhood centred around the idea of something sweet — something we were allowed on special occasions, or as a treat or reward. When I was little, our families would get together to make the sweets for New Year celebrations. Many of the sweets, particularly the milk toffee, would need continuous stirring, so everyone would be there to give the pot a stir, all the while making jokes, playing music and enjoying each other's company. It was a real coming together of the whole family.

I remember the heat of the markets in Sri Lanka, the saris of my aunties blowing in the hot wind as we traipsed from vendor to vendor so they could sift through the sesame seeds to find the best and freshest for their sesame and palm sugar sweets known as Thala guli (page 271), and the crushing disappointment if the sesame seeds weren't super fresh. It was a massive deal, because you gave those sweets away — those sweets were a representation of us, of our home, and of our kitchen. Growing up, such things were sacrosanct.

Many desserts and sweets across the subcontinent typically feature curdled milks, sugar, nuts and spices, while many are deep-fried and coated in sugar. The date palms that thrive in the tropical climate provide a delicate sugar called nolen gur, which is used in desserts such as the dense, fudgy bites of sweetened cheese known as sandesh.

In this chapter I've tried to include a range of desserts and sweets representative of the subcontinent, from sweet and creamy rice pudding, to rosewater-scented sheer pira, to cooling lassis that are sweet enough to double as dessert.

I am sure you will enjoy them.

Tsampa
Apricot, sesame & barley malt balls

These flavour bombs are great for an energy boost. You can add other ingredients, including more dried fruit; you can even soak the dried fruit in freshly squeezed fruit juice, or even rice bran extract — but not too much, just enough to bind it all.

Once rolled, the mixture will firm up during chilling. Just let everyone know these treats are in the fridge and they will disappear very quickly.

REGION Bangladesh | **SERVES** 6 | **PREPARATION** 10 minutes + 1 hour chilling
COOKING 10 minutes | **DIFFICULTY** Easy

100 g (3½ oz/⅔ cup) pepitas
   (pumpkin seeds)
100 g (3½ oz/⅔ cup) sesame seeds
100 g (3½ oz/½ cup) dried apricots,
   finely chopped
100 g (3½ oz/4 cups) puffed rice
60 ml (2 fl oz/¼ cup) barley malt extract

Preheat the oven to 180°C (350°F).

Spread the pepitas on a baking tray and bake for 3–4 minutes, or until lightly toasted. Transfer to a large bowl and leave to cool, then crush them using a mortar and pestle or blender, so they are roughly broken. Place them back in the bowl.

Spread the sesame seeds on the baking tray and bake for a few minutes, until lightly toasted. Crush the sesame seeds using a mortar and pestle, then add them to the bowl of pepitas.

Add the dried apricot and puffed rice and mix together. Drizzle the barley malt extract over the mixture and mix to coat all the ingredients.

Using wet hands, form the mixture into balls about the size of golf balls.

Cover and place in the fridge to firm for 1 hour before serving.

The tsampa should be consumed in a day or two, or the puffed rice will become soggy — but they will still taste great!

TIP Across the subcontinent, dried fruits, including mulberries and green raisins, are used for cooking, snacking and as a sweet treat after meals. Dried plums are a popular cooking ingredient and impart a sweet and sour flavour, while sultanas (golden raisins) make a regular appearance in rice dishes.

Pani pol
Spiced coconut pancakes

WOW is what I think of this dessert. Coconut, palm treacle and spices: these luscious pancakes have all the things Sri Lanka is known for. You can make them beforehand and enjoy them at room temperature, or have them warm with ice cream. They are especially delicious with coconut or vanilla ice cream.

REGION Sri Lanka | **SERVES** 6 (2 pancakes per person) | **PREPARATION** 20 minutes
COOKING 4 minutes per pancake | **DIFFICULTY** Medium

PANCAKE BATTER

2 eggs
75 g (2½ oz/½ cup) plain flour
300 ml (10½ fl oz) milk
60 ml (2 fl oz/¼ cup) rice bran oil,
    plus extra for greasing
a pinch of ground turmeric, to colour
    the mixture

COCONUT FILLING

350 g (12 oz/1 cup) palm treacle
55 g (2 oz/¼ cup, tightly packed) grated
    palm sugar (jaggery)
2 cardamom pods, lightly crushed
2 cloves
½ cinnamon stick
1 vanilla bean, split lengthways,
    seeds scraped
160 g (5½ oz/2 cups) freshly grated
    coconut, or thawed frozen coconut

In a bowl or blender, mix all the batter ingredients together until smooth and lump free; the batter should be thick enough to coat the back of a spoon. If there are any lumps, strain the mixture through a sieve into a clean bowl.

Place a non-stick frying pan or cured cast-iron pan over low heat. Lightly apply some more rice bran oil onto the pan with a paper towel.

Using a ladle, add a thin layer of the pancake batter to the pan. Cook for about 2 minutes, trying not to let it colour, then flip it over and cook on the other side for a further 2 minutes. Transfer to a plate and repeat with the remaining batter, oiling the pan only as needed; the less oil the better.

For the filling, add the treacle, palm sugar, cardamom pods, cloves and cinnamon stick and vanilla bean pod to a small heavy-based saucepan and place over medium heat. Cook, stirring now and then, for about 5 minutes, or until the treacle boils and all the sugar has dissolved. Do not cook too long, or the treacle will caramelise and it will set too hard, into toffee. Remove the aromatics, add the vanilla seeds and coconut and stir until the coconut is warm and well coated with the treacle mixture.

To serve, place a tablespoon of filling into a pancake and roll it up, folding in the sides. Enjoy warm or cold.

TIP Palm treacle is produced from the sap of the flower from the kithul (or fishtail) palm. This delicious syrup is a primary ingredient in the Sri Lankan dessert, 'curds and honey'. It can also be fermented to produce a 'toddy', which is used as a raising agent instead of yeast.

Sweet millet fruit balls

I recently spotted millet growing in an organic garden, among all these beautiful organic vegetables, and it reminded me of a time in Sikkim, in India, where I drank a fermented millet drink, the local liquor in those parts. As I drank it I noticed that a whole lot of grubs were clinging onto the sides of my bamboo cup — so I have never forgotten millet.

Nonetheless, millet is a very healthy grain. Crystal Maymann, an organic farmer on Queensland's Sunshine Coast, told me she only used her millet to feed her chickens, which got me thinking about the various uses for this wonder food, and became the inspiration for these nutritious treats below.

REGION Nepal, Bhutan | **MAKES** 24–30 | **PREPARATION** 30 minutes + 30 minutes chilling
COOKING 25 minutes | **DIFFICULTY** Easy

Preheat the oven to 170°C (325°F).

Rinse the millet and place in a saucepan with the agave syrup and enough apple juice to cover the millet. Bring to the boil, then reduce the head and simmer for about 20 minutes. The apple juice will reduce, and when you can see the top of the millet, it's ready.

Transfer the mixture to a bowl and allow to cool in the fridge.

While the millet is cooking, spread the sesame seeds and pepitas on a baking tray and roast in the oven for 7–10 minutes, or until golden, stirring occasionally. Using a mortar and pestle, grind the roasted seeds to a powder and set aside.

Warm the malt syrup in a saucepan over medium heat.

In a large mixing bowl, mix together the apricots, puffed rice and coconut flour. Add the millet and lime juice. Pour the hot syrup over the mixture and mix until thoroughly coated, using a spoon. Set aside.

Mix the sugar and cocoa powder in a shallow dish. With some of the sugar dust on your hands, roll the millet mixture into balls, around 5 cm (2 inches) in diameter. Keep dusting your hands with more sugar, to help stop the mixture sticking to them.

Refrigerate until serving, and enjoy individually as a healthy energy boost. They will keep in the fridge in an airtight container for several days; you might want to dust them first with cocoa powder if making them ahead.

200 g (7 oz/1 cup) hulled millet
2 tablespoons agave syrup
500 ml (17 fl oz/2 cups) apple juice, approximately
100 g (3½ oz/⅔ cup) sesame seeds
100 g (3½ oz/⅔ cup) pepitas (pumpkin seeds)
60 ml (2 fl oz/¼ cup) malt syrup
100 g (3½ oz/½ cup) dried apricots, chopped
30 g (1 oz/1¼ cups) puffed rice
2 tablespoons coconut flour
80 ml (2½ fl oz/⅓ cup) lime juice
100 g (3½ oz/½ cup) rapadura sugar
2 tablespoons unsweetened cocoa powder

Sheer pira
Afghan rosewater milk fudge

Meaning 'sweet milk' in the Dari language, sheer pera is a delicacy served at Afghan weddings and parties. It will delight your senses, and those of your guests, with its enticing flavours of rosewater, cardamom, walnut and pistachio.

REGION Afghanistan | **MAKES** about 25 pieces | **PREPARATION** 30 minutes
COOKING 15–20 minutes + cooling | **DIFFICULTY** Easy

Place the sugar in a saucepan, add 500 ml (17 fl oz/2 cups) water and stir until the sugar has dissolved. Bring to the boil, turn the heat down to medium and simmer for about 15 minutes, until the syrup thickens and reaches the 'soft ball stage', or 105–110°C (220–230°C) on a sugar thermometer.

Test by putting a small drop of the syrup on a plate; the syrup should be thick, and it should glide very slowly around the plate.

While the syrup is bubbling away, mix together the milk powder, cardamom, rosewater, walnuts and apricots in a bowl. Line a 20 cm (8 inch) square cake tin or another deep heatproof dish with baking paper and lightly grease the paper.

As soon as the syrup is ready, stir it through the milk powder mixture, then pour it into the cake tin or dish. Scatter the pistachios and almonds over the top.

Leave to cool to room temperature. Cut into 5 cm (2 inch) squares or diamonds to serve, garnished with flecks of edible silver leaf if desired.

The fudge will keep in an airtight container for 2–4 weeks; it is best stored at cool room temperature, rather than in the fridge, layered between sheets of baking paper.

440 g (15½ oz/2 cups) caster (superfine) sugar
440 g (15½ oz/4 cups) milk powder
2 teaspoons ground cardamom
2 tablespoons rosewater
75 g (2½ oz/½ cup) roasted walnuts or almonds, chopped
100 g (3½ oz/½ cup) dried apricots, chopped
melted butter, for greasing
70 g (2½ oz/½ cup) finely chopped pistachios
65 g (2¼ oz/½ cup) slivered almonds
edible silver leaf, to garnish (optional)

Banana, coconut & cardamom samosas

Samosas have been around for centuries, in many forms, and probably travelled to India along ancient trade routes from Central Asia, making it as far west as Egypt and Zanzibar, and eastwards to China. While we usually think of them as savoury snacks, in India sweet samosas are common enough too, especially for celebrating festivals such as Holi and Diwali.

These delightful samosas are baked, but they can also be lightly fried in vegetable oil.

REGION India | **MAKES** 10 | **PREPARATION** 30 minutes
COOKING 10 minutes | **DIFFICULTY** Medium

2 large very ripe bananas
60 g (2¼ oz/⅔ cup) desiccated coconut
2 teaspoons freshly ground cardamom
    seeds
1½ tablespoons crumbled palm sugar
    (jaggery) or muscovado sugar
20 filo pastry sheets
100 g (3½ oz) butter, melted, for brushing
icing (confectioners') sugar, for dusting

CHAI CHOCOLATE DRIZZLE
10 pieces of dark chocolate
1 teaspoon salted butter
1 teaspoon spiced chai tea leaves,
    ground using a mortar and pestle

Preheat the oven to 200°C (400°F).

To make the samosa filling, mash the bananas in a bowl, add the coconut, cardamom and palm sugar and mix together well.

Place two filo pastry sheets on top of each other, covering the remaining filo sheets with a tea towel to stop them drying out. Place 1 heaped teaspoon of the banana mixture at one corner and fold the pastry into a triangle, covering the filling. Brush the melted butter on the pastry surface as you keep folding, until you reach the end of the pastry. Stick the loose corners together with a little more melted butter.

Repeat with the remaining filling and pastry, to make 10 triangles, placing them on a baking tray lined with baking paper. Brush the samosas with more melted butter and bake for 3–4 minutes, or until light brown.

To make the chai chocolate drizzle, melt the chocolate in a heatproof glass bowl over a saucepan of simmering water, ensuring the base of the bowl isn't sitting in the water. Stir in the butter until everything is evenly melted, then stir in the ground tea leaves.

To serve, dust the samosas with icing sugar and lightly drizzle with the chai chocolate drizzle. The samosas are best served warm.

Gosh-e-feel
Elephant-ear pastries

Very simple to prepare, this is another Afghan sweet that is served on special occasions. It is made by shaping some dough into the shape of a baby elephant's ear, deep-frying it, and sprinkling with sugar and finely chopped nuts.

REGION Afghanistan | **MAKES** 30–40 | **PREPARATION** 20 minutes + 2 hours resting
COOKING 20 minutes | **DIFFICULTY** Medium

In a large mixing bowl, beat the eggs, sugar and salt until light and frothy, using an electric mixer. Add the milk and rice bran oil and continue beating until smooth.

Add 150 g (5½ oz/1 cup) of the flour to the egg mixture, blending thoroughly.

Blend in another 150 g (5½ oz/1 cup) of the flour.

Sprinkle some of the remaining flour over your work surface, then turn the dough out onto it. Sprinkle the dough with more flour and knead for 10 minutes, sprinkling with more flour as needed. The dough will be somewhat sticky, but with a smooth gloss to it. Cover with plastic wrap and leave to rest at room temperature for 2 hours.

When you're ready to start cooking, pour about 10 cm (4 inches) of vegetable oil into a heavy-based saucepan and heat to 180°C (350°F), or until a cube of bread dropped into the oil turns brown in 15 seconds.

Pull off a piece of dough about the size of a large cherry tomato and roll it into a flat 9–10 cm (3½–4 inch) oval. Take one side of the oval and fold it over to the other side, crimping the edges together, so it resembles an elephant's ear. Repeat with the remaining dough.

Working in batches, add the pastries to the hot oil and cook for 2–5 minutes on each side, until golden, turning to cook them evenly. Remove and drain on paper towel. When cooled, sprinkle with the icing sugar and nuts.

Serve immediately, or store in an airtight container at cool room temperature. The pastries will keep for 3–4 days.

2 eggs
2 teaspoons caster (superfine) sugar
¼ teaspoon salt
125 ml (4 fl oz/½ cup) milk
60 ml (2 fl oz/¼ cup) rice bran oil
375 g (13 oz/2½ cups) plain (all-purpose) flour
vegetable oil, for deep-frying
125 g (4½ oz/1 cup) icing (confectioners') sugar
65 g (2¼ oz/½ cup) finely chopped pistachios or walnuts

Gulab jamun

Literally translating as 'rose berry' ('gulab' means 'rose', and 'jamun' is a dark purple berry native to the subcontinent), gulab jamun is of one of India's most loved sweets. Traditionally the recipe calls for mawa, or milk that has been reduced down to a paste, but we're simply using milk powder for these deliciously soft melt-in-the-mouth sweets. You can serve them warm, cold or chilled on their own, or garnished with pistachios, or stuffed with nuts or a piece of popcorn. I serve them warm, with a scoop of ice cream.

REGION India | **MAKES** 10–12 | **PREPARATION** 15 minutes + 30 minutes standing + 1 hour soaking
COOKING about 5 minutes per batch | **DIFFICULTY** Medium

110 g (3¾ oz/1 cup) full-fat milk powder
35 g (1¼ oz/¼ cup) plain (all-purpose) flour
a pinch of salt (optional)
a pinch of bicarbonate of soda (baking soda)
1–2 tablespoons Greek-style yoghurt
½ teaspoon ghee
10–12 pieces of sweet makhana/elaichi dana (sugar-coated cardamom seeds)
500 ml (17 fl oz/2 cups) vegetable oil, for deep-frying
blanched pistachio or almond slices, to garnish

ORANGE BLOSSOM SYRUP
330 g (11½ oz/1½ cups) sugar
3–4 green cardamom pods, husked, seeds crushed or powdered
a pinch of saffron threads
1 teaspoon orange blossom water or rosewater

To make the syrup, put the sugar and 500 ml (17 fl oz/2 cups) water in a heavy-based saucepan and cook over medium heat for about 5 minutes, until the sugar has dissolved completely, stirring occasionally. Cook the syrup to the 'soft ball' stage, or 105–110°C (220–230°C) on a sugar thermometer. You can test the syrup by drizzling 1–2 drops on a plate. It should be gooey in texture when rolled between your thumb and index finger, or form threads when drizzled from a small height.

Stir in the cardamom seeds and orange blossom water, then remove from the heat.

To make the gulab jamun, sift the milk powder, flour, salt and bicarbonate of soda into a mixing bowl. Add the yoghurt and ghee and lightly mix the ingredients to make a soft, sticky dough. (Don't add too much flour, as it can make the gulab jamun hard.)

Now pinch off a small portion and put a piece of elaichi dana in the middle. Bring the sides up around it, rolling it into a smooth ball about the size of a large walnut. Make sure there are no cracks on the surface, or the ball will break during cooking. Repeat with the remaining dough.

Pour the vegetable oil into a deep heavy-based saucepan and heat to 160°C (315°F), or until a cube of bread dropped into the oil turns brown in 30–35 seconds.

Working in batches, gently slide the gulab jamun into the hot oil and cook for about 3–5 minutes, until golden, taking care not to overcrowd the pan, to keep the oil at the right temperature. The balls will sink to the bottom, then gently rise up. At frequent intervals, slowly turn each ball with a slotted spoon, to ensure they brown evenly.

Drain on paper towel, then soak the gulab jamun in the orange blossom syrup for at least 1 hour, so they absorb and soften in the syrup. (If serving them cold, remove them from the syrup and store them in the fridge in an airtight container.) Serve garnished with nuts.

TIP Before shaping all the gulab jamun, test one by deep-frying it in the oil. If it splits, add a little more milk powder into the mixture; if it is getting hard, add 1–2 teaspoons milk.

Kheer
Rice pudding

Also known as payasam, this recipe was taught to me by a builder on a beautiful island in Fiji in the 1990s. It is a great dessert, and a fun alternative to the standard rice pudding.

REGION India | **SERVES** 2 | **PREPARATION** 15 minutes
COOKING about 1 hour | **DIFFICULTY** Easy

In a non-stick saucepan, warm the ghee over medium heat. Add the chopped nuts, along with the raisins. Cook for about 5 minutes, or until the raisins become plump and the nuts turn reddish brown, stirring often. Transfer to a small bowl and set aside.

In the same pan, toast the rice grains for 2–3 minutes over low heat.

Stir in the milk, increase the heat to medium–high and bring to the boil. Reduce the heat to medium and cook for about 15 minutes, until the milk has reduced by half, stirring regularly, to ensure the milk does not stick to the bottom of the pan. Also take care not to let the milk burn, as even a little burn will spoil the flavour.

Stir in the sugar until dissolved, then add the vermicelli noodles and cook for a further 20–30 minutes, or until the milk has reduced further, and the rice is cooked and has a soft, but not mushy, consistency.

Stir in the saffron, cardamom and half the sautéed nut and raisin mixture.

Serve warm or cold, garnished with the remaining nuts and raisins.

1 teaspoon ghee
1–2 tablespoons nuts — a mixture of almonds, pistachios and cashews
1 tablespoon raisins or currants
55 g (2 oz/¼ cup) short or medium-grain white rice
1.25 litres (44 fl oz/5 cups) full-cream milk
55 g (2 oz/¼ cup) caster (superfine) sugar
25 g (1 oz/¼ cup) broken-up dried rice vermicelli noodles
a pinch of saffron threads
¼ teaspoon ground cardamom

Kulfi
Cardamom iceblock

The subcontinent's favourite ice cream, kulfi is cleansing, cooling and invigorating. It is flavoured with beautiful spices from its Persian origins, and can also contain fruit such as mango or banana. When it is very hot and you need to cool down, the energy hit from this frozen dessert will get you moving again.

REGION Pakistan | **MAKES** 10–12 if using shot glasses | **PREPARATION** 20 minutes + overnight chilling | **COOKING** 15 minutes | **DIFFICULTY** Easy

---

6 green cardamom pods
500 ml (17 fl oz/2 cups) milk
500 ml (17 fl oz/2 cups) thick (double) cream
300 g (10½ oz/1 scant cup) condensed milk
50 g (1¾ oz) blanched almonds, ground
50 g (1¾ oz) pistachios, ground
1 teaspoon ground cardamom
1 teaspoon rosewater
50 g (1¾ oz/⅓ cup) roasted crushed pistachios, to garnish

Remove the cardamom seeds from their pods. Using a mortar and pestle, crush the seeds until they resemble freshly cracked black pepper. Set aside.

Place a heavy-based saucepan over medium heat. Add the milk, cream and crushed cardamom seeds. Bring to the boil, then add the condensed milk, stirring constantly. Add the almonds, pistachios and ground cardamom.

Once the mixture returns to the boil, reduce the heat to low. Cook gently, stirring every 5 minutes or so, for about 10 minutes, or until the mixture has reduced by half. A skin will form on top; just keep stirring it in.

Remove from the heat and stir in the rosewater. Allow to cool for 15–20 minutes.

Slowly pour the mixture into iceblock (popsicle/ice lolly) moulds or shot glasses, then place in the freezer.

After about 30 minutes, when the kulfi is starting to set, place popsicle or ice cream sticks in each mould or glass.

Return to the freezer and freeze overnight, or for at least 8 hours; the kulfi will also keep for a few days, if making ahead.

To un-mould the kulfi, quickly dip each mould or glass in warm water to loosen them, then turn out onto a small plate.

Sprinkle with the roasted crushed pistachios and serve.

Thala guli
Sesame & palm sugar sweets

This is one of my favourite ways to eat sesame seeds, and conjures many memories of my time in Sri Lanka. As a child, I was also in awe of their exquisite presentation — these lovely balls of goodness were usually wrapped in white crepe paper, which was intricately cut to be frilly and beautiful.

REGION Sri Lanka | **MAKES** 10 | **PREPARATION** 15 minutes
COOKING 5 minutes | **DIFFICULTY** Easy

Place the sesame seeds and coconut in a hot dry frying pan. Roast over medium heat, stirring regularly so they don't burn, for about 3 minutes, until they are hot but not brown; the idea is to 'activate' the oil in the sesame seeds.

Crush the palm sugar using a mortar and pestle. Add two-thirds of the roasted sesame seed and coconut mixture to the mortar, along with the salt, and pound everything together until you have a lovely thick paste. Place the remaining roasted sesame seed and coconut mixture in a spice grinder and blitz into a powder, then add it to the crushed mixture. (You can use a blender to grind the entire sesame seed mixture — just take care it doesn't become too fine, as these balls are meant to have lots of texture and bite to them.)

If the texture is too crumbly, add a little more palm sugar and a little more coconut oil to help bind the mixture together.

Take a heaped teaspoon of the mixture and push it into a clean plastic tube, about 5 cm (2 inches) long and 2 cm (¾ inch) wide, pushing down hard so it sticks together, then push it out with a wooden spoon, to give you a nice cylinder of the sweet. Alternatively, use your hands to roll the mixture into a little ball, slightly smaller than a golf ball. Repeat with the remaining mixture.

Serve with a cup of black tea.

The sweets will keep for a week or so, in an airtight container at cool room temperature.

200 g (7 oz/1⅓ cups) raw sesame seeds
50 g (1¾ oz/⅔ cup) freshly grated coconut
100 g (3½ oz) palm sugar (jaggery)
a pinch of salt
1 teaspoon virgin coconut oil (optional)

Cinnamon & cassia
Worlds apart

Cinnamon and cassia are often confused as being one and the same, but these two spices are vastly different in terms of their origin, appearance, health aspects, price and, most importantly, their flavour profiles.

A cross the subcontinent, 'Ceylon cinnamon', or 'true' cinnamon is used, and it is important to source it when cooking these recipes, as it will have a huge impact on the final taste.

Disappointingly, an entire generation of cooks is growing up thinking that cassia is cinnamon. I have seen this in many restaurants, as well as large hotels, where the purchasing manager buys cassia, assuming it is cinnamon, just better priced. I am continually trying to educate people as to the differences between the two.

True cinnamon, or Ceylon cinnamon (*Cinnamomum verum*, formerly known as *Cinnamomum zeylanicum*), grows in Sri Lanka, Madagascar and the Seychelles, while cassia (*Cinnamomum cassia*) comes from Indonesia and China. While they both grow on tropical evergreen trees related to the bay laurel, avocado and sassafras, the two spices are distinctly different — although often sold to us as one and the same.

I do have to ask: if cassia is as good as cinnamon, then why do people try to label it as cinnamon? Just call it cassia! Instead, I have seen cassia labelled as 'Chinese cinnamon', 'cinnamon bark' and even 'cinnamon'! Some countries do understand the difference — in Mexico, where cinnamon is blended into chocolate, they will always tell you that the best cinnamon (or 'canela' as it is known in Spanish) is from Ceylon, as Sri Lanka was formerly known.

Do a taste test and I guarantee you will be able to tell the difference.

TASTE AND SMELL THE DIFFERENCE

Cassia has a very sweet, pungent aroma, and a stronger and more intense flavour than true cinnamon, which is often used for sweetness, whereas cassia is often added for its peppery taste, and becomes almost bitter when used to excess, due to its higher level of cinnamaldehyde.

Ceylon cinnamon is also considered to be safer than cassia as it contains less coumarin, a chemical compound that is moderately toxic to the liver and kidneys.

Cassia is what most bakers use, and what you'd be tasting in their cinnamon doughnuts and apple strudels.

SEE THE DIFFERENCE

True cinnamon sticks (or 'quills') have many concentric layers of paper-thin bark, rolled tightly into cylinders that look a bit like small cigars. They are often about 8 cm (3¼ inches) long and 1 cm (½ inch) in diameter.

Cassia bark can take the form of dark brown slivers, around 10 cm (4 inches) long and a few centimetres (about an inch) wide; the slivers will be smooth on one side and rough on the other. It can also be sold in sticks or quills, which look smooth on the outside; however, they will form a single scroll, unlike the numerous layers of Ceylon cinnamon.

Ceylon cinnamon is tan in colour, while cassia is a darker reddish brown.

Ground cassia and cinnamon look very similar, making it harder to differentiate between them — but if you add a pinch of iodine, pure cinnamon remains unaffected, while cassia takes on a deep blue tint.

APPRECIATE THE DIFFERENCE

True cinnamon, harvested principally in Sri Lanka, comes from the bark of *Cinnamomum verum*, a smallish, shrub-like tree.

Most cassia comes from the bark of taller, birch-like trees also belonging to the cinnamon family, *Cinnamomum cassia*, originally from China, and now grown throughout South-East Asia.

Both kinds of spices are harvested almost entirely by hand, without the use of chemicals. Workers use knives to remove the tree's rough outer bark, and then carefully loosen and peel away the tender, oil-rich inner bark in long, unbroken strips. The inner bark is set out to dry for several days; as moisture in the bark evaporates, the strips curl tightly into narrow quills, which are taken to market whole, broken into chips, or ground to a powder. In some places the rough outer layer is left intact and the bark is sold in thicker, woody pieces.

Harvesting cassia differs from cinnamon in that the whole tree is cut down, before the bark is removed and dried. For this reason, cassia is often seen in many different shapes and sizes, depending on which part of the tree it was harvested from. Large 'chips' of bark come from the trunk and thick branches, while the smaller quills (that many people confuse with cinnamon quills) have come from the small upper branches.

Cinnamon quills are tightly rolled, concentric layers of the very thin underlayer of bark, which has been carefully peeled off cut branches, and then rolled by cinnamon peelers into metre-long quills, like giant cigars, before being cut to size for selling.

NO SUBSTITUTE FOR QUALITY

Ceylon cinnamon is expensive, which is why cassia is often used instead. Unless labelled (and priced) accordingly, cassia cinnamon is the kind your supermarket will most likely stock.

My key advice for cooking is to use the real thing. There is no substitute for the natural sweetness and goodness of true Ceylon cinnamon.

Peray
Bengali cottage cheese dessert

Really sweet and typically Asian, this is a great never-fail recipe. It makes a lovely one-off desert, or another addition to your subcontinental high tea. It is best made a day ahead, to give it time to set.

REGION Bangladesh | **MAKES** 6 | **PREPARATION** 20 minutes + 30 minutes chilling
COOKING 10 minutes | **DIFFICULTY** Easy

250 g (9 oz/2¾ cups) desiccated coconut
150 g (5½ oz/1 cup) pistachios
250 g (9 oz) cottage cheese
250 g (9 oz/2¼ cups) milk powder
240 g (8½ oz/¾ cup) condensed milk
3 drops of pandan extract

In a heavy-based frying pan, over medium heat, roast half the coconut for about 3–5 minutes, until light golden brown, stirring regularly so it doesn't burn. Remove to a plate and leave to cool.

In the same pan, roast the pistachios until lightly browned, then tip them onto a chopping board. Leave to cool, then roughly chop and set aside.

Place the cottage cheese, milk powder, condensed milk and pandan extract in a blender and mix until thoroughly combined. Add the roasted coconut and mix again until incorporated.

Transfer the mixture to a container and chill in the fridge for 30 minutes.

Spread the remaining desiccated coconut on a tray. With wet hands, shape the chilled cheese mixture into golf ball–sized balls and roll them in the coconut.

Slightly flatten them out and push a small dent into the top. Fill each dent with chopped roasted pistachios.

If possible, leave to set overnight in an airtight container at cool room temperature before serving.

Chapter 13
Drinks

I will never forget my first mango lassi. I had just finished my cooking apprenticeship and was backpacking in the Himalayas, surviving on $10 a day for a year and a half.

✵✵✵

My room in Kathmandu was dark and dingy, the opposite of palatial, and the morning trip of getting out onto the streets and into the bazaar for breakfast became quite a ritual.

I can still smell the streets, feel the morning heat, and see how people would listen keenly for the voices of the mobile vendors moving through main streets and alleyways chanting 'Chai!', 'Chai garam!' or 'Lassi!', proffering drinks for a sweet hit or a refreshing bout of sourness. And why not? It was lovely and social, and there was always a theatre and show by the vendors. And a train journey across the Indian subcontinent would not be complete without masala chai — they go hand in hand.

Some people on the subcontinent are so poor they may only have one or two meals a day — and a beverage, be it sweet or sour, or based on thick yoghurt, helps them through the day. And the sweet sugar hit gives them a shot of energy to get back into work, for which they might earn a meagre 10 rupees a day.

This is what is so distinctive about the drinks of the subcontinent — each has its own purpose, whether it is for an energy hit, for a shot of sourness to activate the mouth, a lick of salt to encourage sweating to cool down in the heat, or yoghurt-based to help protect the gut. I wouldn't have understood this had my upbringing been more European; I wouldn't have experienced how the different cultures of the subcontinent attribute meaning to drinks as being nourishing and good for them. They are so firm in the belief that their beverages are healthy. To them, a beverage is not just a drink, but a way of life, steeped in meaning.

The following recipes will, I hope, give you a taste of the sheer variety of drinks on offer across the subcontinent, and their place in everyday life.

Dogh
Yoghurt, cucumber & mint drink

Dogh is an Afghani yoghurt drink that is usually enjoyed either after a meal, or with lunch on a hot summer day. Served cold, it has a crisp, refreshing quality thanks to the cucumber and mint, which beautifully complement the creaminess of the yoghurt.

REGION Afghanistan | **SERVES** 4 | **PREPARATION** 10 minutes | **DIFFICULTY** Easy

400 g (14 oz) plain yoghurt
500 ml (17 fl oz/2 cups) chilled water
1 large telegraph (long) cucumber,
  chopped into small cubes
¼ bunch mint, chopped
a pinch of salt

Mix together the yoghurt and water. Add the cucumber, mint and salt and stir well to combine.

Chill until ready to serve, or serve immediately over ice.

Mango lassi

The first time I had a mango lassi I was listening to Bob Marley and eating a banana pancake. Everything seemed right with the world. It was amazing. I still make mango lassis all the time — they are such a refreshing and healthy way to start the day.

REGION Nepal, India, Sri Lanka | **SERVES** 2 | **PREPARATION** 10 minutes | **DIFFICULTY** Easy

flesh of 3 ripe mangoes, or 2 cups frozen
  mango slices
95 g (3¼ oz/⅓ cup) buffalo curd or
  Greek-style yoghurt
500 ml (17 fl oz/2 cups) milk
1 tablespoon sugar, or 1 teaspoon salt,
  depending on whether you'd like
  your lassi sweet or salty
juice of 1 lime
ice cubes or crushed ice, to serve
2 lemon slices, to serve

Add the mango, buffalo curd, milk and sugar or salt to a blender. Pulse, then blend for 2 minutes, until the mixture is thick but not runny.

Adjust the sweetness or saltiness to taste. Add a squeeze of lime juice and blitz again.

Add some ice cubes or crushed ice to two glasses. Pour in the lassi mixture and serve each with a slice of lemon.

Falooda

Perfect for long hot days, falooda is available all over the subcontinent. It originated in Shiraz, Iran (a country formerly known as Persia), and is one of the oldest drinks we know of. The word 'falooda' means 'shredded', because this olden-day slushie originally contained vermicelli noodles. Traditionally, ice made from frozen sugar syrup was crushed and mixed with rice noodles and rosewater, then topped with lime juice or with strawberry, sour cherry or pomegranate syrup.

My version and many others now have differing ingredients, but the rosewater syrup is the key to this lovely drink.

REGION India, Sri Lanka, Afghanistan, Bangladesh, Nepal | **SERVES** 2
PREPARATION 20 minutes + 3–4 hours setting | **COOKING** 20 minutes | **DIFFICULTY** Medium

1–2 teaspoons sweet basil seeds
250 ml (9 fl oz/1 cup) cold milk
(or camel's milk, if available)

ROSEWATER SYRUP
385 g (13½ oz/1¾ cups) sugar
a pinch of salt
435 ml (15¼ fl oz/1¾ cups) rosewater
60 ml (2 fl oz/¼ cup) corn syrup
(optional, to stop the syrup
crystallising)
3 teaspoons good-quality natural
vanilla extract
a few drops of pink food colouring
(or as much or as little as you prefer)

STRAWBERRY JELLY
1 titanium-strength gelatine leaf
125 ml (4 fl oz/½ cup) moscato or clear
apple juice
1 tablespoon caster (superfine) sugar
1 tablespoon fresh strawberry purée

To make the rosewater syrup, put the sugar, salt and 375 ml (13 fl oz/1½ cups) of the rosewater in a saucepan. Add the corn syrup, if using. Bring to the boil, stirring occasionally to dissolve the sugar. Stir in the vanilla extract. Reduce the heat to low and simmer for about 10 minutes, or until the mixture has a nice thick, syrupy consistency. Remove from the heat and leave to cool to room temperature. Add the remaining 60 ml (2 fl oz/¼ cup) rosewater and stir to combine. Add the food colouring, a drop at a time, and mix until you get a dark pink colour.

To make the strawberry jelly, soak the gelatine leaves in 125 ml (4 fl oz/½ cup) cold water until soft. Meanwhile, bring the moscato and sugar to a simmer in a small saucepan, then leave to cool. Stir in the strawberry purée, add the soaked gelatine leaves (including the water) and whisk until dissolved. Pour into a small container and leave to set in the fridge for 3–4 hours.

Near serving time, soak the basil seeds in 125 ml (4 fl oz/½ cup) water for about 10 minutes, or until they form a gel coating. Drain the seeds and set aside.

Cut the strawberry jelly into 1 cm (½ inch) cubes. (You may not need all the strawberry jelly for this recipe. The remainder will keep in the fridge for several days, to use in your next falooda or other desserts.)

To serve, pour the milk into two glasses. To create a layered effect, slowly pour in the rosewater syrup, using about 50 ml (1½ fl oz) syrup per glass, or to taste. The remaining syrup will keep in an airtight container in the fridge for several months.

Fill the bottom of each glass with jelly cubes. Sprinkle with the reserved basil seeds and serve.

Rose sharbat

'Sharbat' is derived from the Arabic word 'sharbah', meaning 'a drink', and is a syrup made from fruits or extracts of flowers and herbs. The syrup is diluted with water and served with ice. It is a very cooling beverage during the hot summers across India.

REGION India | **SERVES** 2 | **PREPARATION** 30 minutes + cooling + 8 hours steeping | **DIFFICULTY** Easy

Crush the rose petals using a mortar and pestle, to release their fragrance. Place them in a large heatproof bowl and pour the boiling water over them. Pour the mixture into a non-reactive container and add the cardamom seeds. Set aside in the fridge to steep for 8 hours, or overnight.

Line a strainer with muslin (cheesecloth) and set it over a heatproof bowl. Pour the rose and cardamom-scented water through the strainer. Add the sugar to the bowl, then float the bowl in a sink full of hot water until the sugar has dissolved.

Remove the bowl from the hot water. Filter the liquid again through the lined strainer, into a clean bowl. Leave to cool to room temperature.

Pour the liquid into a jug. Add the pomegranate juice, lemon juice and chilled water, stirring well.

Serve straight away, in glasses half filled with crushed ice.

1½ cups freshly picked rose petals; make sure they are unsprayed
185 ml (6 fl oz/¾ cup) boiling water
¼ teaspoon cardamom seeds
75 g (2½ oz/⅓ cup) sugar
170 ml (5½ fl oz/⅔ cup) pomegranate juice
60 ml (2 fl oz/¼ cup) strained lemon juice
1.25 litres (44 fl oz/5 cups) chilled water
crushed ice, to serve

Pulling tea

Wherever you are in Sri Lanka, India or the subcontinent, you're never far from a tea vendor peddling tea or chai — a sweet, milky tea — from trays of steaming glasses. Tea is the second most consumed beverage worldwide, after water.

In the 1800s, the British established tea plantations across India to supply the United Kingdom. For decades, nearly all of India's tea was exported, but in 1881, the Indian Tea Association was formed to promote tea drinking within the country, and Indians embraced it. Today tea is enjoyed extensively — some would say, intensively — across the entire subcontinent.

I recall the ritual of tea from a very early age. My parents in London and later Australia loved their tea, and drank litres of it. Their friend Uncle Roy constantly had tea breath, and there was always a cuppa going. We had tea in the morning with tinned milk and sugar, and then progressed to ginger tea, spiced chai and plain tea; green tea came along much later, with all kinds of lovely infusions.

The making of tea is a soothing ritual, and in the three minutes it takes to brew a cup of tea, I tell everyone to shut down all electronic disturbances, including the phone and TV, and to simply turn to each other and have a conversation. It may be the only time in the day when people can be totally free of distraction and able to communicate with each other in the old way. I love the capacity of tea to bring about conversation.

Food without folklore would be very dull indeed, and in a region of the world with such a prominent tea culture, it's no surprise it also comes with great theatre. 'Pulling tea' — a ritual that was originally designed by the Chinese to cool tea — has been absorbed across the subcontinent. 'Teh tarik', translating literally to 'pulled tea', is a drink made by pouring hot black tea and condensed milk between two containers, from further and further away, until it's blended and frothy — far less aerated than a cappuccino, but with a real layer of foam on top. Tea is poured from one vessel into another and as the maker pours, they 'pull' away from the receiving vessel, creating as much distance as possible between the two vessels while pouring the tea.

Tea pulling is done everywhere in India and Sri Lanka, from restaurants to little tea shops and roadside tea vendors. They all pride themselves on how far they can 'pull' the tea — the higher the better! As a kid, my aunties used to do it for me in our house, and I loved it. It was great fun.

Sura butter tea

Traditionally, butter tea is made by boiling tea leaves in water until the tea is dark brown in colour. The tea is then strained and poured into a special butter churn, along with a large lump of yak butter and some salt, then churned until the butter and salt are well mixed. The tea is then transferred to a kettle, or to a thermos to stay warm as people take it with them on their walks around the mountains. Butter tea is served in a special cup and silver cup holder.

Authentic butter tea is quite an acquired taste. Without yak butter or yak milk it will not be exactly the same, but here is an easy way to get close to the real thing.

REGION Bhutan | **SERVES** 4 | **PREPARATION** 15 minutes
COOKING 10 minutes | **DIFFICULTY** Easy

Bring 1 litre (35 fl oz/4 cups) water to the boil in a saucepan. Remove from the heat and add the teabags or loose-leaf tea. Cover and steep for 3 minutes.

Add the salt. Remove the teabags, or strain if loose-leaf tea was used. Add the milk, return to the heat and bring to the boil for 2 minutes.

Remove from the heat, add the butter and pour into a blender. Put the lid on.

Now, you need to be very careful when blending hot ingredients — so start by putting the lid on, placing a cloth over the lid and pulsing the liquid, then blend on low for about 30 seconds.

Serve the tea straight away, as butter tea is best enjoyed when it is very hot.

TIP 'Half and half', also known as 'half cream' in the United Kingdom, is a simple blend of equal parts whole milk and light cream. It has an average fat content of 10–12 per cent, which is more than milk but less than light cream.

4 good-quality teabags, or 2 heaped tablespoons loose-leaf tea (such as Dilmah English Breakfast)
heaped ¼ teaspoon salt
200 ml (7 fl oz) 'half and half' (see tip) or milk
40 g (1½ oz) unsalted butter

Masala chai

Masala chai is the lifeblood of India. Served in scant shot glasses from dawn until way past dusk, this beverage is EVERYWHERE you look. It's in little makeshift cafes, sold by chai-wallahs at every bus station, train station and street corner, and brewing in every home.

I'll never forget sitting in open-air chai shops in India, drinking creamy, ultra-sweet masala chai. Authentic chai is made with thick buffalo milk, black tea, spices and considerably too much sugar.

Many people refer to this beverage as just chai, but 'chai' simply means 'tea'; not until the beautiful spices are added does it become masala chai.

REGION India | **SERVES** 5 | **PREPARATION** 10 minutes
COOKING 10 minutes | **DIFFICULTY** Easy

10 green cardamom pods, cracked, seeds removed; you'll need about ½ teaspoon cardamom seeds
1 cinnamon stick
4 white peppercorns
2 cloves
500 ml (17 fl oz/2 cups) milk
3½ tablespoons light brown sugar, or to taste
½ teaspoon sliced fresh ginger
⅛ teaspoon salt, or to taste
2 teaspoons good-quality tea leaves (such as Dilmah English Breakfast)

Coarsely crack the cardamom seeds, cinnamon stick, peppercorns and cloves using a mortar and pestle, or a coffee or spice grinder.

Bring the milk to a simmer in a large heavy-based saucepan over medium heat.

Stir or whisk in the brown sugar, ground spice mixture, fresh ginger and salt. Reduce the heat to low and simmer gently, stirring occasionally, for up to 3 minutes to infuse the flavours. Cover and set aside.

Meanwhile, in a large saucepan, bring 500 ml (17 fl oz/ 2 cups) water to the boil. Add the tea and boil for 1 minute.

Pour the tea through a fine-mesh sieve into the hot milk mixture, discarding the tea leaves. Cook over low heat for 1 minute.

Strain the mixture again to remove the ginger. Stir before serving.

Kashmiri chai

Also known as noon chai, this amazingly pink beverage is made from the same tea leaves as green tea, but varies dramatically in taste. A bit salty and incredibly creamy, this chai tea is as unique in taste as it is in appearance. The colour comes from the tea reacting with the bicarbonate of soda.

REGION Pakistan | **SERVES** 4 | **PREPARATION** 15 minutes
COOKING 10 minutes | **DIFFICULTY** Easy

Place a saucepan over medium heat. Add the tea leaves and 185–250 ml (6–9 fl oz/¾–1 cup) water and bring to the boil. Reduce the heat and leave to simmer for about 2 minutes, or until frothy.

Add the bicarbonate of soda and whisk vigorously for about 10 seconds, then add another 185–250 ml (6–9 fl oz/ ¾–1 cup) water and the cardamom seeds. Bring back to the boil, then boil for no longer than 5 minutes, until the tea broth becomes a bright red.

Reduce the heat to medium–low and add the milk, whisking very vigorously to achieve a slight froth. The tea should now be a lovely dark pink. If you add more milk, the colour will soften — the choice is yours.

Finally, add the salt and sugar and stir. Pour into four chai tea cups. Sprinkle with the ground nuts and poppy seeds and serve.

- 2½ teaspoons good-quality Kashmiri tea or oolong tea leaves
- a small pinch of bicarbonate of soda (baking soda)
- 4 cardamom pods, seeds removed and roughly crushed
- 375–500 ml (13–17 fl oz/1½–2 cups) milk
- ¼ teaspoon kosher sea salt flakes
- ½ teaspoon organic sugar
- 1–2 teaspoons ground pistachios and almonds, to garnish
- 1 teaspoon poppy seeds

Cinnamon chai

I have long been friends with the Fernando family from Sri Lanka, producers of one of the world's finest teas, Dilmah. During the planning of a School of Tea, I dropped by Dilhan and Serena Fernando's house for a chat. Serena makes a chai with organic Sri Lankan cinnamon, and it was amazing. The sweetness of the cinnamon really came through, making this one of my favourite chais. You could also put this chai tea into an ice cream machine, for a wonderful ice cream. Thank you Serena.

REGION Sri Lanka | **SERVES** 2 | **PREPARATION** 5 minutes | **COOKING** 10 minutes | **DIFFICULTY** Easy

Pour 500 ml (17 fl oz/2 cups) water into a saucepan and bring to the boil over high heat. When the water is close to boiling, add the cinnamon sticks and leave to boil for 3–4 minutes, allowing the essential oils from the cinnamon to infuse the water.

Add the tea and boil for a further 1–2 minutes, depending on how strong you like your tea.

Strain the tea into two cups and sweeten to taste with condensed milk. Sprinkle with cinnamon and enjoy.

- 2 cinnamon sticks
- 1½ tablespoons good-quality black tea leaves (such as Dilmah English Breakfast)
- 2 tablespoons condensed milk, or to taste
- ground cinnamon, for sprinkling

Yaara thei

Very occasionally even tea tasters develop a yearning for the frothy, milky, sweet tea Sri Lankans know as yaara thei — 'a yard of tea'. It is the perfect weekend tea comforter, just not too often as it is very, very sweet. I used to love it as a kid, as it had a big froth on top when it was handed to me.

If you happen to be in Sri Lanka, Indonesia, India, Malaysia, Kuwait, Brunei or the United Arab Emirates, you can get to a Dilmah tea lounge to have it made for you, otherwise here is the recipe. Be sure to use a double-walled glass so you don't lose the effect of the frothy tea, and to avoid any burns from hot cups!

REGION Sri Lanka | **SERVES** 1 | **PREPARATION** 5 minutes
COOKING 10 minutes | **DIFFICULTY** Easy, but the pulling takes practice

Pour the water into a saucepan and place over high heat. When the water is close to boiling, add the cinnamon sticks and allow to boil for 3–4 minutes, so the oil from the cinnamon infuses the water.

Now add the tea and continue to boil for 1–2 minutes, depending on how strong you like your tea.

Strain the tea and stir in the condensed milk.

Now you can 'pull' the tea, by pouring the tea into a second container from as high as your arms will allow you. Repeat this step three or four times, until you have a nice froth on top.

Pour the tea into a double-walled glass, dust with the ground cinnamon and enjoy.

- 250 ml (9 fl oz/1 cup) hot water (from a kettle)
- 1 cinnamon stick
- 2 teaspoons finest-quality loose-leaf breakfast tea, such as Dilmah T-Series Brilliant Breakfast tea
- 75 g (2½ oz/¼ cup) condensed milk
- ¼ teaspoon ground cinnamon

Sweet basil seed lemonade

*The small black seeds from the sweet basil plant (scientific name **Ocimum basilicum**) have a nice crunchy texture and are widely used in popular sweet Asian drinks such as falooda, sherbet and milkshakes. You can add the soaked seeds to any fruit juice or drink of your choice, including sweet or savoury lassis.*

You can also flavour this lovely lemonade with mint leaves, or the rosewater syrup from the Falooda on page 280.

REGION India | **SERVES** 2 | **PREPARATION** 10 minutes + 15–30 minutes soaking | **DIFFICULTY** Easy

---

1 tablespoon sweet basil seeds
80 ml (2½ fl oz/⅓ cup) lukewarm water
juice of 1 large lemon
2 tablespoons sugar or honey, dissolved
    in 60 ml (2 fl oz/¼ cup) warm water
pinch of salt
½ teaspoon black salt
ice cubes, to serve
mint sprigs, to garnish

Clean the basil seeds of any grit or small stones. Wash the seeds and place in a bowl. Add the lukewarm water and leave for 15–30 minutes, or until the seeds begin to swell. When you observe a transparent jelly-like coating over the seeds, they are ready to use.

In a bowl, combine the lemon juice, sugar or honey syrup, salt and black salt, mixing well. Add 600 ml (21 fl oz) water and the basil seeds, along with any leftover water from soaking the seeds. Mix well.

Pour into two glasses and serve with ice cubes and mint.

Fresh green herb elixir

I can't publish this recipe without mentioning the person who gave it to me: my friend Dharshan Munidasa, restaurateur and co-owner of three of Sri Lanka's most famous restaurants, Ministry of Crab, Nihonbashi and Kaema Sutra, two of which are rated in Asia's top 100 restaurants.

Make this healthy, energising drink part of your morning ritual. It is simple to prepare and so nutritious. There is really no substitute for a fresh king coconut, because of its amazing flavour; the next best option is to use a good coconut water that still contains some of the coconut flesh, although the flavour will never be the same.

REGION Sri Lanka | **SERVES** 2 | **PREPARATION** 10 minutes | **DIFFICULTY** Easy

---

1 thambili (orange-shelled king coconut)
    with the flesh, or 300 ml (10½ fl oz)
    coconut water with flesh
juice of 1 lime
2 cm (¾ inch) knob of fresh ginger, peeled
½ cup vitamin-rich green herbs, such as
    pennywort, flat-leaf (Italian) parsley
    or kale

Place all the ingredients in a blender and whiz together until thoroughly combined.

Strain into two glasses and serve immediately.

Index

Acknowledgements

I would like to thank my publisher, Diana Hill, for her confidence in me and all the meetings and encouragement over the last four years. This has been a long journey. What started as a Mexican cookbook came to a grinding halt when we realised that another was coming out at the same time. Diana could have just cut me loose, but instead she showed great confidence in me and with her encouragement we settled on this beautiful book.

Thank you to Jane Price for managing the book and to Hugh Ford for his design. This book looks beautiful because of their efforts.

A special thanks to my editor, Katri Hilden. She and I have spent nearly a year communicating via email and phone to ensure you, the reader, gets a book that is written well. Katri has taken my chef's thoughts and turned them into beautiful words which reflect my thoughts and feelings about all that is in this book.

Alan Benson, Vanessa Austin and Ross Dobson helped put the soul into this book. Alan's photography and Vanessa's styling bring warmth and honesty, while Ross and I worked on cooking the food for them to photograph. I have never left half of the recipe preparation to someone else during a photo shoot, but Ross did an amazing job during the second week of the shoot. He was my tester and it was really good to hand the recipes to someone else to cook. It gave me confidence that the recipes worked and were real.

To be in the warm embrace of people who have faith in you is an amazing and uplifting feeling.

Published in 2018 by Murdoch Books, an imprint of Allen & Unwin

Murdoch Books Australia
83 Alexander Street,
Crows Nest NSW 2065
Phone: +61 (0)2 8425 0100
murdochbooks.com.au
info@murdochbooks.com.au

Murdoch Books UK
Ormond House, 26–27 Boswell Street,
London, WC1N 3JZ
Phone: +44 (0) 20 8785 5995
murdochbooks.co.uk
info@murdochbooks.co.uk

For Corporate Orders & Custom Publishing contact our business development
team at salesenquiries@murdochbooks.com.au

Publisher: Diana Hill
Editorial Manager: Jane Price
Designer: Hugh Ford
Editor: Katri Hilden
Food Editor: Katrina Meynink
Photography: Alan Benson (except author photograph page 6, by Ian Waldie)
Styling: Vanessa Austin
Food preparation for photography: Ross Dobson
Production Director: Lou Playfair

The publisher would like to thank TeraNova Tiles and Design Tiles for use
of their products in the photography of this book.

ISBN 978 1 74336 511 3 Australia
ISBN 978 1 74336 512 0 UK

A cataloguing-in-publication entry is available from the catalogue of the
National Library of Australia at nla.gov.au
A catalogue record for this book is available from the British Library

Colour reproduction by Splitting Image Colour Studio Pty Ltd, Clayton, Victoria
Printed by C&C Offset Printing Co Ltd, China

TABLESPOON MEASURES: We have used Australian 20 ml (4 teaspoon)
tablespoon measures. If you are using a smaller European 15 ml (3 teaspoon)
tablespoon, add an extra teaspoon of the ingredient for each tablespoon.